TOUGH STUFF

THE MAN IN THE MIDDLE

To Dick

I hope you enjoy Tough Stuff.

Sam Huff

TOUGH STUFF

THE MAN IN THE MIDDLE

SAM HUFF
with Leonard Shapiro

Introduction by Tom Landry

St. Martin's Press

NEW YORK

Design by Robert Bull Design

Library of Congress Cataloging-in-Publication Data

Huff, Sam.
  Tough stuff.

  1. Huff, Sam. 2. Football players—United States—
Biography. I. Shapiro, Leonard   II. Title.
GV939.H84A3   1988   796.332′092′4   [B]   88-18163
ISBN 0-312-02302-2

First Edition

10 9 8 7 6 5 4 3 2 1

To Vicky, Jennifer, Emily, and Taylor, the great joys of my life, and to my father, my hero.

To Sam Jr., Cathy, and J. D., and to my grandchildren, may they truly understand my life and times and know that hard work, not cleverness, is always the answer.

ACKNOWLEDGMENTS

The morning after the New York Giants had dismantled the Denver Broncos in Super Bowl XXI, I bumped into Sam Huff in a terminal at the Los Angeles airport.

We were both scheduled on the same flight back home to Washington, D.C., but a snowstorm back East changed all of that. Not long after we arrived, we were told our flight had been canceled.

I've known Sam since my days as a reporter covering the Washington Redskins in the 1970s, and we decided to go to the Los Angeles Marriott to have breakfast and plot strategy on how to get back home.

Over scrambled eggs and coffee, Sam regaled me with story after story about the old New York Giants. Thirty years had passed since the Giants had won the NFL championship with a baby-faced rookie starting at middle linebacker, a kid named Sam Huff. And as Sam spoke, he was constantly interrupted by a stream of Giant fans who recognized his face and just wanted to say hello, how are you, what did you think about the game?

Sam has always thought a lot about the game, and over the next two days, I found that out firsthand. That's how long it took us to get home, with an overnight stop in Dallas when our connecting flight to Washington was wiped out by the snowstorm.

But it was time well spent. Sam definitely likes to talk,

and at one point high in the sky, after another marvelous tale had been told, I asked him if he'd ever considered doing a book about his life.

"Nah," he said, "never had the time."

"Want to try now?"

"Yes."

And so, with a healthy assist from Mother Nature, *Tough Stuff: The Man in the Middle* began to take shape. Over the next fifteen months, many other people contributed to the project, with bits of information, with scrapbooks and yearbooks and old Giant programs, with encouragement, with suggestions on the editing and writing.

Thank you all.

In particular, there was my agent, Esther Newberg, the best in the business, bar none, whose patience and perseverance will never be forgotten. Nor will the great efforts of my editor at St. Martin's Press, George Witte, who gave me the opportunity to tell Sam's story, then did wonderful work with the words.

Thanks to Don Graham, Ben Bradlee, Howard Simons, and Len Downie, for everything.

Thanks to my colleague, and dear friend, George Solomon, for his boundless enthusiasm for the project and for helping provide the time to do it.

Thanks to Joe Browne and John Wiebusch of the National Football League for their invaluable advice and assistance in getting this book published; to Joe Horrigan of the Pro Football Hall of Fame; to Ed Croke of the New York Giants and Greg Aiello of the Dallas Cowboys, all of whom provided research material and fabulous photographs for the book. And to Tom Landry, for taking the time and effort to write the perfect introduction.

My gratitude also to Sam's good friend, Don Smith, who rummaged through his attic and sent box after box of old clippings, scrapbooks, and photographs from Sam's days with the Giants.

From West Virginia, I received great help in the research from Buck Basile, Tony Constantine, John Manchin, John Victor, Blair Wolfe, and John Veasey.

From great Giant fans and my friends, Elizabeth Cale, Alan Stypek, and Sean Burke, came books, scrapbooks, old programs, and fond memories, a treasure trove of information. Dave Klein of the *Newark Star-Ledger* and Rich Rosenbush of *The New York Times* offered advice, telephone numbers, and more old clippings.

Thanks also to my dear friends Helen Wiley, Emily Clarke, Michael Sussman, Joe Goldstein, Jura Koncius and Morgan Dodd, Nance and Hank Minchin, Budd and Audrey Fenton, to my parents, Joseph and Julia Shapiro, and my in-laws Dr. Charles and Naoma Moon, for their never-ending enthusiasm, encouragement, and support. And to all of my colleagues at *The Washington Post* for more of the same, especially Ken Denlinger, Tony Kornheiser, Tom Boswell, John Feinstein, Sandra Bailey, Christine Brennan, Don White, Sally Jenkins, Mike Wilbon, Bill Gildea, Shirley Povich, Don Beard, Martie Zad, O. D. Wilson, Mike Trilling, Mark Asher, Bill Brubaker, and Angus Phillips.

This book could not have been produced without the dedicated and remarkable efforts of Olwen Price, who transcribed the tapes and typed the manuscript faster than I thought humanly possible, and Carol Van Horn and Carol Leggett, who helped out in a pinch.

Thanks to Del Nylec, Sam's secretary at the Marriott Corporation, for putting up with so many phone calls, answering so many questions, and rounding up a mother lode of photographs; to Carol Holden, for her patience through it all, and to Mary Jane Hill, for tending to baby Taylor while his dad typed away upstairs.

And finally, thanks and much love to my wife, Vicky Moon, for her patience, her understanding, her encouragement, and her great advice every step of the way.

Leonard Shapiro
April 1, 1988

INTRODUCTION
By Tom Landry

I've known Sam Huff for thirty-two years. I coached him. I coached against him. I was the presenter at his Hall of Fame induction. Now I'm writing the introduction to his book.

Sam and I have a good thing going. We're friends. And that's saying something when you consider the two teams he's so closely identified with are the Giants and Redskins.

You see, I've been with the Cowboys so long now people forget I was a Giant for ten years. Ten great years of my life. That's how I met Sam.

It was the summer of 1956 in a little town outside of Burlington, Vermont, called Winooski. That was the Giants' training-camp site in those days. I had just retired as a player after the 1955 season and was beginning my first year as a full-time coach. I had been a player-coach in 1954 and 1955.

My job was to coach the defense—all of it, which I had been doing for two years already while also playing cornerback. Football was a little simpler in those days. You could fit an entire coaching staff into a compact car. Now you need three or four limousines. So I coached the defense. Vince Lombardi had the offense. And Jim Lee Howell was the head coach.

Our third-round draft choice that year was an offensive guard from West Virginia named Robert Lee Huff, nicknamed "Sam." He was a pudgy, baby-faced kid. Kind of soft-looking. Not particularly impressive to look at. Looks can be deceiving, of course, and in this case they were. Sam turned out to be one of the toughest, most competitive players I've ever seen.

It wasn't smooth sailing all the way, however. That's not Sam's style.

I remember that first camp when Sam and another rookie, Don Chandler, were upset about the shabby treatment of rookies by Giants veterans and coaches. Huff and Chandler decided they were quitting, but Ed Kolman and Vince Lombardi, both assistant coaches at the time, talked them out of it.

Sam stayed in camp, and good thing for me he did. Soon I was going to need a middle linebacker, and the coal miner's son from Farmington, West Virginia, was going to be quite a choice.

Middle linebacker was a new position in pro football in the 1950s. I had been developing the "4–3" defense for the Giants in those couple of years before Sam's arrival. The main defense of the early fifties was the "Eagle" defense, named after the Philadelphia Eagles, the dominant team of those years.

The "Eagle" defense consisted of a five-man line with two linebackers playing over the ends, who lined up tight in those days. Bucko Kilroy was the middle guard, or nose tackle as it's called today, playing over the center. On passing downs, Bucko would sometimes stand up and drop into pass coverage like a linebacker. This was the forerunner of the "4–3" defense (four linemen, three linebackers) and the middle linebacker position. It was also a few pounds ago for Bucko, who once was a scout for the Cowboys and now is vice-president of the New England Patriots.

This new middle linebacker position required a combination of lineman and defensive-back abilities. He had to be big and strong enough to handle linemen and running backs on the line of scrimmage, but also fast enough to pursue and drop into the secondary to cover the pass. And he had to be smart because the middle linebacker called the defensive plays. He was the quarterback of the defense.

Sam had all the right qualities. He was an offensive lineman with size and strength. He was mobile. He was smart. So in that 1956 training camp we decided to move Sam to middle linebacker to back up the guy I was grooming, Ray Beck, another converted offensive lineman. That's probably why we thought of switching Sam to linebacker in the first place.

It wasn't long before Sam moved into the lineup. Ray Beck got hurt early in the season and suddenly Sam Huff, a rookie, was our starting middle linebacker.

It turned out to be a fantastic year. We won the NFL championship, beating the Bears 47–7 in the title game at Yankee Stadium. And the defense became the heart of the team.

Sam and I developed a special relationship that year. My wife Alicia and I lived at the Excelsior Hotel in New York City on Eighty-first Street and Central Park West along with several other players, including Sam and his wife Mary.

Sam was eager to be successful, so every night after practice I would call him and go down to his apartment and teach him how to play middle linebacker. Sometimes we watched film, but mostly I would draw plays and show Sam how to recognize what the opposing team was doing, how to call the right defenses, and how to fill the right gap to make the play. We went through those things over and over again.

I was teaching a new way to play defense. Instead of reacting to the play and pursuing, we used a coordinated defense that plugged all the gaps along the line of scrimmage. "Gap control" is what we called it. It was the same philosophy I took to the Cowboys that became known as the "Flex" defense. It required great discipline, especially from the middle linebacker. Sam made it work because he was a great student.

During games, I used hand signals to flash the defensive plays to Sam. He called the plays in the huddle and he called the automatic adjustments based on how the offense lined up. Sam always made the right move. That's why we won.

Because I was young and still felt as much like a player as coach, Sam and I became good friends. We went out with our wives to the great New York spots like Toots Shor's and a place called The Anchor on Fifty-ninth Street. I was very close to that defensive team. I kind of grew up with those guys. I was their only coach for many years. Some of my best friends to this day, like Sam, are from that team.

Sam went on to become a legendary Giant. In his eight years in New York, he played in six NFL championship games, was named All-NFL four times, played in five Pro Bowls, and was named to the NFL's All-1950s Team. He never missed a game.

More memorable, though, was his role in changing the way football fans viewed defense. We won with defense in those days and the fans knew it. They loved that old Giant defense. They would chant, "De-fense, de-fense!" and we would go out and win 6–3 or 7–6.

Sam, not being the bashful type, used to irritate the offense something terrible. He would come off the field and as he passed the offensive players, he would say, "Hold 'em, guys," or "Don't let 'em score." Something endearing like that. Sam was a cocky, proud leader of a great defense. He became the first glamour middle linebacker on the first glamour defense, playing in New York City at the dawn of television's love affair with pro football.

All those factors—his talent as a player, his name, his personality, the success of the team, the city, the TV explosion—converged at the same time in Sam Huff, a new kind of football star. He was on the cover of *Time* magazine. CBS made a famous documentary about him called "The Violent World of Sam Huff." His individual battles with Jim Brown and Jim Taylor were promoted like heavyweight title fights. It was quite a time.

I know how hurt he was when the Giants traded him to the Redskins in 1964. But Sam made the best of it. Not surprisingly, he became a success in Washington, first on the football field, then with the Marriott Corporation. He's also an analyst on the Redskins' radio network. Has been for years. So I always see Sam at least twice a year when he comes to our locker room with his little tape recorder before each game to ask me questions about how I plan to beat the Redskins.

Come to think of it, didn't Sam's Redskins just win the Super Bowl again? Probably so. But that's the Sam Huff I've known for thirty-two years. Always a winner.

1

They called it Number Nine.

I wasn't born there, but I grew up in Number Nine, a mining camp a few miles outside Farmington, West Virginia, just west of the Monongohela River Valley in the soft coal hills at the northern end of the state. I was the fourth of six kids in the family, and they named me Robert Lee Huff. "Sam" came later, and to this day, I have no idea how I got my real name, or the nickname.

I spent the first few years of my life in another coal camp not too far from Number Nine, a place called Edna Gas. I don't remember much about that. I was born in 1934, right in the middle of the Depression, and as we all knew, times were hard. My dad was Oral Huff, and like his father before him, "Orly" Huff worked all his life in the coal mines, from the age of thirteen until he died in 1970 at the age of sixty-three from a series of heart attacks and black lung, too. Everyone in the mines had the black lung— they'd come home coughing up black mucus every night. It's one of the reasons I knew I could never be a coal miner; in fact, it made me work that much harder in everything I did to avoid having to live that kind of life.

My dad was not a very big man, maybe five feet seven and 150 pounds. But he was tough, strong as a bull until the heart attacks and the black lung got him. He ran what they called a "loading machine" in the mines, but people tell me he could do almost anything, any job they had. He was great with his hands, he could fix any piece of machinery, and he loved coal mining as much as I loved football.

We were not very much alike. He liked to go down in the mines; I was scared to death of them. He loved to hunt and fish; I always hated guns and killing. Maybe that goes back to Edna Gas. The earliest memory I have is of when I was three or four years old. I had a pet dog and somehow he got loose. The dogcatcher actually shot my dog, and I saw it happen. It's a very vague memory, but I truly believe that's why I shy away from guns and hunting to this day.

My dad had a tough life, but he never complained. By the time we got to Number Nine, he was working regular shifts. Back during the Depression, that was not always the case. Sometimes you'd work a few days, then not at all, but my dad managed to hold the family together. By the time I was in school during World War II, the coal mines never stopped; back then you had three eight-hour shifts, and my dad worked all of them at one time or another, and sometimes back-to-back so he could have a little extra time off to go hunt or fish.

We lived from payday to payday. You got paid every two weeks, and, just like the song said, you owed your life to the company store. The house we lived in was owned by the company. You went to the company store for your food, your clothes, everything you needed. We had an old car that my dad took care of, and the big outing for him and my mother, Catherine, was a trip into Fairmont about ten miles away to do the grocery shopping. I remember once seeing my dad's paycheck, and it was thirteen dollars after they had taken out the rent and store money. It didn't leave much for anything else, but I never felt like I was poor. Maybe it was because everybody had exactly what we had, which wasn't very much. But we didn't know any better.

As a kid, I only had one pair of shoes and wore them all year. They'd put taps on the heel and toe so they wouldn't wear out, and in the spring, you'd take off those shoes and go barefoot until it turned cold in October.

Our old house is still there, but the mine is closed now, has been since seventy-eight people were killed in a terrible tragedy in 1968. My sister still lives on the same street in Number Nine, and nothing has changed much except for the indoor plumbing. We lived in a rowhouse, on a dirt road. You'd walk up a set of stairs into the living room. We had a sofa, a big chair, and potbellied coal stove that heated the whole house. There were two bedrooms—my mom and dad had one and my brothers and sisters shared the other. I slept in the same bed with my older brother Don all the time I was growing up. There was no running water, just a community pump for water and an outhouse about fifty yards up the hill behind the house. I'll always remember that place for the cold linoleum floors. We had no rugs, just bare linoleum floors. It's funny, all the kids today like those hardwood floors. I'll take wall-to-wall carpeting any time.

My mother ran the house. Her life was not easy, either. I can remember my dad coming home from a day in the mines with coal dust all over him so that all you could see were the whites of his eyes. He'd be filthy, and he'd cough and spit up all that coal dust in his lungs. When he walked in the door, he'd get into one of those big tubs my mother used to wash the clothes in. He'd sit down in a tub of hot water, and that water would turn black after just a few seconds. I think that bath was the real highlight of his day. The rest of us had to wait until Saturday—that was bath day—but my dad took a bath every day of his life.

Dad was an easygoing kind of fella, but he was also a disciplinarian. He carried a razor strap with him in the mines, and he wouldn't hesitate to use it on us if he had to. My brother and I were responsible for the garden we had planted near the house. Don liked to play softball and I was always playing sports, and invariably we'd put off spading that garden until the last minute, or we'd forget to do it altogether. When my dad came home and saw we hadn't done the work, out came the strap. To be truthful, Don got it more than I did, maybe because he was older. I can also tell you that belt hurt. He'd hit you so hard he'd raise welts on your body. Then we'd go to my mother, and she'd rub Vaseline on them and try to soothe us. But don't get me wrong; it wasn't done out of cruelty. That's how people disciplined their kids, and we got whacked in school, too, if we were out of line. My father was not a mean man; but that's how it was done.

My mother kept it all together. She was the manager of the family, handled all the money and the bills. She'd go to that A&P store in Fairmont and come back with everything she needed to keep us going. We got our vegetables from the garden and she would can them for the winter, too. She'd buy a big old beef bone or ham hock and make soup that would last all week. She baked the best bread I've ever tasted to this day; my mouth waters just thinking about it. She'd buy a pound of oleomargarine and add some kind of orange coloring and make it look like butter. She'd cook a big mess of hamburger, then leave the grease in the pan and fry potatoes in it. It wasn't fancy, and it probably wasn't very healthy either, but nobody knew much about cholesterol back then. Between the coal dust and cholesterol, no wonder so many of those people had bad hearts.

My brother Don was four years older than me and, quite honestly, we never did get along very well. We constantly seemed to be at each other. Of course he was always bigger than me, and I always wanted to hang around him and his friends and he'd shoo me away. We fought almost every day of our lives as kids, and they were the toughest fights I ever had, including my days in football. He'd just beat the hell out of me, but I never wanted to give up. I'd throw anything to get back at him—rocks, sticks. Once I found a pistol—there were a lot of guns around—and pulled the trigger. It happened so long ago and I can't remember if I was fooling around or truly meant to kill him. I just thank God it never fired.

Don was a pretty good athlete in high school, but he never dedicated himself to sports. He liked to hunt and fish, too, and when he was sixteen, like a lot of kids back then, he quit high school and went to work in the mines.

My brother died when he was thirty-five years old, out in a field, hunting with my dad. It was kind of ironic the way it happened. My dad had a bad heart from the mines, and we tried to watch him pretty closely. One day, Don and my father went hunting. Don was about six foot three and weighed over 250 pounds. To get a day off to take my dad, he worked three straight shifts in the mine. They went up to Romney, West Virginia, and they were walking in a field when he told my father he was feeling pain in his chest and arms. He collapsed right there. My dad knew immediately what was wrong. He'd had a couple of heart attacks himself by then, and he went for help. By the time they got back, though, it was too late. Don was gone.

Hunting and fishing weren't for me, but I always did love sports. There was always time for baseball and football at Number Nine. We didn't have a lot of equipment. We made our own baseballs. You'd get an old sock and stuff it with newspaper and straw, then wind this thick black electric tape around it until it was round and pretty hard. We'd use broomsticks for bats. We made our own footballs, too.

The outside world came to us through the radio, just like for a lot of other people back then. I spent a lot of time listening to the radio. I was always bugging my parents for a pony because my favorite shows were Roy Rogers and Gene Autry. I still love horses to this day, and I really think the radio was responsible for that. I followed the Pittsburgh Pirates—Ralph Kiner was an early hero—and of course I'd listen to the West Virginia football games and knew all the players. Frank Gatski was another hero. Like me, he grew up in Number Nine, then went on to play college ball at Marshall University and had a long career as a lineman with the Cleveland Browns. Made the Pro Football Hall of Fame, too, a couple of years ago: two guys in the Hall from little old Farmington High School.

My whole life centered around Number Nine. I went to elementary school there with about a hundred kids. There were three or four teachers, including the principal, Blair Wolfe, who is still a good friend. He was a firm believer in teaching the basics—reading, writing, and arithmetic—and his teachers followed the program. You'd have first and second grade on one floor, third and fourth on another, and fifth and sixth on the top floor.

The teachers were allowed to hit you if you misbehaved, and I still remember getting whacked on the knuckles with a ruler when I was trying to write my alphabet letters. If you didn't do it right, you got smacked. I guess I was a pretty good student, but to tell you the truth, I usually did just enough to get by. Education was not a high priority around my house or anyone else's in the neighborhood. It wasn't emphasized and nobody ever talked about going to college. We were too poor to think about it.

The favorite part of the day was recess, of course, and Mr. Wolfe usually took us outside to play ball. We couldn't really play in the schoolyard—it was a dumping ground for waste materials in the mines. They'd dump the slate anywhere they could, and the school was surrounded by these slate fields. You'd rip your clothes to shreds if you played on it, and who could afford to do that? We all had the basics, a T-shirt, a couple of pairs of bib overalls, and a heavy coat for winter. Kids wear those bib overalls all the time now because they think they're cool. We weren't making any fashion statements; it was all very practical. No frills. The first time I ever felt like a grown-up was when I put on a pair of regular jeans with a belt in high school.

Anyway, Mr. Wolfe would take us out to a pasture and we'd play baseball or football, depending on the season. Back then, my best friend was a kid named Leo Coceano. His family came to this country when he was four or five years old, and when I first met Leo, he couldn't even speak

6

English. His dad worked in the mine with my dad, and Leo and I became great buddies. We still talk occasionally—he became a school teacher in New Jersey—but back then, we were almost inseparable.

We also became great rivals. We both were pretty good athletes, and he'd always be the captain of one team and I'd be the captain of the other. If we played on the same team, we'd always win. Our games were always competitive. Blair Wolfe likes to remind me about the time he was umpiring one. I was pitching and I was getting a little hot over some of his calls. Finally he called a pitch a ball that was right over the plate, and I lost it. I called him a cheater and a lot worse, I guess. Well, he came right up to me, picked me up by the shirt, and popped every button he shook me so hard. He tells me it was also the last time he ever umpired a game for us.

We never really played any kind of organized sports, at least not until we got to high school. We had our own school, about 700 kids, in Farmington a few miles from Number Nine. If you were a boy and grew up in a coal camp, you were expected to play football. If you were a girl, you tried out to be a cheerleader, or you played in the band. Mary Fletcher, whom I met in the seventh grade and married in my senior year of high school, played the French horn. She played in the band: I played football and baseball and a little basketball until I was thrown off the team for swearing in the ninth grade by the coach, John Victor. He likes to tell people he was the only coach ever to kick a Hall of Famer off his team. At the time, it really hurt me, and I never played organized basketball again.

There were no blacks in the school. Even though our fathers worked side by side in the mines, the blacks lived in their little community in Number Nine and we lived in ours, and they went to separate schools until desegregation in 1954. But when I was in high school, from 1947 to 1952, I never played against a black athlete in any sport. It wasn't that we didn't get along, it was just not done back then. No one thought anything about it, and when they did finally desegregate the schools, it was done calmly and peacefully as far as I can recall, at least in that part of the state.

I went out for the football team when I was a freshman, about fourteen years old, and in that first year, I almost quit. The coach was a man named Ray Kelly and he was a real stickler about conditioning. He'd run us until we literally dropped, and there were times that first year I really didn't think I was going to make it.

Mr. Kelly had gone to Farmington High himself and had fought in World War II. He came back in 1946 to teach and coach and he was a wonderful man, a guy you could go talk to and get straight answers. We probably had a hundred kids out for football and only two coaches, Mr. Kelly and Mr. Victor. They'd let the seventh and eighth graders come out for the team, too; you'd play on the junior varsity until your sophomore or junior year.

My first goal in football was just to get a uniform. There weren't all that many to go around. That first year, I was playing on what they called second team, or junior varsity. I'd play in those games and they'd let me dress for the varsity games, but I never got to play until my sophomore year. I went both ways, offensive guard or tackle and defensive line. I never really played linebacker until I got to the pros. Practices were tough. One time, we lost a game and some of us were talking to each other, saying Coach Kelly would probably keep us out at practice until the moon came out. Well, he overheard us and said, "Boys, I wouldn't want to disappoint you." Needless to say, we practiced until the moon came out.

We played basic single-wing football, and almost everybody played on both sides of the ball. I never had a desire to carry the football. I didn't have great speed and we had some excellent running backs. I also enjoyed the contact on the line. Leo Coceano played right next to me on defense at end, and by the time we were seniors, most teams avoided running toward our side of the field.

I had other goals. I always wanted to have one of those letter jackets, the kind that said all-county on the back. Then I wanted to get an all-state patch. That motivated me. And the more I learned in school, the more I knew I wanted to graduate from high school and go to college to become a football coach like Ray Kelly.

We had a pretty close-knit school. Everybody took the bus, but I usually had to hitchhike home after football practice. The principal was a tough old bird named Joseph C. Cotrel. He'd been teaching at the school since 1924 and became principal in 1930, and he wouldn't think twice about giving you a paddling if you were screwing up.

He got me good once, and I was totally innocent. My locker was located near the gym, which in reality was the stage of the auditorium. Right below my locker was the boiler room, and that's where guys would go to sneak a smoke. I have never smoked in my life; it just doesn't do anything for me. But one of my buddies came out of the boiler room that day with a cigarette in his hand. He wanted to go shoot some baskets up on the stage, so he handed me the cigarette. Just as he gave it to me, Mr. Cotrel turned the corner, and I was guilty. No trial, no appeal, just the death sentence. I took a few licks in his office, and for some reason he really seemed to enjoy giving it to a big old football player.

Actually, I wasn't all that big in my sophomore year. I guess I weighed about 150 pounds, but then a funny thing happened. I had my tonsils taken out between my sophomore and junior year, and by the time I was a senior, I was up to 210 pounds. Actually, I was lucky to be alive.

The tonsillectomy was routine. I spent a couple of days in the hospital, and then they sent me home. I was still laid up in bed the next weekend, and all of a sudden I started to get a nose bleed. That had never happened before, so I did what I thought you were supposed to do—I lay down. For some reason, my parents weren't home that day, and I was there alone. Fortunately, the doctor who had taken my tonsils out decided that afternoon to go for a ride with his wife through Farmington. For some reason he figured that as long as he was in the neighborhood, he might as well stop by and see me. As it turned out, my little nose bleed was a massive hemorrhage. He got me into his car and took me back to the hospital. At first, they weren't going to admit me unless my mom or dad could sign me in. But the doctor raised so much hell, Fairmont General finally let him operate on me to stop the bleeding. He told me later that if he hadn't been passing through that day, I probably would have bled to death on the couch in the living room.

My junior year, we had a pretty good football team, even though we were one of the smaller Class B schools in the state. We'd travel all around the area and most of our games were against Class A schools, with bigger enrollments. We played the big boys because we needed the money. Our own school didn't even have bleachers. The field was cut into a little valley, just like everything else in West Virginia, and spectators had to sit on the banks of the hills to watch us play.

Most teams didn't want to come to our field, so we usually played away. We'd have caravans, four or five players to a car with our fans following behind. That's how I met John Manchin, a man who played a major role in my life and one of the best friends I've ever had. He owned a furniture business in Farmington, gave me my first job and bought me my first suit and my first car. When I went to West Virginia University, he gave Mary a job and I worked for him on weekends and vacations. A very special man.

In Fairmont, we'd play at East-West Stadium, sometimes under the lights. I guess we'd draw as many as 3,000 people, and I swear, even now, it seems like it sounded louder than anything I ever heard at Yankee Stadium in the glory days with the Giants.

I guess the first time I ever had an inkling that I was any good came in the first game of my junior year, against Benwood Union. I remember one of their coaches yelling on the sideline, "Run the ball away from where Huff is." That told me something about myself that no one ever had. Maybe I could play this game.

Late that season, I got in trouble with Coach Kelly. I had gone to a birthday party for a friend and I had a heck of a time catching a ride back home. We had an early curfew, and I probably didn't get home until two or three in the morning. Well, somehow Coach Kelly found out about it and he decided that I wasn't going to play the next game against one of our biggest rivals, Monongha. I was upset, even the teachers were upset about it. One of the history teachers, J. W. Thomas, went to Kelly and said, "If you hold Sam out, even the goalposts won't be safe." But Kelly wouldn't change his mind.

Now, we were playing Monongha and I was on the bench. They were moving the ball up and down the field, fortunately not scoring, and late in the first quarter, Coach Kelly walked up to me and said, "Well, Sam, I hope you've learned your lesson." He put me in the game. Monongha had a great quarterback, Benny Salopek, and the first series I was in there, he dropped back to pass. He jumped up to throw that old jump pass that was so popular back then, and I just unloaded on him. I hit him so hard he had to come out of the game. He went back in but he couldn't throw after that because his shoulder was injured, and we won the game, 13–7. I think they found out later he had a broken shoulder.

Now we were back in the locker room, and the Monongha coach, Jim Feltz, came in and started yelling at me about going after his quarterback. He called me every name in the book, accused me of playing dirty, which was not true. I hit that kid a perfectly legitimate shot, and Coach Kelly finally got Feltz out of there. To this day, it's something I'll never forget. I was surprised Coach Kelly didn't haul off and hit him.

That year, we finished 6–3 and I was named to the second team all-conference. I also was starting to get some notice. One of the West Virginia University coaches, Harold Lahar, came over to scout one of our games. He was looking at a halfback on our team, Rudy Banick, a real quick little runner, and another guy who played for Rivesville High School, one of our big rivals, a fullback named Bob Toothman. After the game, Coach Lahar went up to Ray Kelly and told him I had impressed him quite a bit and that he would be keeping his eye on me the following year. Of course they never told me that, but by my senior year, West Virginia wasn't the only school that was interested.

After the tonsillectomy, I started to grow. I don't know if it was a coincidence or my mother's good cooking, but by the time I was a senior, I weighed in at about 210. In their annual preview, the Fairmont newspaper downplayed our chances because we had lost fourteen seniors to graduation. "The gridders in general are medium-small, except for big and agile Huff," the story said. "This six-one husky stars for Farmington's sandlot baseball contenders [I was a pretty decent catcher in those days], shows no awkwardness for his age and runs like a truck. . . . An all-conference choice in our book."

He was right about me, but wrong about our team. We started off the season with a pair of ties, then won seven straight games and finished undefeated. In the last quarter of my last game in high school, I picked up a fumble against Romney High School, another big school, and ran 20 yards for a touchdown, the only score in a game we won, 6–0. They had a complicated point system that determined who would play in the state championship, and we just missed out. But it was a memorable season for a lot of reasons.

For one, Mary and I got married. We were both too young, but then again, it was not that uncommon back then. We'd known each other since the seventh grade and dated steadily through high school. I never had much money, so when I knew Mary was going to the movies, I'd wait until she paid her way in and bought some popcorn, then I'd pay to get in and mooch her food. That's about all I could afford.

I was a better than average student, but never really applied myself. I was president of our letterman's club and even participated in our school play, a production of *We Shook the Family Tree.* In our class yearbook, *The Lincolneer,* I was described this way:

This good looking boy is our muscle man.
At football he is great.
Sammy used his brains as well as brawn.
He made first team, Class B, All State.

I also was being recruited by a couple of schools. Army was interested, until they found out I was married. That was definitely against the regulations. Florida was interested, too. I took my first ride on an airplane to visit their campus and when I got to the airport, I was picked up by one of their players, Haywood Sullivan, the quarterback. Haywood drove me over to campus, but I never saw him again that weekend. He went on to play professional baseball and now owns a piece of the Boston Red Sox. To this day, I kid him about that weekend. I always tell him the money he was supposed to have spent on me on that visit probably went toward buying the Red Sox.

Really, though, there was no other choice for me but West Virginia. Morgantown was thirty miles down the road. I had grown up listening to their football games on the radio, broadcast by Jack Flemming. I knew all their players, read about them in the papers, and when they said they wanted me to come there, it was the happiest moment of my life. After all, I was the first kid in my family ever to go to college.

The coach at West Virginia was Art (Pappy) Lewis, a big man with these great big bushy eyebrows and a great reputation as a recruiter. Joe Marconi, a fullback from Pennsylvania and my best friend at West Virginia, used to tell me he couldn't get Pappy out of his house until he agreed to go to West Virginia University. He said Pappy would put his feet up on the coffee table and eat and drink. "What's for dinner, Momma?" he'd ask Joe's mother. And when the food ran out, he'd just have another beer with Joe's dad.

Pappy always used to ask recruits, "You coming up here with me, son?" He called defensive players "hunters and walking dogs," and when he scouted running backs, he asked, "Does the boy like the brier patch?"—another way of saying can he handle contact inside or does he run to the water cooler?

In those days, schools could bring you onto campus in the spring of your senior year of high school and give you a tryout. They had already offered me a scholarship and I'd already signed a letter saying I was going to attend. But I guess they wanted to get a little closer look at what they had, so I went down to Morgantown one weekend in the spring. They gave me a sweatsuit with WEST VIRGINIA written across the front, and I was proud as hell walking around Morgantown. I probably never even took it off the whole weekend.

At the tryout, Pappy Lewis called me over. He was with another coach, Gene Corum, and they wanted me to hit a blocking sled. I'd never even seen a blocking sled in high school. We'd block and tackle each other; we didn't have machines because we couldn't afford them. Coach Kelly sold candy and cakes out of his office at lunchtime just to make money to buy our uniforms.

Anyway, Coach Lewis was a very big man, over 250 pounds, and he and Corum were standing on this big sled. I'm thinking to myself, *I'm gonna kill that sled, just break it in half and impress these guys*. Well, I threw myself into it and the spring recoiled and just shot me back ten yards.

Now I'm lying on my back on the ground, and Coach Lewis, the biggest man I've ever seen in my life, is standing over me. Then he turns to Corum and says "Aw, hell, Gene, there goes another wasted scholarship."

2

When I left home for the start of summer practice, I really had no idea what I was getting into. But when I left West Virginia University four years later, I had been a part of the greatest football team in the history of the school.

Despite my problems with the blocking sled, I knew I could play the game, but now I was at a much different level. In high school, I was probably the biggest kid on our team. In college, I was just another big old country boy Pappy Lewis had brought to the state university.

Pappy was a big old country boy himself. He was born and raised on a farm in Middleport, Ohio, just across the Ohio River from West Virginia. When he graduated from high school, he spent two years working in the mines before he decided to go to college. He was a twenty-one-year-old freshman at Ohio University, and that's when people first started calling him Pappy. He played one season of professional football with the New York Giants in 1936, then took a meandering road to West Virginia. He worked as an assistant coach in the pros, took three years off to go fight World War II, then came back as a head coach at Washington and Lee and then head line coach at Mississippi State. He was named head coach at West Virginia in 1950, and by the time I got there, the team had gone from winning two games in 1950 to 5–5 the year before I arrived. Just as important, though, old Pappy was establishing himself as one of the country's best recruiters. For years, some of the state's best football players would wind up playing everywhere but West Virginia University. Pappy changed all that. He'd go into a kid's house, recruit the hell out of your parents, and when he'd ask, "You coming up here with me, son," how could you say no? The team that he assembled in the summer of 1952 was made up mainly of native Mountaineer sons.

By the time I left in 1956, we had something very special. In fact, people still call my years there the "golden age" in West Virginia football. Over the four years, we were 31–7, had a number of guys make All-American, and became the only West Virginia team to go to a major bowl— the Sugar Bowl in 1953, my sophomore season. Lewis, in fact, had more wins than any coach in West Virginia history, with the exception of the current coach, Don Nehlen, even though he was fired in 1959. After my class graduated, things started to go downhill for Pappy, and there was even talk that he'd been let go because he had a serious drinking problem. It was sad, because a lot of the people who had jumped on the bandwagon when we were going so well criticized him viciously when the team started losing. A lot of the newspaper guys he used to pal around with even turned on him. He wound up as an assistant coach with the Steelers and died in 1962. The man definitely deserved better.

When I showed up for the start of summer practice, I had no inkling of what to expect. Mary was back in Farmington, living with her folks and working for John Manchin. In fact, she stayed in Farmington most of the four years I was in college. Sam Jr. was born during my freshman year, and we really couldn't have afforded it any other way.

In those days, Pappy took the whole football team to a summer training camp called Jackson's Mill, a beautiful 4-H camp in the north central part of the state. We'd stay in these bunkhouses and practice twice a day. It was the perfect spot because there was nothing around to get you in trouble. We practiced on a field that was also a landing strip. Just getting there was an adventure because you had to cross a creek on one of those old swinging bridges.

Five of us freshmen made a major impact on the football team that year and we formed its nucleus for the next four years. Freddy Wyant was a cocky little left-handed quarterback from Weston, West Virginia. His high school team had won only two games his senior year and on the night Lewis scouted him, they got creamed, 26–7, by another little school down the road. But when Pappy came back to campus, he told one reporter he'd "just seen a boy who will make me a great coach some day." Pappy Lewis wasn't wrong.

Pappy also brought in Bruce Bosley, a big strong tackle from Greenbank who played fullback in high school. I remember going to Morgantown my senior year to see the state high school basketball tournament and watching Bosley play. At the time, he was the best-built human being I had ever seen. He must have weighed 240 pounds, and it was all muscle. I mean the guy looked like L'il Abner on the basketball court. People would try to get by him on the baseline and just kind of bounce off him out of bounds.

Pappy also brought in two great running backs that year, Bobby Moss, an all-state kid from Huntington, and Joe Marconi, a 220-pound fullback from Fredericktown, Pennsylvania, about thirty miles from Morgantown. Marconi became my best friend in college; we roomed together for most of the four years and took most of our classes together. He didn't come to camp right away that freshman year because he had decided to go to the University of Maryland. The coach at Maryland, Jim Tatum, told him when he recruited him that he was the only fullback he was going after that year, but when Joe showed up at College Park, there were seven other guys ahead of him on the depth chart. He called Pappy, who had recruited him real hard anyway, and Joe made it to Morgantown in time to start the season for us.

He was one of the lucky ones. What I remember most

about that first year was the training camp. Lewis was a stickler for conditioning just the way Coach Kelly was, and we were on that practice field all day and what seemed like half the night. He'd also bring teams in from the outside to scrimmage us. The Quantico Marines always had a team and they'd come in there with all these guys who'd played college ball and it really was men against boys. I suppose I did all right because I was always practicing with the first or second team and I played a lot my freshman year.

We opened up against Furman, a team we were supposed to beat, and made about a million mistakes. We lost it 23–14, but late in the game, Lewis decided to give Wyant a chance. Freddy came in and threw a long touchdown pass and drove us to another score in the fourth quarter. It was too little, too late, but Lewis had himself a quarterback for the next four years. Freddy ran the split-T offense, with a fullback and two backs and the lineman taking big splits. We were a run-oriented team with a lot of option stuff, and mostly we just overpowered people. We did lose to Penn State, 34–21, early in the season, mainly because we couldn't stop their tight end, a big tough guy named Jesse Arnelle, but that was the last time we lost to Penn State while I was there, and also the last game we lost that season. We won our final six games and finished 7–2. That year the rules allowed two-platoon football and I spent most of the season playing middle guard on defense and some tackle on offense. By 1953, they had changed the substitution rule, and everybody played both ways.

My life at West Virginia pretty much revolved around the football team. That first year, I lived in the men's dormitory, and I wasn't crazy about that. It was two to a room and a bathroom shared with a couple of other guys. Lewis didn't believe in keeping his athletes together and away from the regular student population, like a lot of schools do now. There were times, though, when I wished it were just football players. One night about four o'clock in the morning, a kid from the next room came into our room and pissed on my foot. He'd gone out and gotten drunk and he thought my room was the bathroom. Let me tell you, that kid sobered up real quick, because I almost killed him. He doesn't know how lucky he is to be alive. You hear all these stories about the big rough tough football players wreaking havoc wherever they go, but it wasn't really like that for me at West Virginia. I wasn't a fraternity man. I hated the fraternity guys. I got to campus and I heard all this stuff about pledging, and I didn't even know what the hell they were talking about. Then I saw all these guys walking around campus with their little beanies and carrying their silly paddles, and I thought they were crazy. I didn't have time for that.

Pappy Lewis was a stickler about players going to class. I was no scholar in college, but Marconi and I hardly ever missed a class. I was a physical education major, and I thought I wanted to go back and teach and coach football. Pappy would tell us, "Now, boys, I can do a lot for you if you play here at West Virginia for me, but if you don't go to class, I can't help you, and I don't want you around." If you messed up, he would say, "If you don't like it, you can go get yourself a good ole number three shovel and go back to the mines."

There were no prima donnas, no spoiled-brat athletes, and none of us were being paid off. You hear all these horror stories about places like SMU, where kids take a pay cut when they go to the pros. Well, I don't think that happened when I was there. Don't get me wrong, people did things for the athletes. There was a guy named Freddie Cavallaro, who's still in Morgantown, and he had a little bar with some pinball machines we were always playing. That's where we'd go and Freddie would feed us chili and cheeseburgers. Jack Hines, the Goodyear tire dealer, would do things for the athletes. Once, Mary and I were driving back from New York to West Virginia on bald tires and she wouldn't even let me replace them until we got home and saw Jack. There was another guy named Harry (Has'em)

Goldsmith. He was called Has'em because he owned a clothing store and he had everything you needed. If you were picked as player of the week by the coaching staff, you could go to Harry's shop and pick out a new tie or a belt or a shirt. And he'd put your picture in the window. If you went to a movie, the guy at the door would let you in free. If you didn't have enough for a soft drink, the guy at Chico's Dairy Bar would serve you for nothing. Now all of that stuff was and still is against the rules, which is ridiculous. I'm not saying you have to pay the players, but there are times I believe the NCAA people are not realistic. They won't allow athletes to have jobs during the season, so why shouldn't a football player get a free hamburger at Roy Rogers? The NCAA expects kids to stay clean, and it's never going to happen, especially in this day and age.

All I was paid at college was room, board, and tuition and about ten dollars a month to do my laundry. Bobby Moss came from a big high school and was one of the most highly recruited backs in the country. I always thought he dressed a little better than the rest of us, always looked a little neater, so I figured he made a little extra money on the side. But I wasn't sure, and it's not something you'd ask. Hell, I roomed with Don Chandler for eight years on the Giants, and in all that time, I never asked him how much he was making and he never asked me. Nowadays, they print it in the newspapers; back then, it was nobody's business but your own.

I also know there weren't a lot of fat-cat alumni hanging around our locker room after the games. In fact, I didn't hang around there much after games myself. The only time I could get home was on the weekends, so I'd get dressed and hitch a ride to see Mary. Sometimes I'd leave a game and go over to the Manchins' grocery store and help Mary close up for the day. A few hours after the game, the big football hero would be stocking shelves or sweeping the floor while his wife added up the day's receipts. I had virtually no social life on campus. During the week, you went to class and then you went to practice. On the weekends, I went home. You had your fun playing intramural basketball or softball. The football players always got together a basketball team, and with me and Bosley playing forward, I guarantee you no one ever tried to come up the middle for a lay-up.

After my freshman season, I went home to Farmington. By this time, Mary and I had rented an apartment above a little grocery store about a block from Mary's parents' house. Living away from the in-laws worked out a lot better. Her father and I never got along. He had retired from the mines on a disability and he never really liked me very much. I have to admit the feeling was mutual. But when we moved out on our own, at least we had some privacy and a little room to breathe. Of course, it was only about a block from Mary's folks, so we had built-in day care for Sam Jr. while I was off at school and Mary was working. Through all four years of college, I kept working for John Manchin. Mary worked in his grocery store and I worked in his furniture business. I sold it, I moved it, I carried it up the stairs when I delivered it. I got paid minimum wage, and sometimes if times were tough in the business, I didn't get paid at all, but John was always there when I needed him and I like to think he says the same about me. In 1968, his furniture store was gutted in a fire. He lost everything. At the time, I wasn't exactly making a whole lot of money, but I sent him $10,000. I couldn't really afford it, but it didn't matter. John eventually paid me back, and that's the kind of relationship we've always had. In fact, my last three years at school, I lived with three other football players in a trailer John owned in Morgantown. Dormitory space was tight, and we saved a few dollars in the trailer. There wasn't a whole lot of space and four guys shared two double beds, but at the time, it was the best we could do.

Joe Marconi and I are still known back at West Virginia as the "gold dust twins," probably because we were always trying to make a little extra money on the side.

When we were at West Virginia, Hot Rod Hundley was

the big basketball star, and he'd pack them into the field-house every time they played. There were two parking lots on each side of the fieldhouse, and they were always reserved for the media.

Most of the time those lots were pretty empty. So I worked out a deal with the building superintendent. Joe and I worked at a dollar an hour as maintenance men keeping the place clean, sweeping up after games. We were on the clock anyway, so I told the superintendent we'd go out and supervise the parking lots for him.

Joe went to one lot and I went to the other, and we charged two dollars a car for people to park there. If a reporter showed up, he'd park free, but everyone else paid, and we got to keep the money. I also got to know the state trooper who was watching the door, and we worked out a deal where he'd let people in at five dollars a head to stand and watch Hot Rod. One night, between the parking lot and the standing-room-only crowd, we split about three hundred dollars. All of it was in one-dollar bills, and when I took my cut home to Mary and threw all those bills on the bed, she asked:

"Where'd you get all that money?"

"Robbed a bank," I told her, and she started crying. She really believed me.

One night, Barbara Schaus, the wife of Fred Schaus, then the basketball coach, now the school's athletic director, drove up to our lot. I didn't recognize her, and I asked her for two dollars.

"I'm the coach's wife and you're going to charge me two dollars?" she asked indignantly.

"No, ma'am," I said, "you just park wherever you like."

She parked her car, but she wasn't happy. The athletic director heard about it, and before long, not only did we lose our parking-lot concession, we also got fired from our fieldhouse maintenance jobs. It was nice while it lasted, and if the NCAA had ever found out about it, I suppose we would have been in deep trouble. Hell, we were just two poor kids trying to make a buck.

You spent so much time with the team that most of your friends were football players, and that was fine with me. One of my best friends was Tommy Allman, who played fullback for West Virginia and is still very active in the letterman's club. Today he sells insurance. Back then, he made a lot of guys wish they'd had a policy.

Jesse Arnelle was one of them. In my sophomore year, Allman hit Arnelle so hard he stood him straight up and broke his nose. I don't believe Arnelle was ever the same football player after Tommy got through with him that day.

Allman came from Charleston, West Virginia, and he was a character, a barroom brawler who liked to have a good time. He never lifted a weight in his life, but he could still take on any of today's players and whip 'em in arm wrestling. He was always in the coach's doghouse because he wasn't a great practice player, but Pappy loved him because he came to play on Saturdays.

They would never let us practice on the Mountaineer Stadium field because they wanted it perfect for game-days, so they'd put us on a bus and drive us out to a field on another part of campus. One day, Tommy decided he was going to try warming up bare-footed. Unfortunately, while he was prancing around out there, he stepped on a piece of glass and just tore up his foot, three days before we were supposed to play Pittsburgh, one of our biggest rivals. They sewed him up, and somehow Tommy managed to start the Pitt game. But after a few plays, he came out and hobbled up to our team doctor, an old guy named Sam Morris who'd graduated from Maryland in 1912. "Doc," he said, "my foot's killing me, you gotta give me something for the pain."

So old Doc Morris pulled off his shoe and Tommy's sock was just all blood. Doc said, "Well, son, I've got to pump a little painkiller into that foot." So he took a needle that looked to be about a foot long out of his medical bag and just jabbed Tommy with it, right through the sock. That's right, on the sidelines, in full view of thousands of people, and he didn't even take the sock off. How Allman didn't get blood poisoning, I'll never know, but I'll be damned if he didn't get his shoe back on and finish the game. That's how tough Tommy Allman was.

He also had a sense of humor. For some reason, we always had trouble with equipment managers. They constantly gave the athletes a hard time and always thought they were the most important people on the team. The equipment room was their little kingdom, and they made sure you knew it. One day, Tommy got into an argument with Soupy Roberts, the equipment manager. Soupy gave Tommy an old pair of shoes for practice, and Tommy didn't like the way they fit, so he asked for a new pair. Soupy wouldn't do it. "You can't have a new pair because we don't have any for you right now," he told him.

So Tommy found a big cardboard box and went around to each player's locker. He put every pair of shoes he could find in that box, carried it right past the coaches' offices and out the door. There was a river near the school and Tommy crossed the bridge and just threw all those shoes over the side. Everybody got a new pair of shoes. The hell of it was, Tommy never even got in trouble for it. I really think some of the coaches were scared of him. He was absolutely—and still is—the toughest guy I have ever known.

One day he got me in a heap of trouble with Art Lewis. In my sophomore year, Pappy had gotten upset with the team after a couple of so-so performances and decided to bench me, more for psychological purposes than anything else. But I was steaming. We were at practice, and I was pouting, jogging at half-speed through the workout and not paying much attention because I was so mad. My good friend Allman knew I was burned up and yelled across the field, "Hey, Sam, how's come you're not running?"

I yelled back at him, "When you play second team, you don't need to work, you don't need to run." I knew

Pappy heard me, I wanted him to hear me, and oh boy, did he get mad. He ran over to me, grabbed me by the shirt, and said, "Let me tell you something, Huff. You'll run when I say run, and you'll shut up when I say shut up. Now when I put you down, you better run." I said "yessir" and that big old bushy-browed man put me down and I ran.

But Art Lewis always used to tell his players, if you thought you were better than the guy playing ahead of you, "Come and tell me and we'll arrange to see who should be playing." So that's what I did. "Okay," he said, "we'll do the nutcracker drill tonight at practice." The "nutcracker" meant you took two blocking bags and put them side by side, with about three yards between them. The players face each other in that three-yard space and go one-on-one, head-to-head. The guy still standing won the starting spot. So Pappy matched me up that night against the man who was ahead of me on the depth chart, a senior named Frank Federovitch. I didn't like him much anyway because he was one of those fraternity guys—a beanie and paddle man. Well, I outweighed him by about twenty pounds, and I destroyed him in the nutcracker drill, just dominated him. Pappy was true to his word, too. I started the next game.

The 1953 team may have been the greatest in the school's history. We won our first five games, including a 17–7 win in the opener over a Pitt team that the following week tied the great Oklahoma Sooners coached by Bud Wilkinson. I was starting at defensive guard and offensive guard—they moved me to tackle my senior year—and by midseason, the bowl scouts were descending on Morgantown.

The Sugar Bowl people became very interested after we beat Penn State, 20–19, when Bosley blocked a punt and recovered in the end zone for the winning touchdown. Penn State also had a great team that year, including a huge, 290-pound defensive tackle named Roosevelt Grier. Years later we became teammates and good friends on the Giants, but when we were in college, there was no love lost. He also was the first black player I'd ever gone up against, but when you had to play Rosey, you didn't think in terms of black and white—you just worried about getting through in one piece.

We had an outstanding line coach at West Virginia, Russ Crane, and every spring practice, he would work with Bruce and me on blocking and tackling technique with Rosey in mind. Russ had studied the films and decided the best way to block Rosey was to always hit him low. Rosey never liked that very much, and it was always effective against him. There were times I felt like a sand crab out on the practice field, but it worked. Russ also taught me how to grab a guy and still not get caught for holding. Pappy and Russ Crane always told us the key to beating Penn State was controlling Rosey Grier. Before that game sophomore year, Pappy Lewis told me that if I could handle Grier, he'd get me a suit of clothes. So I called him on it after we won, and he delivered. Only it was one of his old suits, like a size fifty-two with these big lapels. It looked like something the Godfather would wear. Some football players get money; I got a used suit that was three sizes too big.

Allman ran 55 yards in the last quarter the next week to help us beat Virginia Tech, 12–7, our seventh straight win of the season and thirteenth in a row over two years, but we couldn't stand prosperity. The following week, we had a record 31,000 in the stadium, but that didn't stop South Carolina from beating us at home, 20–14, on a fourth-quarter punt return. But the Sugar Bowl took us anyway, matching us against a Georgia Tech team with Pepper Rodgers at quarterback.

The Sugar Bowl should have been one of the great experiences in my life. Instead, it was one of the most embarrassing and miserable experiences I've ever had.

For one thing, we treated it like a big holiday. They flew the team down there, including the wives, and that was a mistake. It should have been just another game on the road, a regular business trip. But we had to go down early, and we were headquartered in Biloxi, Mississippi, about sev-

2 6

enty miles from New Orleans. We were practicing at the local high school field and nothing was the same as it usually was. Georgia Tech, meanwhile, was doing it the right way. We went down there on December 20, almost two weeks before the game. Tech came in the weekend of the game. For a lot of us, it was a totally new experience. Even Pappy seemed a little concerned. "Some of these boys have never been out of the hills and you can't tell what will happen when they get to this part of the country," he told a New Orleans quarterback club luncheon a few weeks before the game. "But no matter what happens, they'll be hitting hard on New Year's Day."

It was not a pleasant experience away from the practice field either. Mary came down and she was not happy. She was homesick. They'd take us all on these silly tours of Bourbon Street and things like that. I was going crazy. We really couldn't afford her trip; she was in the room crying and I was going batty. We had a real bad argument one night because she wanted to go see a show at the Roosevelt Hotel in New Orleans and I didn't want any part of it. She stormed off and went anyway, and I stayed in the room. If I'd had any money, she would have flown back home.

Actually, a couple of nights before the game I did get some money. It was the only illegal cash I was ever paid. We were having a team banquet and Pappy Lewis got up and said, "Boys, I want you to look under your plates right now." So we looked under our plates and every player got a brand-new twenty-dollar bill. It was the first twenty I'd ever had to call my own.

There was another first on that trip. I learned to like eating shrimp. In West Virginia, we used shrimp for bait when we went fishing. Now I'm at a banquet in Biloxi and they're serving us shrimp cocktail and I'm saying are you crazy, there's no way I'll eat that fish bait. Well, someone talked me into it and, thanks to the mustard sauce, I survived that terrible ordeal. I can't say the same for the football game.

Tech was coached by the great Bobby Dodd, and he had a good quick team that liked to throw the football. We always had trouble with good passing attacks because our defense was designed to stop the run, and with Rodgers, Tech had one of the best quarterbacks in the country. That day he proved it. He completed 16 of 26 for 195 yards and three touchdowns and Tech murdered us, 42–19.

The game left a bitter taste in my mouth for years—in fact, it still does. Two things happened that made a major difference. For one, we were down, 14–6, when Marconi dropped a touchdown pass from Wyant in the end zone. Number two, Allman took a pitchout, went to the outside, and ran 60 yards for a first-quarter touchdown. Just as he broke clear, the umpire looked right at me, threw his handkerchief down, and said, "You're holding." Hell, I never even blocked the guy, and when we looked at the films afterward, there was no holding anywhere along the line. Call it sour grapes, but I believe the fact that we were a Northern team playing against a Southern team in the South just might have influenced that umpire. Officials play such a big part in a football game and I even see it today. Sometimes they may even have a favorite team. They're normal, they're human. In the 1953 Sugar Bowl, there's no doubt in my mind that official cheated when he brought back that touchdown.

The next season, we won eight out of nine games, including a 19–14 win over Penn State, but didn't get a bowl bid. After the egg we laid in New Orleans, the major bowls were reluctant to give us another chance, even if we did have a great football team. They should have, because we'd had bowl experience and probably would have handled it differently. But you lose an opportunity like that and it's very hard to recover. The biggest bowl game West Virginia's been to since was a Gator Bowl in 1982. You blow a bowl game like we blew the Sugar Bowl, and it stays with you forever.

By 1955, we were being touted for a top ten finish in the polls and maybe even another bowl game. In addition to the usual cast of characters—Bosley, Wyant, Moss, Marconi, and me—we also added a sophomore linebacker named Chuck Howley. Chuck went on to star for the Dallas Cowboys, but back then, he was better known around the state for being a talented gymnast. At West Virginia, he'd even perform at halftime of the basketball games.

The season was memorable for several reasons. For the third straight time, we beat Penn State, something I believe no other school had ever accomplished. I know we made an impression on a young assistant coach for the Nittany Lions. A few years ago, I was doing the radio broadcast for an Alabama-Penn State game in the Sugar Bowl and I introduced myself to Joe Paterno, who was an assistant to Rip Engel at Penn State when I was playing. I held out my hand and said, "Coach, I'd like to say hello, I'm Sam Huff." He looked at me and said, "Number seventy-five."

"No, sir," I said, "number seventy," which is what I wore in the pros.

"Not at West Virginia you didn't," he told me. "You know, Sam, we had another assistant who did the scouting for us and when he gave the team his report, he'd always give everybody's number. I'll never forget this scout telling us that everybody talks about the left tackle, number seventy-seven, Bruce Bosley, but that Huff, number seventy-five, he's the guy who's killing everybody. Nobody talks about him, but he's the guy you better watch out for." Joe Paterno definitely made my day.

There was another first in my senior year. I was knocked out for the first time in my life, against mighty Marquette, of all teams. We were playing in Milwaukee, and all of a sudden, someone turned the lights out on me. I woke up on the sidelines, and nobody could tell me what had happened. Then we watched the film the next week and it became very apparent what had happened. The guy I had been playing against just hit me in the jaw with his fist. I found out later he was the school's heavyweight boxing champion, and I could understand why. He just flat-out cold-cocked me. And I have no memory of that game.

I do have a lot of memories about the Syracuse game that year. We had to play it without Wyant and Howley, both on the injured list, but that's not what made it so memorable.

This was the first of many meetings between me and Jim Brown, and there was no question who came out ahead this time.

Syracuse had a good football team that year; any team that had Jim Brown on it was a good football team. Russ Crane had scouted them and he came into a meeting and said to us, "Gentlemen, I want to tell you something. They have a guy who's the best damned football player you've ever seen. His name is Jim Brown and he wears number forty-four. And he has the ability to go all the way every time he touches the ball. You better keep it away from him. Don't even kick it to him." Well, we had a good team, too, and we were kind of cocky. What the hell, we were kids, we were football players, and we didn't pay all that much attention to the opposition. In this case, that was a very big mistake. Now it was game day, and we were in our huddle before the opening kickoff. I had a pretty good leg back then and handled the kickoffs. So Wyant said to me, "Don't kick it down there, Jim Brown's down there."

I looked down the field, and there was the biggest running back I'd ever seen. He had huge shoulders and arms, no hips, and huge legs, the perfectly built human being. But Mountaineer Stadium is a horseshoe and the wind was blowing in my face from the open end and I said to Wyant, "Don't worry about it, I can't kick it that far."

Or so I thought. For one of the few times in my life, I really nailed that kick, and of course it went right to Brown at the goal line. He caught that ball and went through us like we were not even there, guys bounced off him left and right until he was in the open field. *Phoooom.* Bobby Moss managed to catch him from behind at the ten and now it was the first play from scrimmage, and my friend Joe Marconi was playing linebacker. Brown came through the hole and ran right over poor Joe, just flattened him and scored. But they called it back on a penalty. They scored a few plays later, and Brown had definitely made an impact on our football team. Even so, we were still leading, 13–7, at the half, but when we came out on the field, Jimmy said to me, "That was your half, baby, but this one's ours."

Now it was early in the third quarter, and here came Jim Brown through a hole and there I was to meet him. I hit that big sucker head-on and my head gear snapped down and cut my nose and my teeth hit together so hard the enamel popped off. He broke my nose, broke my teeth, and knocked me cold.

I woke up in the training room with an ice pack on my head and my nose bleeding. My teeth were killing me. I always took great pride in those teeth, in fact people always used to tease me about my nice, big smile. Well, it wasn't so nice anymore. I was lying there and my tongue was going over all these rough edges and I was screaming, "My teeth are gone, my teeth are gone."

It wasn't quite that bad, but it's a day I'll never forget. He got the best of me that first time. But believe me, over the next ten years, I more than paid him back.

3

A few weeks after our season ended at West Virginia, the National Football League held the first part of its player draft. They were concerned about competition for players from the Canadian league, so in December they chose the first three rounds and immediately tried to get the best guys under contract. Nowadays, the NFL makes a major production out of the draft. There's a big buildup in the newspapers, everybody wonders who's going to take who and in what round, and they put the whole thing on television, which to me is sort of watching the grass grow.

Back then, I didn't really know much about the draft, or pro football for that matter. It did not dominate the sports pages the way it does now and quite frankly, the prospect of playing professional football never really intrigued me. I had listened to the Pittsburgh Steelers games on the radio as a kid and I knew that Frank Gatski from my hometown of Farmington was playing for the Cleveland Browns, but I really thought that when my senior year ended, my football career was probably over. I was more concerned about getting my degree, and I just figured I'd be getting into coaching or teaching when I left Morgantown.

In those days, there was nothing very sophisticated about the draft. There weren't that many scouts and a lot of teams just took the All-American lists and tried to get those guys on draft day. Bruce Bosley and I had made most of the All-American teams; the ones he made, I didn't, and vice versa. Somebody told me once the reason we both weren't consensus All-Americans was that most of the writers didn't want to pick two guys from the same team at the same position. Somebody else told me Bosley probably made a couple of teams ahead of me because his name started with B and the writers saw his name first on their player lists. Bosley got most of the press coverage in our senior year, but I never paid much attention to that; it never really bothered me because I knew he was a great football player. I loved the game and I was happy just to be out on the field. I later found out the reason the New York Giants got interested in me in the first place was because of Bosley. They sent one of their personnel men, Al De-Rogatis, to Morgantown to check Bruce out. Al had been a starting lineman for the Giants back in the early 1950s before knee injuries ended his playing career and he went on to become one of the best network football analysts years later. After he retired as a player, the Giants used him to scout the colleges part-time, and when he saw us play in the fall of 1955, he wrote in his report that "Bosley is great . . . but there's another guard down there who will be even greater. His name is Sam Huff."

I'm told that on the strength of that report, the Giants made me their third-round draft choice that year. Bosley was drafted number one by San Francisco and Marconi number one by the Los Angeles Rams. But none of us really knew what to make of it: hell, the Giants didn't even ask me to come to New York after the draft. I read that they picked me in the newspaper.

My first contact with the Giants came a few weeks after the draft. I had been selected for the *Look Magazine* All-American team and the magazine flew us all in to New York for a picture session. It really was a big deal. *Look* actually sent a plane around the country to pick up all the guys. They hired a young up-and-coming actress named Kim

Novak to serve as our hostess and of course Paul Hornung immediately tried to put the moves on her. Hornung was only a nineteen-year-old junior quarterback at Notre Dame, but he was first-team All-American, and a first-team skirt-chaser, too. Like the man says, you have to practice, practice, practice. No one got very far with Kim Novak, who was kind of stuck up and aloof, I thought, but we had an interesting time in New York. There were some great people on that *Look* team: Hopalong Cassidy, a fine running back from Ohio State; Earl Morrall, a crew-cut quarterback at Michigan State; Jim Parker, a huge guard from Ohio State, and Rommie Loudd, an end from UCLA who later went on to own a franchise in the World Football League before they indicted him and sent him to prison on a cocaine charge.

Anyway, we were in New York for about a week. They had a big dinner for us at Gene Leone's Restaurant, gave us a Lord Elgin watch, and even put us on the Jackie Gleason television show. We were staying at the Hotel Lexington in Manhattan, and one day, Wellington Mara, then and now the owner of the Giants, called and said he wanted to talk to me about joining the team that summer. He said he wanted to discuss a contract and I was agreeable, though I have to admit I really didn't understand what this contract business was all about. In those days, nobody thought about having a lawyer or an agent represent you. If you had tried that, the owner wouldn't even have talked to you. There was no such thing as playing out your option and becoming a free agent. If anyone had done it, they'd have been frozen out of the league. Nobody would admit it, but there was a gentlemen's agreement among the owners not to sign anybody else's players. If you didn't like what they offered, you could hold out, but that didn't work very often.

Mara came over to the hotel one afternoon and at some point in our conversation he offered me $5,000 for the year. I may have been a country boy from West Virginia, but I told him I didn't think I could play for that, not with a wife and child to support.

"Well, what will you play for?" he asked me.

I told him $7,000, and he said that might be possible. Before I left Morgantown, though, I had promised Art Lewis I'd call him before I signed anything, and I told Wellington Mara I still had to run it by Pappy. So I found a telephone and phoned him.

"Mr. Mara wants me to sign for seven thousand, what do you think?"

"Son," he said, "that's like stealing money. You get right back over there and sign that contract before he changes his mind."

So I agreed to my first professional contract on the spot. Then Mara asked me if I needed any money. I told him that Mary and I had just bought some furniture and we owed about $500. "No problem," he said, and wrote me a check for $500, which I thought was a bonus. Later on, when I made the team and we got our first paychecks after the first game of the 1956 season, I opened the check and $500 had been deducted. So I went to Wellington and asked him what was going on, why was I shorted $500? "That's an advance I gave you when you signed the contract," he told me. "You gotta learn, Sammy, in this business, there's a big difference between a bonus and an advancement."

I never did get that $500 back, but it taught me a very important lesson about professional football and the people who held the power in the game. It's the same kind of lesson a lot of players learned last year during the NFL strike. Sure it's a game on Sunday, but bottom-line it's a business, buddy, and don't ever forget it.

Believe it or not, that meeting with Wellington Mara was my last contact with the Giants until I got a letter telling me when and where to report for training camp the next summer. It was nothing like the system they use now. A college kid today starts getting attention from the pros the day he walks on campus as a freshman. The scouts come to the practices, they weigh you and time you and poke you and ask people about you and watch hours upon hours of film. Then when they draft you, they bring you right in for classroom work, put you on a conditioning program, and start teaching you their system long before you go to training camp in July. They have minicamps for rookies alone, then more minicamps for the rookies and regulars. There's virtually no off-season, and a lot of guys simply stop going to classes after their college season ends because they figure they'll never be able to finish their course work after they're drafted, so why bother?

After my senior season, I played in a couple of all-star games over the holidays—the North-South game in Florida and the Senior Bowl in Mobile, and that was it for football. I hardly ever missed a class, and the prospect of not graduating on time never even occurred to me. Hell, the fact that I was the first kid in the family to get a college degree was more than enough incentive to keep me going.

The North-South game was a miserable experience. Pappy Lewis was coaching the North team, so he picked five of us to play in the game—me, Bosley, Wyant, Marconi, and Moss, and all the players drove down together. That's what made it so miserable. I don't know how, but Wyant had a car, and he was just learning how to drive. Freddy was a great agitator; he'd tease you and make fun of you and give people a hard time, but he couldn't take it himself. So we were driving down the road, giving him a hard time about his driving, and he was getting madder and madder and started to floor it. We're going around curves and it feels like we're on two wheels he's going so fast. I was so scared I actually crouched on the floor preparing for the inevitable crash. Freddy finally calmed down and we made it there in one piece. When we got into Florida, Bosley was fascinated by the orange and grapefruit groves and made Freddy stop so he could pick the fruit. I don't remember much about the game, but I'll never forget that drive.

A few weeks later, I went to the Senior Bowl in Mobile, Alabama, and that was a first-class operation. They flew me down, and even better, they paid me $500, the first time I'd ever been paid to play football, other than the Sugar Bowl $20.

The rest of my senior year was spent trying to finish up my classes and graduate. That spring, I played catcher on the West Virginia team and I did well enough to attract some attention from the scouts. In fact, I wasn't able to walk across the stage and graduate with my class because I was signed to play minor league baseball by the Cleveland Indians. I had played baseball all my life, and in college, I played some semi-pro all around the state. Wyant and I spent a lot of time playing for the Swaney Coal Company team, and the scouts were always coming around. I can't tell you how much I signed for, other than to tell you it wasn't a lot. I figured I could play ball until pro football started in August, and the Indians signed me and assigned me to their Class A team in Reading, Pennsylvania.

Mostly it was a waste of time. I spent most of the games that summer warming up pitchers in the bullpen. The manager was a guy named Don Heffner, and he never let me play, never put me in a game. One day I went up to him and asked him why I couldn't get into a game. He told me he wanted to throw a good pitcher at me in batting practice to see how I'd do. So the next day, we took batting practice and I was knocking the ball out of the park fairly consistently; I was a big strong guy and had pretty good power. Then Heffner came up to me and said, "We think you can hit, but we don't think you can catch good enough to make it in the majors."

At that point, I said to myself, "Let me outta here." I wasn't crazy about baseball life anyway. You'd get on a bus and ride forever, then they'd put you in these fleabag YMCAs and you'd spend all day eating greasy cheeseburgers waiting to play a night game. It was terrible, especially if you weren't playing. To this day, I'm not sure why the

Indians wasted their time on me. Baseball seemed so political; the best guys definitely weren't on the field on our team, though we did have a couple of pretty good pitchers. That's where Jim (Mudcat) Grant started his career, and Gary Bell, too. And that's where my baseball career ended. In a hurry.

It was all for the good because by early August, I had to report to practice for the College All-Star game. Bruce and I were both on the All-Star team, and we drove from Morgantown to Evanston, Illinois, in yet another memorable trip. Bruce took his wife Barbara and they had a baby, Brucie, and he came, too. I spent the entire trip in the backseat of the car, taking care of little Brucie.

The College All-Star game was canceled a few years ago because it really was no contest. You'd take a bunch of college players from all over the country, work them out together for a couple of weeks, then make them go out and play the defending world champions in the first exhibition game. It was usually no contest, and the year I played in it, we got slaughtered, 26–0 by a very good Cleveland Browns team.

Still, I thought it was a very big deal. You played the game for the *Chicago Tribune* charities, and we practiced at Northwestern University in Evanston. Every day you'd see crowds of reporters hanging out, and fans would come by the hundreds to watch us practice. Our coach that year was Curly Lambeau, a dapper, well-dressed guy who always smoked a cigarette with a holder. He looked very Park Avenue, and not at all like a football coach. To tell you the truth, he didn't do much coaching. We did a lot of basic stuff, nothing fancy, and they put me on offense at guard. I didn't even practice with the defense. That was okay with me. When I went to Evanston, I just had one goal in mind: I wanted to be introduced with the starting team, and I was. That's always been a motivation for me. I don't know why, but I had this burning desire to be somebody; I wanted to be noticed, I wanted to be recognized.

Some guys will deny it, but that's what they're playing for. Nowadays, you're recognized for how much money you make, and I think that's wrong.

Anyway, I was recognized plenty in the All-Star game, mostly by the referees. I was playing against a veteran lineman named Don Colo, and as one writer at the time suggested, he gave me an instant introduction to submarine warfare. I got penalized three times for a total of 45 yards for throwing punches. I just plain lost my temper. He kept giving me these head slaps, which were legal, and my ears were ringing all night. I also learned that game that it's always the second guy in a fight who gets caught, because that's exactly what happened. I'd be damned if I was going to take it, that's just not my nature. But the thing I had to learn about football was that it was controlled violence. It's definitely a violent game, but you have to keep your emotions in check or you'll get thrown out every time.

When it was over, we knew this had been another case of men against boys. You just can't expect a bunch of twenty-two-year-old kids to be able to hold their own against seasoned pros, especially a team that won the world championship. I wasn't that upset about losing the game—after all, it was only an all-star game, just an exhibition. But I was beat up physically, just battered and bruised all over. There truly would be no rest for the weary.

The day after the game, five Giant rookies on the All-Star team—myself, Jim Katcavage, Don Chandler, Henry Moore, and Hank Burnine—had to fly East to join the Giants in training camp.

Back then, the team spent the summer at St. Michael's College in Winooski, Vermont. To this day I'm not sure why, except that the climate was a little cooler than New York would have been in August, and the Maras liked being associated with a Catholic school. When we broke camp, in fact, we also trained at Fordham. Wellington Mara always liked to have a priest or two around, and what the hell, how could it hurt?

We all arrived at the Giant training camp stiff and sore and not knowing what to expect. We were rookies, we had no idea what was about to happen to us, and the Giants didn't help very much. In fact, two days after getting battered by the Browns, we were all expected to take part in the team's regular scrimmage on Sunday. The veterans had reported about two weeks earlier, and we were some fresh meat.

At our first dinner, we met the coach, Jim Lee Howell, a tough old bird from Arkansas and a man I disliked almost from the first minute I met him. He let us all know who the boss was right away; he laid out all the rules, talked about curfews and fines, and tried to put the fear of God into all of us. He also told us about the scrimmage, and he said whichever team won would get the next day off.

So we dragged ourselves into the scrimmage and they let me play a little defense. I'd played middle guard in college, and that's where they put me, nose guard straight up on the center. It was almost like playing middle line-backer because you can hit and pursue and go where you have to go. Well, I made a lot of plays that day, really got off to a fast start. The best thing I did, though, came late in the scrimmage. Chandler went back to punt and I slipped the center and came in on him all alone. I just picked the ball right off his foot and ran about 60 yards for a touch-down. My team won the scrimmage, and I was really looking forward to a day off to ease some of my pain.

It never happened. Despite what Howell told us, we had to practice the next day, and that did not sit right with me. I've always believed that what a coach tells you ought to be the law. I don't like people who lie to me, and I didn't like Jim Lee Howell.

He also liked to pick on rookies, and I was a prime target. I really think Howell hated rookies. I'd be out there running and hustling and busting a gut and he'd yell across the field in that Arkansas drawl, "Huff, you're not run-ning." He'd push you and work you to death, which is okay. Some coaches can do that and then build you back up. Vince Lombardi was like that. He was the Giants' offensive coach that year, and despite everything you've ever heard, he knew when to stop driving and let a man breathe. Howell never knew how to do that. He never knew how to put his arm around you and get you back.

Truthfully, there were times I got so angry with him that I wanted to kill him. I'd hold onto my helmet and I had visions of just taking it and smashing him over the face with it if he said one more thing to me. I would have beaten him to a pulp, and to this day, I don't know why I didn't. Years later, after the Giants traded me in 1964, I told him that, told him how close he had come to dying. I told him how much I'd hated him and asked him why he'd done it. He just shook his head and said he didn't realize he'd been that way.

The veterans were not exactly friendly either. With only thirty-three guys on the whole team, they all knew we were there for one reason: to take their jobs. There was no camaraderie between the vets and the rookies like there is now. We definitely didn't sing our school song at the dining hall.

One of the first days of practice, I was walking onto the field and saw an old, gray-headed guy with a baseball cap on. I had done some kicking in college and I wanted to practice some place-kicking, so I asked him, "Hey, Coach, where's the kicking balls?" That was no coach, that was Charlie Conerly, the Giants' veteran starting quarterback. Dumb old country Sam made an immediate impression on one of the team's star players, and he was not amused. He just turned around and glared. "Don't you ever call me a coach, you smartass rookie," he said, and he wasn't joking. We can laugh about it now, years later. Back then, it was not funny.

In fact, there was nothing amusing about the situation. I was hurting, I was homesick, I was being yelled at by the head coach every day and they still didn't know where they wanted me to play, offense or defense, the line or line-backer.

Not too long after I got to camp, we played our first exhibition game in Boston against the Baltimore Colts. I'd spent most of the week working on the offensive line and, being a rookie, I was on most of the special teams, too. The Colts had a little guy named Buddy Young, all of five foot four, but that man could run with the football, and he was especially dangerous on punt returns. When I was at Farmington High School, Ray Kelly used to teach me that when you were running down on punts, you always followed the ball, which of course was exactly the way you're not supposed to do it. But no one had ever told me any different. So on the first kick of the game, I followed the flight of the ball, not looking at how the blocking was forming in front of me. Buddy got the ball, took a couple of steps, and wheeled around to go to the other side of the field. As he reversed his field, I got hit from the blind side and my knee buckled.

It was the first time in my life I'd ever had a knee injury, and I was sitting on the sidelines in a lot of pain. One of the Giants linemen, Walt Yowarsky, saw me sitting there with the ice on my knee and said, "Hey, rookie, you're supposed to be out there, now we gotta do it all," meaning that the veterans had to go down on the special teams. If I could have stood up, I would have slugged him, too.

When it was time to go back to Winooski after the game, we traveled by train, and those guys wouldn't even let me have a lower berth. I had a knee that was just killing me and I had to get into an upper; that tells you how much anybody cared about the rookies. I got no sympathy on the practice field, either. If you were hurt, you had to show up no matter what. Try standing around two-a-day practices holding 235 pounds up on crutches sometime.

Anyway, it didn't do much for my morale. I was feeling pretty low, to say the least, and so was my roommate, Chandler. About that time, there was a very popular song

4 2

playing on the radio called "Detroit City," and one of the lyrics really got to us. Every time we heard "I wanna go home" Chandler and I would tell each other if we heard it one more time, we were definitely goin' home.

Sure enough, I had no more than said it when that damned song came on the radio. "That's it," I said. "Let's go." And Chandler was more than willing.

We figured we had to turn in our playbooks. I was still practicing with the offense, and I went looking for Howell, but I couldn't find him. But Lombardi was lying on his bed, taking a quick nap between practices. We went into his room and woke him up. "Hey, Coach, we wanna turn in our playbooks." That was the first time I had ever seen Lombardi angry. He jumped out of that bed and just lit into us, called us every name in the book. Chandler got out of there, but I was on crutches with the bum knee and I could hardly move. Finally Lombardi calmed down and I left, still determined to go home. I went back up to the room and started packing. A few minutes later, there was a knock on the door and Ed Kolman, our line coach, came in.

"They tell me you're homesick and want to leave, Sam, is that right?" he asked. "Yes sir," I said. I also told him I couldn't take Jim Lee Howell anymore, I was tired of his picking on me and yelling at me.

"Sam," he told me, "you can be a star in this game. You can be a great player, but you've got to stay in camp and stick it out. If you stay, I'll talk to Jim Lee and get him off your back. But I want you to stay."

I said, "For you, I'll stay." But Chandler still wanted to go. There was no way Lombardi was going to coddle a homesick rookie, so Chandler talked me into going to the airport with him. He knew I was staying, but I guess he wanted some company. There was another kid there from Ohio State who had a car—Ohio State must have been paying more than West Virginia—and we rode to the Burlington Airport. We were sitting in the waiting room because there were no planes arriving or leaving, and all of a sudden, Vince Lombardi came stalking into the waiting lounge. Having raced to the airport in a team station wagon, he came right over to us and talked Chandler out of leaving.

Lombardi had a special thing for Chandler, really liked him and even traded for him when he left the Giants and went to the Packers. From that day on, Jim Lee Howell left both of us alone, but I have to say this: that man hurt some good football players. I just thank God I stuck it out.

4

When I first met Tom Landry, I don't believe he liked me very much. It was nothing personal; he was just not about to spend a lot of time with a raw rookie, especially a guy they couldn't even find a position for.

At 235 pounds, I was what you'd call a "tweener," too small to play on the offensive line and a little too big for a linebacker, so they kept playing me at both offense and defense in training camp before I was finally assigned to Landry full-time late in the summer.

The regular middle linebacker was Ray Beck, an All-American at Georgia Tech and a veteran known for his intelligence. Landry was in his first year as a full-time assistant coach after a great career as a defensive back for the Giants and several seasons as a player-coach after Howell got the head job in 1954. But now he was totally in charge of the defense, and Howell left him alone, just as he left Vince Lombardi alone with the offense. Tom was starting to develop what is now known as the 4–3 defense with Beck in mind, because he was a very mobile guy and a real student of the game.

Though my knee was getting better, I didn't play in most of the preseason games that summer. In those days, you played six exhibition games because that was all extra gravy for the owners. There was no billion-dollar television contract, so they scheduled games for us all over the country, many of them in cities that did not have an NFL franchise. Their player costs were minimal—hell, all you got was ten dollars a week in training camp. No health benefits, disability, or life insurance, and if you didn't like it, too bad, you could always go home.

As a player back then you essentially had no rights.

We had a tough offensive tackle named Dick Yelvington on the team, and one year, we were on our West Coast exhibition swing staying at a very nice hotel in Berkeley, California. We were going to be there for a week, and in those days, a lot of the hotels didn't have free TV in the rooms. So a few guys decided to rent TVs, thinking the team would pick up the extra expense because we were on the road. It was a dollar a day, and when we got our paychecks the next week, anyone who had rented a television had that money deducted. We were hardly getting enough money to tip the bellboys, and Yelvington was not happy about it.

That day, as he got on the bus to go to practice, he saw Wellington Mara, and he said something like, "I had a cup of coffee in the coffee shop, Wellington, why didn't you take that out of my paycheck, too?"

Wellington never said anything, but not long after that Yelvington was traded.

Once again, we all knew who had the power in the National Football League.

I'll tell you how tight the purse strings were. In camp, the equipment manager would put all the practice uniforms in boxes—jerseys in one box, jocks in another, sweat pants in another. One day I got there a little bit late and I went over to pick out my gear. Wellington Mara was right behind me because he used to like to change into sweats and cleats and be on the field with us for every practice. So I picked up a pair of sweat pants, about the only ones left, and the crotch was worn out they were so old. I started to think that maybe Mara would come to my rescue, tell me that they had some new ones coming in; after all, you couldn't expect the owner to wear these old rags. Was I ever mistaken. "Hey, Sam, that's all we've got to work with," he said to me. "Just put a pair of shorts on underneath, they'll be okay."

Our locker room was under the chow hall at St. Michael's. Each guy had a little cubicle in what amounted to the furnace room. You'd come off the practice field on a hot summer day and walk into a shower room that was probably twenty degrees warmer. You'd get in a shower—there weren't that many to begin with—and by the time you got dressed and walked outside, you'd be soaked in sweat. If owners tried to do that to players today, they'd have a revolt on their hands. These guys nowadays have no conception of what we put up with; they're spoiled.

I missed most of the exhibitions because of my bad knee, but Ray Beck was also hobbling on a bum ankle. We were supposed to play the Chicago Cardinals in Memphis, Tennessee, late in the exhibition season, and early that week, Landry asked me if I'd ever thought about playing middle linebacker. I told him I hadn't really, but he asked me to give it a try.

I had always played middle guard or what people now call nose tackle in college, so it wasn't that unusual to find me in the middle of the defense. In fact, while the Giants were experimenting with the 4–3, they also worked on the 5–2, and I'd been practicing at nose guard most of the summer. When I made the move, though, it just seemed so natural. Before, I had always had my head down looking right into the center's helmet. Now, I was standing up and I could see everything, and I mean *everything*. I always had outstanding peripheral vision—I can still see things out of the corner of my eye. Sonny Jurgensen kids me now about being able to see the whole field from the radio booth, but it's true. I really believe it's one of the reasons I was so perfectly suited for the position. Anyway, that night against the Cardinals, I had a great game. I was making tackles left and right, which was another ability you have to have to play the position, especially the way Landry designed it with the plays funneling to me. I had also been drilled to death on tackling by Russ Crane at West Virginia. Every night Bosley and I were out there with that tackling dummy, and very few people had that kind of background.

I was feeling pretty good about myself after the Cardinal game, but Landry was not about to start me in the season opener the next week against San Francisco. Beck's ankle had improved, so Landry went with the veteran. But he got hurt again, and I got in for a few plays. Nothing spectacular, but I did make a contribution in a big win over a San Francisco team with Y. A. Tittle at quarterback.

Now we were going to Chicago for our second game. Back then, the Giants were always opening on the road because the Yankees were still playing baseball. Actually, 1956 was our first season at Yankee Stadium after the Maras decided to leave the ancient and somewhat decrepit Polo Grounds. They had gotten a million-dollar offer to sell the team from a syndicate that wanted to move the Giants across the East River to Yankee Stadium. They rejected the buy-out, but liked the idea of playing in a more modern park. They especially liked the idea of 67,000-plus seats.

Beck was still hurt for the Chicago game, but Landry was leery about starting me at middle linebacker. He decided to move Harland Svare from an outside position into the middle, but Harland never could master the middle, and this day was no exception. The Cardinals also surprised us because they came out in a split-T offense centered around a great running back, Ollie Matson. He was a big man and he could fly, and the Cardinals tore us up. I didn't even play that day, except for the special teams, and it was very frustrating. The Cardinals had something else up their sleeve, a little electronic hanky-panky. Their coach, Ray Richards, was using transistors to communicate with his quarterback and his defensive captain to call all the signals, and we lost, 35–27. I'm not sure the transistors were totally responsible, but we went into our next game with a few gadgets of our own.

Jim Lee didn't believe in that stuff, but just in case, we had a little transistor trick ready. The Browns, under Paul Brown, also were using transistors to communicate with the quarterback, but somehow we were able to tune into their wave length. We had a rookie end named Bobby Topp sitting on the end of our bench listening to Brown call the plays. He'd relay the information to Landry, and Landry would tell us what plays were coming. Unfortunately, it didn't last very long. The Browns had the usual capacity crowd for their home opener, and their quarterback, George Ratterman, couldn't hear Brown over the roar of the crowd. So they scrapped the radio stuff and we went at each other just like we always did.

Beck came back to start that week, but he was hurt again early in the game and Landry sent me in to replace him. Paul Brown didn't get to the Hall of Fame for being stupid; he knew if there was a rookie middle linebacker out there, he was going to take the play right to him.

The Browns always liked to give the ball to a big back, and this year it was Ed Modzelewski, the older brother of my teammate Dick. We lined up in that 4-3 defense, and it seemed like every time I looked up, here was Big Mo coming right at me. He'd plow through there, and I'd meet him head-on, play after play after play. Andy Robustelli, who joined the Giants that year in a trade from Los Angeles, did his part by sacking Ratterman six times, and we won the football game, 21-9.

In all honesty, it may have been the finest football game I ever played. From that day on, I was the starting middle linebacker for the New York Giants, and Tom Landry began paying a lot of attention to me. A bunch of us were living together at the old Excelsior Hotel on Eighty-first Street right off Central Park on the West Side of Manhattan. Nobody wanted to give you a short-term lease for an apartment, and almost everyone went home after the season anyway, so a lot of the players, and even some of the coaching staff, stayed in this apartment-hotel. Landry lived there, too, and most every night that year, he'd come down to my apartment or I'd go up to his and we'd talk about defense, discuss philosophy, situations, how to react to what was going on.

That's really how we developed the 4–3 defense. It was kind of simple when you think about it. We'd have the inside 4–3 where the defensive tackle would shut off the middle and the linebackers would pursue to the outside, or we'd go to the outside 4–3, where the tackle would angle outside and I would come up the middle and make a play in there, or catch the play from behind. All the years we played, that's all I ever did. We got so good at it, it became almost second nature to everyone on the unit. That first year, Landry called the signals. If he had his hand on his hip, we'd go to the inside 4–3. If he put his hand on his belly, we'd throw in a blitz.

At first, he wanted me to play off the center, and then try to pursue. But that caused some problems because I'd get caught in traffic and I couldn't get there to make the tackle. So I said to him, "Why don't you let Mo and Rosey Grier take care of the middle and let me go with the flow of the backfield?" He put them both in a four-point stance, which they weren't crazy about, and they plugged up the middle and let me roam sideline-to-sideline.

Landry was one of the first people to set up his defenses against the strength of the formation. Every offensive formation has its strength and its weakness, and every defense has its strengths and weaknesses. So Tom would meticulously set up the defense to play against the strength of the offense. We would always line up in a 4–3 and give the offensive team the same look, but once the ball was snapped, we had all kinds of looks, depending on what we keyed on. Before Landry, teams would line up in that 4–3 and just go after the ball. But Tom would tell us to watch the way the backs lined up, to watch what side of the field the tight end and the flanker were lined up on. Those were the keys to what the offense would do. So we would roll our zone defense to the strength of the formation and react accordingly when the ball was snapped. It really was a very simple concept, and when you watched it on film, it was a thing of beauty.

Landry was a genius then and now. In effect, he made me the first designated hitter in sports. He was a very methodical guy, and that's always been his great strength. He would also treat his players like professionals. His theory was don't expect me to pat you on the back and tell you what a great job you did. You're a pro, we expect you to do a good job, that's what we pay you for. Even today, if you watch him on the sidelines, when a guy scores a touchdown, or kicks a field goal, or makes a big play on defense, he never even looks at him coming off the field.

Because of that, a lot of people think Tom Landry is unemotional, that he doesn't care about people. His own players have said that; Duane Thomas and that "plastic man" crap. That's because they don't know him. If they really did, they'd know he cares very deeply about his players—always has, always will. I even asked Tom about it once, and his answer said a lot about the man.

"Sam," he answered, "I believe my team reacts the way I react, so if I give in and get upset when one of my players gets hurt or goes down and I become too emotional, I think the other players would see that and maybe lose concentration on what they're supposed to be doing. I never want emotion to break my concentration on the task at hand."

Landry's great strength was as a planner. In fact, his whole life has been to plan, plan, and plan some more, and that's why I believe we were so successful in New York. We were prepared for every eventuality, and that's how you win football games.

Of course, we also had some very talented people to work with. In addition to me and Chandler, the Giants that year had drafted defensive end Jim Katcavage out of Dayton, a guy I believe is probably one of the most underrated players in the history of the game. In the off-season, the

Giants had also put some other pieces of the puzzle together.

The Robustelli deal was really important. Andy grew up in Connecticut and had gone to a small school there, Arnold College. He was drafted by the Rams and made All-Pro with them several times. But when he asked for permission to report to camp a couple weeks late because his wife was about to have a baby, they gave him a hard time. Robustelli threatened to sit out the season, but Wellington Mara called him and asked if he'd be interested in playing for the Giants. Robustelli was living in Stamford, Connecticut, and jumped at the chance. So Mara made the trade and we got a guy who helped draw some fans from his home state, never missed a game in all the years I played with him, went on to be a player-coach, and eventually became the team's general manager. Not a bad deal.

We had also made a trade with Pittsburgh to obtain Big Mo's little brother, Dick, an immediate starter at defensive tackle. He played next to Rosey Grier, my old pal from Penn State, and Katcavage and Yowarsky shared the other end. The linebackers were Svare on one side and Bill Svoboda on the other. Svoboda had joined the team in 1954. Pound for pound, he was one of the toughest guys I've ever known on the football field. He weighed only 215, but everybody on our team was scared to death of him because even when we practiced without pads, he prided himself on not letting the offense run around his end of the field. He would deck anyone who tried—Frank Gifford, Alex Webster, Kyle Rote, it didn't matter how big a star they were. He liked to play without a face mask, and his face always looked like a bloody mess. But he seemed to prefer it that way, and nobody—I mean *nobody*—ever gave Svoboda a hard time. That guy could have taken on the heavyweight champion of the world and held his own.

Our defensive backfield got a big lift when Mara got Ed Hughes from the Rams to go along with a future Hall of Famer named Emlen Tunnel, Jimmy Patton, and Dick Nolan, and it wasn't too long before our defense received the recognition it deserved.

Of course the offense wasn't half bad either, not with Conerly at quarterback, Gifford and Webster at halfbacks, and Kyle Rote on the end, all of them coached by Lombardi.

Howell used to tell people all the time that he didn't have to do a thing except to keep the chalk sharp for Lombardi and Landry and blow up the footballs. At the time, people thought he was just being funny; truth was, that's exactly how it worked. In all the years I was there, I never once saw him draw a play on a blackboard. He just stayed out of the other coaches' way and gave them their head, which might have been his greatest strength—recognizing talent and letting that talent do the job. Howell was more of a disciplinarian, the drill sergeant.

Our lifestyle away from football was pretty simple. You'd spend most of the day practicing or in meetings and at night, when I wasn't talking with Landry, a lot of the players would hang out at Toots Shor's or P. J. Clarke's, a downtown bar. Toots was a great guy who always treated athletes right. He'd get you seated up front with the celebrities; if you were an athlete you got treated better than the Vice President of the United States. He called everyone a crumbum and was a very generous guy. One night my first year, he had a whole stack of World Series tickets and gave all the players a couple. For some reason, I didn't go, and wouldn't you know it, Don Larsen went out and pitched a perfect game against the Dodgers, the only perfect game in the history of the World Series.

But it wasn't a very glamorous life. Television was still in its infancy, so no one really knew what we looked like. No one had any endorsements or shoe contracts athletes get today. You'd walk the streets and pretty much go unrecognized. That first year, I didn't even have a car and had to go everywhere by taxi or subway. One day my rookie year I tried to get to practice at Yankee Stadium and hopped on a subway with Little Mo. He was a veteran and I figured he knew his way around, which was a big mistake. Turned out, he'd never been on a subway either. Both of us just figured that every subway had to stop at Yankee Stadium. We got on one that didn't and we finally got off in someplace called Washington Heights. We had gone so far into the Bronx, it cost us a twenty-dollar cab ride just to get back to the Stadium.

Finally, after beating San Francisco and Chicago on the road, the Giants played their home opener on October 21, 1956. Almost 50,000 people came out to watch us, and I was in awe of the place. Two weeks earlier, Larsen, Mickey Mantle, Yogi Berra, and Whitey Ford had won a World Series sitting right at these very same lockers. And now, here we were in the most famous stadium in America.

If we were nervous, it hardly showed. Before the largest opening-day crowd in the team's history, we killed the Steelers, 38–10, as Gifford ran wild and Conerly had a terrific day. We beat the Eagles and the Steelers in our next two games, and now it was time to play the Cardinals again, with their split-T and big Ollie Matson. This time it was no contest. Landry had me keying on Matson—a preview of the same kind of style we wound up using when Jimmy Brown joined the league the next season, and Matson was held to 43 yards rushing in only 13 carries. We won the game, 23–10, with over 62,000 in the stands, and now we were 6–1 and in sole possession of first place in the NFL Eastern Conference.

We had a little late-season slump, losing to the Redskins and tying the Bears when their receiver, Harlon Hill, made one of the greatest catches I've ever seen. We had him double-covered, but he got behind Jimmy Patton, tipped the ball at his own five, tipped it again at the three, then dove into the end zone and caught the ball, just stretched out for the touchdown that tied the game.

For most of the season, Howell was using two quarterbacks. He'd usually start Don Heinrich for the first quarter, then bring in Charlie Conerly, like a relief pitcher, and Charlie would take it the rest of the way. I never could quite figure it out, and neither could Heinrich. To this day he's got to be wondering why Howell hardly ever let him finish what he'd started.

Conerly was never a great pure passer, but he was a precise, control-type quarterback, methodical and with a great feel for the game. He was a quiet guy, too, always roomed with Frank Gifford, and he was definitely a leader on that team. But he led out on the field, not with his mouth, and he was the toughest old bird you'll ever see. Actually, he was kind of a grump; he could go six weeks at a time without even saying as much as hello, like he was in another world. People misunderstood that, thinking he wasn't friendly, but Charlie just was not an outgoing person. Out on the field, though, he was in complete control. At that point, he was thirty-six years old and he'd taken an awful lot of punishment over the years. In fact, at one point after the 1953 season, they had to convince him not to retire.

The year before, the Giants had lost nine games, with Conerly getting blasted almost every week. The offensive line was inexperienced, Charlie was getting beat up, and the fans were really on his case. When Howell took over for Steve Owen in 1954, the first guy he went to talk to was Conerly. He promised Charlie he'd try to get him some more help on the line and Conerly agreed to come back.

Anyway, back to the Redskins. They were breathing down our necks, and we had to have the second game against them. The defense played well, while Gifford ran for three touchdowns and threw for another in a 28–14 win. We shot ourselves in the foot the next week in a 21–7 loss to the Browns and we were 7–3–1 for the year. The Redskins were 6–4. We had to beat the Eagles to win the Eastern title, and that's exactly what we did. Heinrich started the game, and for a change, finished it, too. We won, 21–7, on touchdown runs by Gifford, Rote, and Webster, and we won the division. It had been a long season, and now we were on the brink of a world championship.

To tell you the truth, I was in a daze a good part of that year. I still wasn't exactly sure what all of this meant. I knew we were playing in big games, but I was still only twenty-two years old and fresh off the campus. That doesn't mean I didn't take it seriously; any time I'm out on a football field it's serious business. But when I think about that season, everything still seems like one big blur in my mind, even the championship game.

I do remember the cold, however. The week before the game, the New York area felt like the North Pole. The Yankee Stadium field, even with a tarpaulin on it, was frozen solid. Wellington Mara recalled that the day the Giants had won their first championship in 1934, also against these big bad Bears, the team had been outfitted in basketball sneakers. A few days before the game, Andy Robustelli, who owned a sporting goods store in Cos Cob, Connecticut, was talking to a salesman for Keds, who told him about a new line of shoes that had great suction on gym floors. With Mara's blessing, Robustelli ordered enough pairs of shoes for the entire team, just in case, and when we got to the stadium and saw the field conditions, a couple of guys tried out the sneakers and came back raving about their ability to move around, despite the icy footing. So we all wore the sneakers, and the Bears were using regular shoes. Everyone said the sneakers were the reason we won the football game, but there was no doubt in my mind that we had the better team.

Lombardi decided to keep the game plan simple, and most of the day our quarterbacks just handed the ball to our big fullback Mel Triplett. He ripped the Bears to shreds, and so did everyone else.

Gene Filipski started us off with a 53-yard kickoff return to Chicago's thirty-eight, and two plays later, Triplett, a 220-pounder with the biggest thighs you'll ever see on a football player, went off left tackle, bulldozed the umpire, Mike Wilson, and carried three Bears across the goal line on a brutal 17-yard touchdown run. We got two quick field goals from Ben Agajanian, then Webster scored from three yards out for a 20–0 lead.

The Bears, meanwhile, with Ed Brown at quarterback, simply could not do anything right. I spent a good part of the day keying on their fullback Rick Casares, another hard-nosed, punishing ball carrier, and our defense was in control all afternoon. There was one slight scare, when Emlen Tunnell fumbled a punt and Casares converted it into a touchdown to cut our lead to 20–7 in the second quarter. But then we drove 72 yards for another Webster 1-yard run, and we put it away for good when Ray Beck blocked a punt and another rookie, Henry Moore, our first-round draft choice, fell on it in the end zone for a touchdown and a 34–7 halftime lead. In the second half, George Halas sent George Blanda into the game, but when you know a guy is just going to stand back there and throw, it makes defense even more fun. We just teed off on Blanda, and Conerly threw touchdown passes to Rote and Gifford.

Final score, Giants 47, Bears 7, and I had the distinction of becoming the first rookie middle linebacker ever to start on a world championship team. At the time, I just didn't realize the importance of that. I had never played on a losing team, not in high school or college, so here I was on another winning team. It just didn't seem that big a deal, certainly not the way people today carry on when they win a Super Bowl.

Of course the stakes were a little different, too. The winning player on the Super Bowl team last year made about $80,000. Our payday for the NFL championship in 1956 was $3,779.19. We voted on playoff money and the meeting was incredible. You had to vote to pay guys who had come and gone or got hurt, and you had to decide which coaches got how much. And if the head coach didn't like the way you voted, he'd let you know about it. I can still remember Jim Lee Howell yelling at us, "I don't like that vote, now get the hell back in there and vote again.''

The people in charge of the team had all the power, and it was very obvious who the hired help had to answer to. Significantly, the week before that championship game, there was another historic occasion for professional football. That's the year the players got together and started the NFL Players Association. Rote was one of the organizers, and it took a lot of guts to do that. Some of the owners, in particular George Preston Marshall of the Redskins, flat out told their teams that if anyone showed up for the meeting, they'd be playing elsewhere the following year. Eddie LeBaron did represent the Redskins, but when it came time to call a press conference and let the photographers in, Eddie was long gone.

The owners had a good thing going, and they knew it. Think about it. In 1956, I played on a world championship team, and I made less than $11,000, including my ''bonus''—$500 worth of furniture, courtesy of Wellington Mara.

5

When a team wins a Super Bowl these days, life becomes a year-long celebration for the players and coaching staff. It's a nonstop victory tour of banquets, personal appearances, commercial endorsements, "The Today Show" and Johnny Carson. When the Giants won it in 1986, eleven different books came out profiling the team, the coach, the season.

After we won the 1956 National Football League championship, most of us scattered across the country to our home towns with almost no fanfare. In fact, after a short vacation, I was back in Farmington, bagging groceries in a local supermarket. That's right, bagging groceries for whatever they would pay me. I couldn't even work a forty-hour week because I wasn't in the union, but I'd show up anyway on Saturdays when they were real busy and they'd ask me to help out.

I was a college graduate, but I couldn't teach or coach because half the school year was over and those jobs were filled. Mary was still working for John Manchin and I'd help him out whenever he needed me, too. I just wanted to have an extra paycheck coming in; I've always been that way. I always knew football was not going to last forever, and I wanted to have a little money in the bank just in case.

Nowadays, these kids sign their big contracts and the first thing they do is go out and buy that shiny new Mercedes. In 1956, I bought a used two-year-old green Chevrolet. I'm sure people thought I was making a lot of money as a professional football player, and in that neck of the woods, the money I'd earned the year before was a hell of a lot more than any kid a year out of college could have made. But I've never been real loose with a buck, and I did not want to have people look at me in a big flashy car and say, "There goes that rich pro-football player flashing around his big money." So I had a '55 Chevy, and people were probably saying, "There goes that cheap SOB driving a used car."

That car almost got Mary killed one day. By this time, we were renting a house in Farmington and it was up on top of a very steep hill. She was coming down the driveway, turned the wheel, and the steering shaft literally broke. To this day, neither one of us knows how she managed to stop that car. It was a very close call.

I stayed in West Virginia for the entire off-season. There were no minicamps for veterans; hell, they didn't even give you a workout program. Hardly anyone lifted weights; you just tried to stay active, run a little or play some basketball, and watch what you ate so you wouldn't balloon up.

Even as a veteran, the Giants would never talk to you or even communicate with you in the off-season. They'd just send a contract in the mail and it usually arrived about a month before camp was set to start. They didn't want to give you a lot of time to think about it, and certainly they didn't want to negotiate. They wanted you to sign that contract and mail it back.

In 1957 I didn't sign it. I had been the first starting rookie middle linebacker on a championship team, and I thought I deserved a decent raise over the $7,000 I had earned the year before. Wellington Mara had other ideas, however. The contract he sent me was for $7,500; that's right, a $500 raise. I sent it back, unsigned, and told them I'd talk about it when I got to camp in a few weeks.

About two weeks into training camp in Winooski, Wellington initiated talks with me. So I went over to his office and he said, "We want you to sign this contract." I told him I wanted $8,500, and then I really made him mad. I told him I wanted to negotiate with his brother, Jack, who handled the business side of the club and did negotiate some player contracts. Absolutely not, Wellington said. "You can't talk to Jack because he has his favorite ball players and I sign all the tough guys." Finally, he offered me $8,000, but I really thought I deserved $8,500 and kept pressing the point.

But Wellington was not going to budge, and then he got furious with me. It was the first time I had ever seen the man get really angry and this was no act. His Irish temper was up, the veins on his neck were sticking out, and his face was just blood-red. At one point, he stood up and grabbed all the papers on his desk and just threw them every which way. Then he looked me right square in the eye and said, "You *will* sign this contract or I'll trade you so fast you won't even know where you landed. *Now you sign this contract!*"

I was twenty-two years old and I really did want to play for the New York Giants. I liked the team, I liked my teammates, and I loved playing before those big crowds at Yankee Stadium. So I told him I'd sign for $8,000 because the extra $500 just didn't mean that much to me, at least not enough to have him come down on me like that. It's something I will never forget as long as I live, though, and I never wanted to make Wellington Mara angry again.

Another guy you didn't want to cross very often was my good friend Alex Webster, a tough running back who later became head coach of the Giants. Alex was a street-brawler type from New Jersey who never saw a fight he didn't like. He'd fought for everything in his football life and got to the Giants in a roundabout way. He'd been drafted out of North Carolina State by the Redskins, who tried him as a defensive back, then cut him a few days before the start of the 1953 season. He wound up playing in Canada for two years and just tore up the league in 1954, winning their MVP award. Al DeRogatis, the same guy who had spotted me at West Virginia, was still doing some part-time scouting for the Giants and convinced the Maras that Alex was the big, bruising back they ought to sign. So Webster came down in 1955, scored three touchdowns in the first two exhibition games, and was so good Howell decided to start him at right halfback and move Kyle Rote and his wounded knees out to end.

By 1957, Alex had become one of the leaders of the offense. There was always a rivalry between the offensive team and the defensive team. In training camp, when you're playing in real hot weather and you've been out in that brutal sun for a few hours, friendly rivalries more than occasionally turn into blood feuds. We used to fight among ourselves quite often in camp, guys swinging at each other, even if we were wearing helmets. One year Wellington said I wasn't going to get a raise because he'd counted five different fights I'd been in with my own teammates. I told him he was wrong about that; it was only four.

Our defense was so good that many times we simply controlled the offense in practice, wouldn't let them do anything. That used to get the offensive guys ticked off, and Lombardi would get so angry he'd keep the offense out on the field long after Landry had let the defense go to the showers.

One day, Landry sent us in and most of our unit had already showered and changed clothes by the time the offense trudged in. We had an end named Ken MacAfee on the team—his son went on to be an All-American tight end at Notre Dame—and Ken always had a way of saying the wrong thing at the wrong time. He was a nice, friendly guy from Alabama, but he was always putting his foot in his mouth. As I was standing there drying off at my locker, the offense came into this hot furnace room that doubled as our locker room after working overtime. Lombardi had been on their backs all day and no one was in a mood for joking around, except MacAfee. He said to Alex, "You know, Webster, if you ever learned your plays, we wouldn't have to stay out there so long."

Wow, you couldn't believe the scene that followed. Webster was on the other side of the room, and immediately bodies were flying through the air, lockers were tumbling down, and Webster was like a crazy man trying to get at MacAfee. I was knocked flat on my back, stools were flying, and if about five guys hadn't gotten hold of Alex, MacAfee would not have made it out of the locker room alive and there wouldn't have been any future Notre Dame All-American.

Training camp was never very much fun, then or now. They take you to these remote places, work you twice a day, and then schedule meetings all the time. You're away from your family, and in those days, you were constantly on the road playing exhibitions. The Giants by this time were pretty much a veteran team and nobody really took the exhibitions very seriously. You just wanted to play and not get too banged up. As a result, the Giants were never really very successful in the preseason, and 1957 was no exception.

Anyway, we were back practicing in the New York area late in the preseason and we had just lost a game, hadn't played well at all, and one day, Jim Lee Howell just unloaded on Frank Gifford.

By this time, Gifford was an NFL superstar. He'd always been kind of a golden boy from Southern Cal, had married a Miss California—Maxine—and they were just the perfect couple. He was a handsome guy with movie-star good looks and she was gorgeous. Frank really was a man about town. They were regulars at Toots Shor's and P. J. Clarke's, and Frank always had his name in the gossip columns. But he also knew exactly what he was doing. He knew just where he wanted to go and how he was going to get there. He had goals in the business world. He knew he wanted to be a broadcaster. He wanted to be a movie star, even if he couldn't act much. And he didn't waste time. He didn't sit in the bar until two or three in the morning talking about football. He knew who the powers were at the Giants radio station, WNEW, and worked for them part-time during the season. He knew who the powers were at CBS where he first went to work in television after he retired. And I admired that; in fact, I learned from him. I learned how to hustle, how to use football to open other doors. We weren't great bosom buddies—I've never been to his house for a drink and he's never been to mine—but I consider Frank a friend, and I hope he'd say the same about me. I also know he feels the same way that I do about Jim Lee Howell, especially after this one incident in 1957.

Frank had just come off a great season. He had been named the National Football League's Most Valuable Player after we won the championship, but that wasn't good enough for Jim Lee. Frank wasn't playing particularly well in the preseason; he never did. There were enough running backs on the offense that he could take a blow now and then, and it seemed dumb to leave your game out on the field in August and have nothing left when the regular season started. Of course the guys on defense didn't have the luxury of cruising through the preseason. There were only fourteen of us, so you had to play all four quarters and special teams, too.

Anyway, we were back in New York practicing at Fordham University. Every day after practice we took laps around the field, then came back for one of Howell's little talks before he'd let us get dressed. On this day, Jim Lee just lit into Frank. He said, "You guys were just terrible out there; you look like you've never played the game before. And then there's Mister Hollywood; number sixteen, the Most Valuable Player in the National Football League. Right now he is the worst player on this football team. He hunkers up [that was Jim Lee's favorite expression] when he's supposed to be running with the ball."

It was absolutely embarrassing, and it got worse. Frank was obviously very upset about it—I do believe there were tears in his eyes—and all of us were just squirming, not really knowing what to do. Finally Jim Lee shut his mouth and Frank managed to regain his composure. The whole thing was totally uncalled for and while Frank may be too diplomatic to talk much about it, I can tell you that he never forgave Jim Lee Howell for that, and neither did I. Hell, everybody on that football team knew that when the chips were down, Frank Gifford was going to be there to make the big plays and be the big star.

We had a lot of guys like that on our offense. Webster was the same way; impossible to keep out of the lineup, even if he was probably in the worst shape of any athlete I think I've ever played with or against. He was always getting ear infections and his knees were constantly banged up because he took so many shots trying to gain those extra few yards. Alex was a slow, plodding kind of back, but when you needed that third and one, he got the ball, and usually he got the first down. I always wondered how good he would have been if only he'd taken care of himself; God, what an off-season conditioning program could have done for that guy. He smoked all the time. He was the only man I've ever seen who would sneak smokes on the sidelines during a game in full view of thousands of people. He'd get one of those capes you used to keep warm and huddle under it, puffing away so hard the smoke would be coming out the top of the cape.

I always said he was so slow the defenders would run off and leave him behind. But he also was a smart football player; he knew exactly where he had to go to get a first down, how many steps it would take to get there. Our whole team was like that—basically intelligent people who wanted to succeed.

We studied everything, even the officials. I always wanted to know how they would call certain things, how much they'd let you get away with. Today, most of the players couldn't tell you anything about the officials, except how they blew a call. Hell, I knew their names, their wives' names, their kids', because I always made it a point to talk to them, try to get friendly with them. I always figured that if they knew you, they might not throw that handkerchief down so fast. I even socialized with them off the field. Once I was invited to a retirement party for an official named Sam Palazzi, and I considered that a great honor. After I sat out the 1968 season and came out of retirement to play for Lombardi and the Redskins in 1969, when I ran out to the middle of the field for the first game that year, the officials presented me with a yellow flag that said "Welcome Back, Sam." The field judge that day, Fred Swearingen, said to me, "Sam, you're so damned old, anything you see out there just go ahead and call."

Another intelligent guy on that team was Kyle Rote, the captain of the offense. Smart and loved by everyone.

Kyle has had some serious health problems in recent years, but back then he was another one of those All-American-boy types. He had come out of SMU almost a national hero after a stunning, though losing, effort against a heavily favored Notre Dame team in his senior year. He was the first player taken in the 1951 draft, but always had knee problems that finally forced Lombardi to move him outside when Webster came along.

Kyle was a wonderful guy, handsome, with a beautiful family. His son, Kyle Jr., went on to become perhaps the most famous American professional soccer player in the 1970s. His dad was the perfect captain. Oh, he'd drink a little and smoke a little and played some poker like the rest of us, but he was such a gentleman. It seemed like any time a kid was born to a player, if it was a boy, they'd name him Kyle. Jim Patton had a son named Kyle. Frank Gifford named a son Kyle. I used to joke that everybody named their sons Kyle and their dogs Sam.

He was our captain and he took the role seriously. If somebody had a death in the family, Kyle would make sure to collect the money and send flowers. When it came time to take care of the clubhouse boys for shining your shoes and taking care of your locker, Kyle made sure every guy kicked in. He'd collect the tip money for the college kids who served us meals at the training camps.

He was also kind of a ham. Whenever we had get-togethers with the families, Kyle would get up and lead the singing. He loved the song "Tears on My Pillow" and would sing it every chance he got. The Giants in those days truly were run like a family. On Saturdays, all the players brought their kids to practice. It was funny because Wellington Mara brought his children, too, and most of the time his kids were on one side of the field in their white shirts and bow ties and the players' kids would be on the other side in their Levi's and plaid shirts. Before long, someone would throw them a ball and they'd all be playing tackle together. At Thanksgiving, the Maras would give all the players turkeys or big hams and they'd put on a Thanksgiving dinner for the players and their families at the Grand Concourse Hotel near the Stadium, where a lot of guys lived during the season.

Players like Rote helped perpetuate that family atmosphere and I truly believe it was one of the reasons we were so successful over the years. Despite my contract hassles, I really did feel part of something special, and there was nothing phoney about it. At least that's what I thought until the Giants traded me in 1964, but we'll get to that soon enough.

Unfortunately, there was nothing particularly special about the 1957 Giants, not after we had a chance to win the division, only to lose our last three games and finish second to a Cleveland Browns team with a rookie fullback named Jimmy Brown.

Incredibly, Brown was not the first player chosen in the draft that year—that distinction went to Len Dawson, a future Hall of Fame quarterback who was picked by the Steelers. But I knew all about Brown from my days at West

Virginia, and before that season opener against Cleveland, I made sure my teammates knew, too.

A lot has been made over the years about how we would set our defense to stop Jim Brown, and as the years rolled on, we did do a lot of that. But in the first game, we pretty much stayed in our basic 4–3 defense, and both teams had a hell of a defensive effort.

The game was in Cleveland, and we opened up by scoring with a Ben Agajanian field goal. Later in the game, we had a chance to go up 6–0 after Agajanian kicked another field goal, but the Browns were offside on the play and Howell decided to take the points off the board and try to score a touchdown. Well, the offense moved the ball inside the fifteen, but Agajanian missed the field goal this time and we still only led 3–0. The Browns tied it up at 3–3 and then with twenty-one seconds left, Lou Groza kicked a 47-yard field goal and we lost, 6–3. I'll always remember that game for two reasons: it taught me that you never, and I do mean *never,* take points off the board because it will always come back to haunt you. Also, it was the first of many confrontations with Jim Brown. He "only" gained 89 yards on twenty-one attempts, but after that game, our defenses always focused on stopping the big guy.

There were other memorable events that season. My daughter Cathy was born during the season; Mary had stayed back in Farmington to have the baby and I roomed with Don Chandler and Bill Svoboda at the Grand Concourse. I also was credited with what some people say may have been one of the greatest tackles in the history of professional football.

We were playing the Forty-niners later in the year. Y. A. Tittle was the quarterback, and on one play, he dropped back about eight yards and threw a little screen pass to Hugh McElhenny, San Francisco's great running back. I looked up the field and here came McElhenny running behind my old teammate Bruce Bosley and another big guard, Lou Palatella, about 550 pounds just bearing down on me. All I wanted to do was strip the interference and let someone else make the tackle, so I just plowed into the two guards, Bosley and Palatella. I hit both guys in the chest and in doing that, my momentum took me right into McElhenny. All three of them went down. This was at Yankee Stadium, right in front of their bench, and the crowd went wild. I meant to get the blockers and I got 'em *all*. Was it lucky? Of course, but I also was playing a defense designed to always have me in the right spot, and that day, I was exactly where I was supposed to be.

We lost that game to the Forty-niners because of a play Tittle made famous. It was called the alley-oop, and Tittle would simply lob the ball toward R. C. Owens, a six-foot-three receiver who was a great leaper. He'd just outjump any defensive backs near him, and he hurt us badly that day.

The next week, we were upset by the Pittsburgh Steelers. So the Browns, who also lost that day to the Lions, had replaced us as champions of the East, making our final game at the Stadium against Cleveland meaningless. But try telling that to our fans. They sold 50,000 tickets by midweek, the largest advance sale in the history of the franchise to that point, and the largest crowd of the season, more than 54,000, came out for the season finale.

They definitely got their money's worth, even though we lost, 34–28. The game ended with us driving deep into Cleveland territory before time ran out and our season ended. It had been a disappointing year, but it also was a learning experience for our defense, especially in how to stop the greatest runner in the history of professional football. At this point, Landry had begun setting his defenses to stop Brown, and my assignment was to key on him. Wherever Brown went, I'd be right there with him. That's really how Brown versus Huff started, and as the years went on, it was a rivalry that kept getting built up and up and up.

Brown basically became my responsibility because I

was always going with the flow of the play. Landry would tell us, "If you hold Jim Brown to four yards a carry, we'll beat Cleveland." Now, it doesn't take a genius to figure out if he gets four yards a carry, three downs multiplied by four yards in West Virginia math is still a first down. But that's how much respect we had for the guy. After all, he averaged 5.2 yards a carry for his whole career.

What made Jim Brown a great back? Everything. He had size, he had speed, and he had strength. He also was one of the smartest players out there; I'm not talking about his IQ, I'm talking about his football mind. He knew where to go and what to do, how to use his blocking and how to save his strength. He ran straight up and he let you hit him, if you could get a shot. He was so fast and so strong, and he only wore these little shoulder pads and never any thigh pads, unless he put a little piece of cardboard in there. You'd hit him and it was like hitting a tree; nothing would give. Three or four of us would gang-tackle him and think we had him, and all of a sudden he'd feel like he was going down. You'd relax a little to brace yourself for the fall, and he'd just gather himself and go into a gear nobody else has ever had—before or after, I guarantee it.

He was the finest football player I have ever seen, and on the field he also was the best sportsman I have ever played against. He'd actually compliment you. I'd hit him with everything I had and he'd get up real slow and say, "Nice tackle, big Sam." He was always that way. He was so nice he'd almost take the edge off your competitive spirit. I used to try to find reasons to dislike players so I would have no hesitation in creaming them. But Jim Brown would take that away from you. The respect was mutual. Even to this day, when guys from my era talk about Jim Brown, they just refer to him as "The Big Man." You don't have to say his name, you don't have to give his number, you just talk about The Big Man.

And he also could make you look very bad. I remember one time I flew into a hole, hit him, and he kept on going for a 17-yard gain. When I got to the sidelines a few plays later, Landry met me coming off the field and asked, "What happened, were you late getting in the hole?"

"No, Tom," I said, "he just ran right over me."

Of course I had a lot of company around the league in that regard.

My teammate, Dick Nolan, one of our defensive backs who is now an assistant coach with Landry in Dallas, will always remember Jim Brown, too.

On one play in 1957, their center got hold of my ankle and I couldn't get back to fill in the hole. Brown just flew through there and Nolan, who weighed about 175 pounds and was called "Sticks" because he was so skinny, came up to meet him. Nolan hit Brown and they both went down. Brown bounced right up, but Dick didn't move. I went over to try to help pick him up and looked at him and his eyes had kind of rolled back in his head.

"Great tackle," I told him somewhat sheepishly. "Geez, Dick, I'm really sorry I didn't get there in time, somebody picked me off."

He kind of looked up at me and his eyes still weren't very focused.

"Great tackle, hell, Sam," he said. "I couldn't get out of that son of a bitch's way."

6

When we started out the 1958 season by losing five of our six exhibition games, then split our first four regular-season games, no one on the football team could possibly have imagined that before the year would end, we'd wind up winning the Eastern title and participating in what is now commonly referred to as the greatest game ever played—the 1958 championship between the Giants and Baltimore Colts.

Despite our awful record in the preseason, a lot of us felt that Wellington had really improved the football team in the off-season, especially in the secondary. We traded Dick Nolan and Bobby Joe Conrad to the Chicago Cardinals for cornerback Lindon Crow, and almost as an afterthought, the Cards threw in a veteran kicker named Pat Summerall. Rosey Grier was back from the Army after missing the 1957 season, and we also added veteran defensive back Carl Karilivacz and drafted a pair of pretty good backs, fullback Phil King from Vanderbilt and halfback Don Maynard from Texas Western. Maynard got cut after that year but later moved out to wide receiver and became Joe Namath's favorite target with the New York Jets and went on to be voted into the Hall of Fame. Back then, he was sort of a "rhinestone cowboy" type, wore cowboy boots and talked with such a thick accent that none of us could understand him.

One thing we could understand, though, was Landry's defense. This was our third year with it, and with Rosey back in the middle, we figured we could dominate teams. That year, we *had* to dominate because the offense just wasn't that strong. For the whole season, we averaged only twenty points a game, our average margin of victory was about five points, and the throw-in, Summerall, scored twenty-five percent of our points on field goals and placements.

But it didn't matter, because our defensive unit was truly something special. We'd been together for a few years, we were all close friends, and we were developing into the crowd favorites of Yankee Stadium. People actually would start chanting "Robustelli, Robustelli, Huff-Huff-Huff" or "Dee-fense, Dee-fense." I used to get chills up my spine when I heard it, and it only made us play that much harder. We were also the first defensive unit to get introduced before the game.

It was a defense made up of some rather unique individuals. Dick Modzelewski taught me that you always had to have a character on your football team, a free spirit who could make you laugh and make you cry.

Though he was only about six-one and 255 pounds, Dick was one of the strongest people I've ever seen, almost impossible to move out, just a little tank who would not budge. He couldn't see very well and always wore contact lenses, but managed to get the job done. He also liked to have a good time. In training camp, Howell would have us finish off our calisthenics with a couple of laps around the baseball diamond. On one side of the field there was a big old wooden backstop, and we'd run around that. Mo would duck down behind the boards after the first lap. We'd all be huffing and puffing coming around for the second time and old Mo would pop up and lead the whole group to the finish line, fresh as a daisy because he'd only done one lap.

Howell fell for it every time. He'd be yelling " 'Atta way to go, Mo, way to lead 'em in,'' and we'd all break up.

No one ever minded because that was the kind of personality Mo had. He liked to eat, he loved to tell stories, and he loved to sing Polish folk songs. He came from the Pittsburgh area and every time the team would play the Steelers, he'd take a couple of guys over to his mother's house and feed them these huge meals. When we went to Cleveland, we'd wind up at his brother Ed's restaurant where you ate so much you could barely get up from the table.

Rosey Grier was also a big eater; in fact, it's one of the reasons the team eventually traded him. He had a terrible time controlling his weight. In the off-season, he could go as high as 340, so they'd put him at the weight watchers' table in camp, making him eat salad and Jell-O. Then he'd sneak out at night and eat anything he could get his hands on.

Rosey probably had as much talent as any football player who ever played. He and Big Daddy Lipscomb of the Colts could run as fast as any big men I've ever seen and catch people from behind. But he had a hard time staying in shape; he was always asking us to call time so he could catch his breath. When Rosey made up his mind to get the quarterback, not many people could stop him. Some of the fiercest battles I ever saw, though, happened on our own team. Rosey would go one-on-one in the nutcracker drill against Jack Stroud, one of our offensive linemen. Jack was one of the few guys back then who believed in weight-lifting, and he was a very strong man, probably the strongest guy on the team. One day after practice, we were sitting in the dressing room and Rosey said to him, "You know, Stroud, when I play against you, I'm playing for my life."

Everyone loved Rosey. He really was a gentle man, and he loved to pick on a guitar. Couldn't play it worth a damn, but he'd always be clanging on it. During training camp, when you'd be trying to get a little sleep between two-a-day practices, Rosey would be picking on that guitar and driving everyone crazy, but no one was about to tell this

7 4

guy to keep it down. One year, after we had moved our camp to Fairfield, Connecticut, somebody stole a tube out of Rosey's amplifier. He was using an electric guitar by then, and now he couldn't play it. At lunch the next day, he stood up and said, "Gentlemen, I want to tell you, somebody took the tube out of my amplifier and it better be back tonight or I'm gonna take each guy one at a time and find out who did it." Thank goodness, the tube mysteriously found its way back into that amplifier.

Jim Katcavage, the defensive end who joined the team the same year I did from Dayton University, had as much heart as any football player I've ever seen. He only knew one speed—all out—whether it was practice or a game. In 1963, we were practicing for the world championship against the Bears. This was on a Thursday, and our coach, Allie Sherman, had us out there with helmets and shoulder pads, but it was not a full-gear workout. So we were in a drill, defense against the offense, and Sherman said, "I want you guys to go half-speed." Well, Katcavage never knew what that meant, so he came barreling through there rushing the passer and just slammed into our quarterback Y. A. Tittle, who at this point was no spring chicken. It may have been the hardest shot Y. A. ever took; he just got knocked ass over teakettle. Sherman was not very happy, and when we got back into our defensive huddle, I said to Katcavage, "Kat, for God's sake, what the hell did you do that for? He's an old man, and we need him healthy on Sunday."

He looked at me and said, "Sam, you don't understand. I have to battle that offensive tackle every day to get to the quarterback, every day. So I get through and he's standing there with the ball. What am I supposed to do? I've got to hit that quarterback."

I understood exactly what he was talking about. "Kat," I told him, "if you get through, just hit him, go ahead and get him." You just can't knock that. You never want to discourage that kind of aggressive thinking in a good defen-

7 5

sive football player, because he'll always lay it on the line for you.

That was never a problem with Kat. In 1959, we were playing the Eagles, and Kat hated them because he was from the Philadelphia area and always wanted to do well against the hometown team. On the first play of the game, he filled a hole, took on the guard, and broke his collarbone, one of the most painful injuries there is. But he wouldn't leave the game. Played three quarters with that injury, then had it X-rayed afterward and found out he'd have to miss the rest of the season. Talk about tough. I've played hurt myself, but not with a broken collarbone.

Andy Robustelli, the other end, was a cerebral player. He wound up coaching the defense after Landry left to coach the Dallas Cowboys in 1960. He'd been in the league for a long time and knew exactly how to pace himself. He had surprisingly deceptive strength and great hands and was always a guy who would come up with the big play for you. It would be third and seven and he'd be in the huddle saying, "Okay now, we gotta get 'em right here," and damned if he wouldn't bust in there and sack the quarterback or block a field goal and make a big play.

He also was a hustler. He was in so many businesses you couldn't keep up with him. He had that sporting goods store; he had travel agencies; he'd sell clothes by mail order. Once he got all of us to buy sports coats that came from Hong Kong. There was one small problem: they had never dealt with people our size, and we all got these beautiful cashmere coats that none of us could wear. I finally gave mine to a little running back, Bobby Epps, and he couldn't even get it on. Another year, Andy was in the shirt business, so we all bought his shirts. In "The Violent World of Sam Huff," the 1960 CBS documentary, all of us were wearing these striped shirts that made us look like we just got out of prison. Kat, Mo, Rosey, Andy, and I wore Andy's shirts so he could get a little free advertising.

Andy eventually went on to the Hall of Fame, in fact

three of us on that unit were voted in. The third was our safety, Emlen Tunnell, just an amazing football player with an even more amazing story. He had gone undrafted out of Iowa in 1948 because he missed his senior year with an eye injury. He hitchhiked to New York from his home near Philadelphia and showed up in the Giants offices unannounced to ask for a job. The team's general manager at the time, Ray Walsh, recalled his name from Emlen's Iowa days and the team invited him to camp. Once he got out on that field, there was no doubt Tunnell belonged in the NFL. He was the first black player ever signed by the Giants. He also was the first black assistant coach in the NFL, the first black in the Hall of Fame, and the first player ever taken by the Hall because of his defensive skills. To top it off, Emlen was an incredible punt and kickoff return man.

He was the hardest-hitting guy in the league. He would hit people so hard they'd be afraid to catch a pass in front of him; catch a pass in front of Emlen Tunnell and usually you didn't finish the game. He was a big safety, about six foot one and 210 pounds, and he had the softest hands. He'd catch a punt, and you wouldn't even hear the ball land in those hands. And he loved the game, loved playing it, and always told everyone it was an honor to play for the New York Giants. He believed that. He never played the game for money. When he died after a heart attack in 1975, he was broke. He'd given away all his money to his friends. He was always buying tickets for people; you'd walk into a bar with him and he'd buy the house a round, then another round and walk out with nothing in his pocket.

He was always after me to go with him to a place in Harlem called the Red Rooster, but I'd never go because I knew he'd make me buy drinks for the house. One day Chandler and I walked into a place called Jim Downey's, a famous old bar on Broadway, and Emlen was already there. "C'mon, you guys," he said, "come on and have a drink." So Emlen bought us a drink and then he bought everyone in the place a drink. There must have been seventy-five people there standing at the bar. Then he looked at us and said, "Okay, it's your turn." We told him we'd be happy to spring for a drink for a teammate. "No, Sam," he said, "you buy everyone a drink." Chandler and I just shook our heads and finally I had to tell him no way. Chandler's from Oklahoma and I'm a country boy from West Virginia, and we weren't about to buy anybody drinks except our friends. He laughed and bought another round himself.

Later in his career in New York, Emlen had slowed down a little and he was having some difficulty playing Landry's defense. Emlen usually played Emlen's defense, and finally, he was asked to retire. But he couldn't really quit because he had no money, so Emlen asked to be put on waivers. In Green Bay, Lombardi saw his name on the waiver wire and immediately grabbed him because Lombardi loved him and he was certainly better than anything they had up there.

That summer, we were playing a preseason game against the Packers in Bangor, Maine, and Emlen was playing safety against us. Conerly threw a little swing pass over the middle to a running back, Joe Morrison, now the head coach at South Carolina, back then one of the more versatile guys on our football team. Up came Emlen and you could hear the hit a mile away . . . *thwaaaaaack*. I mean a shot. I didn't even have to look up, I knew who'd made that hit, and Emlen knocked Joe cold. I also remember Jim Lee Howell yelling at Emlen, "You never hit like that when you were with us!"

Wellington Mara was on the sidelines that day and he heard what Howell had said. Emlen was one of Wellington's favorite players. He was also a favorite of Wellington's father, Tim, the original owner of the team. I think I met Tim Mara a total of about ten times in all the years I played for the Giants, and he could never remember my name. But he knew Emlen and, like his son, he also had a special feeling for Tunnell. Wellington turned to Howell and said, "Don't you ever say that about Emlen. He played hard for you, and he was one of us. He was a great player, don't you ever put the knock on that guy.''

Despite his difficulty with Landry's defense, Tunnell was a main character on that 1958 team. As it turned out, the championship game against the Colts would be his last as a Giant player.

When I look back on it now, thirty years later, it's amazing the Giants got that far considering how much of a hole we'd dug ourselves early in the season. But after ten games, we were 7–3 and the Cleveland Browns were 8–2. It took a few bizarre games to get us to the championship.

In our next game, we played the Detroit Lions, knowing we had to win to stay alive. We thought we were dead late in the game when the Lions held a 17–12 lead, but their coach, George Wilson, made one of the more bonehead calls in the history of the league to let us off the hook. The Lions had a five-point lead and the ball and were facing fourth and twenty-one at their own forty-four. Wilson got the punting team on the field, but then called for a fake and a run by his kicker, Yale Lary. We tackled him for a 1-yard gain and took over with great field position. Conerly completed a pass for 34 yards to Bob Schnelker, and on fourth and two, Gifford ran over for a touchdown and a 19–17 lead. We weren't home free until Harland Svare and Robustelli worked a stunt that allowed Svare to block a field goal from the twenty-five in the final seconds that saved the game and the season.

We escaped that week and knew that in order to win a championship, we had to beat the Browns the next Sunday to force a playoff, then beat them again to play the Colts.

Once again, things looked bleak when Jimmy Brown went 65 yards for a touchdown on the first offensive play of the game. But on a snowy, miserably cold day, we recovered our composure and eventually tied the score at 10–10 in the fourth quarter when Gifford threw a halfback option pass to Schnelker for a 6-yard touchdown. Now it was time for our throw-in kicker to go to work. He did, but Summerall missed a 31-yard field goal with four and a half minutes to play. Actually, no one really expected him to kick at all that day because he'd been nursing a sore knee all week and couldn't even practice.

Summerall got another chance when the defense, as usual, stopped the Browns on three straight passes, and the Giants got the ball back at midfield. By now, the snow had obliterated the chalk lines and visibility was down to whatever you could see two feet away.

Webster managed to get open on second down but dropped a long pass from Conerly at the five that would have certainly settled the issue. Two plays later, Howell stunned the stadium and Summerall himself by sending the kicker out on the field to try what has officially been called a 49-yard field goal. But that 49 yards had to be an estimate because no one really knew where the ball was spotted. To this day, Summerall tells people he could not believe Howell wanted him to kick. Most of the guys wanted another pass play. I'm glad that for once, Jim Lee made the right call. Summerall kicked that thing into the snow and it floated through the goal posts for the game-winning points. Some people say it had enough distance on it to go 60 yards. Whatever, it was one of the greatest kicks in the history of professional football.

Now we were tied with the Browns and we had to play the same team again the following week. Howell had his doubts. "This is a great team emotionally—the greatest," he said. "But how many times can you do this?"

As it turned out, one more time.

The next week at Yankee Stadium, we had perhaps the finest defensive effort we ever had against Jim Brown. We held him to 8 yards rushing on 12 carries and held Cleveland to 86 yards of total offense. On one play, Jimmy took a pitchout and slipped. Mo hit him low and I whacked him high and kind of dazed him. I thought I knocked him out, but to this day he says he was never out cold because he never stayed down.

We scored our only touchdown that day on a very

strange play. It was a double reverse—a handoff to Webster going left, another handoff to Gifford around the right end, and then a little twist Lombardi had put into the offense that week. Just as he was about to be hit, Gifford pitched the ball back to Conerly who was trailing the play, and he scored. Summerall added a field goal in the second quarter, and that's all the points we needed in a 10–0 victory that clinched the East title for us.

Now it was time for the Colts, and to tell you the truth, we knew we were in trouble. We had gone through the wringer to get this far, we were banged up after playing an extra game, and now we had to play one of the most potent offensive teams in the history of the game. The Colts were murdering everyone that year. John Unitas was throwing to people like Raymond Berry and Lenny Moore and could also give the ball to a bruising fullback named Alan (The Horse) Ameche, while the defense had guys like Gino Marchetti, Art Donovan, and Big Daddy Lipscomb. Before we'd go into a game against the Colts, Landry always used to say, "The score is seven to nothing, and we haven't even kicked off yet." We knew the Colts were going to score on us, and we knew we couldn't afford any mistakes.

We knew it, but we couldn't keep mistakes from happening. Gifford fumbled twice in the first half and we trailed at the half, 14–3. Early in the third quarter, the Colts really had our backs to the wall with a first and goal at the Giant three. Back in the huddle, we were starting to get steamed up. We were acting like crazy men, and the feeling was there was no way we were going to let them get in and turn this thing into a rout. Ameche gained 2 yards to the one, but Unitas tried to sneak it in on second down and we stopped him. Ameche came at us on third down and Rosey and I tackled him short. On fourth down, Unitas got cute. He thought we'd be expecting Ameche up the middle; instead he threw him a pitchout to the right side. Cliff Livingston smelled it coming and stopped Ameche for a 4-yard loss, and the offense took over.

On the next series, we had third and two on our own

thirteen when Conerly crossed the Colts up by calling for a long pass after a fake pitch to Gifford. Rote was wide open over the middle and just kept running. Though he was caught from behind at the twenty-five and had the ball stripped, Webster, my friend the big-play man, was trailing the play. He scooped the ball up on the dead run and made it down to the one. From there, Mel Triplett, our fullback, bulled in for the score, and we were back in the game, trailing 14–10. Early in the fourth quarter, Gifford atoned for his earlier fumbles by catching a 15-yard touchdown pass from Conerly, and Summerall's extra point gave us a 17–14 lead. But with Unitas around, everyone in the stadium knew it was hardly the time to breathe easy.

We turned up the pressure again on defense and Unitas couldn't move his team. Late in the period, Unitas had a second and six at our twenty-seven, but Robustelli beat his man, Hall of Fame tackle Jim Parker, and sacked Unitas for an 11-yard loss. Then it was Mo's turn. He came up through the middle and got Unitas again for a 9-yard loss. On fourth and twenty-six, the Colts had to punt, and all we needed were a couple of first downs to wrap up our second NFL title in three years.

We got one of them on a 10–yard pass to Webster. But on third and four at our own forty, the game turned. Gifford took the ball from Conerly and was moving wide to the right up the field. He was tackled by Marchetti, and as they went down, Lipscomb came over and fell on the pile. The impact was enough to break Marchetti's ankle, and he was on the field screaming and writhing in pain. In the confusion, the ball was spotted about six inches short of the first down. I've seen the films and there's no doubt in my mind that Frank got that first down. But the referee picked up the ball and actually moved it back, and now Howell had a tough decision to make. The crowd was going crazy; they wanted him to go for the first down, but Howell sent in the punting team, and I do believe it was the right decision. We had the lead, we had Chandler, the best punter in the league, and we had the best defense in the game. There wasn't much time left, so you figure there was no way they could score a touchdown, and Steve Myhra, their kicker, wasn't very good; he'd only made four of his ten field-goal attempts all year and was hardly known as a pressure kicker. Howell clearly made the right choice, no question in my mind about that.

Chandler's punt got the ball to the Colts fourteen, and we thought we were sitting pretty when Unitas fired two incomplete passes. But on third and ten, he found Moore open for an 11-yard gain, and the drive stayed alive.

At that point, we were playing a little looser, trying not to give them anything deep. Unitas took full advantage of that. On second and ten, he found Berry open over the middle with single coverage by Karilivacz and hit him for a 25-yard gain to midfield. Next play, same combination, Unitas to Berry for 15 yards, Karilivacz trying futilely to defend. First down at the thirty-five, and Unitas went to Berry one more time, for a 22-yard gain to the thirteen. Poor Carl, he blamed himself for years for that loss, but it wasn't all his fault. Hey, we were playing a great offensive football team—four guys in the Hall of Fame—Unitas, Moore, Berry, and Parker. Anyway, Unitas had moved them 62 yards in the time it takes to blink, and Myhra surprised everyone in the stadium and probably himself, too, when he kicked a 20-yard field goal to send the game into sudden death.

At that point, a lot of us knew we were in very deep trouble. We were exhausted from that last series and Unitas and Berry were just on fire, and there didn't seem to be anything we could do about it. His linemen were blocking as if his very life depended on it. Our offense didn't help us on the first series after we won the coin toss. Maynard bobbled the opening kickoff and recovered it and brought the ball out to the twenty, but Conerly couldn't get anything going and Chandler came on to punt.

The Colts took over at their own twenty, and never gave up the ball again. Twice we had Unitas in third and long situations on the drive, and twice he found receivers open—first Ameche for 8 yards, then 21 yards to Berry for a first down at the Giant forty-three. The next play was the killer. Unitas called a trap and gave the ball to Ameche. He rumbled up the middle for 23 yards to our twenty, and four plays later, Unitas crossed us up one last time by throwing a pass to his tight end Jim Mutscheller on second and goal from the seven that carried to the one. From there, in one of the most famous pictures of all time, Ameche got the ball and bulled over for the touchdown that gave the Colts the game and the title.

Why was it the greatest game ever played? Well, you had one of the most prolific offensive units in the history of the league playing against one of the most dominant defenses. There were Hall of Famers everywhere you looked on both sides of the line. It was the first time a championship had been decided by sudden-death overtime, and there were fifty million people watching on national television. A lot of people say that game was responsible for getting people really interested in professional football. It had everything—great offense, great defense, a lot of controversy. Hell, I even got in a fight with the Colts' coach Weeb Ewbank, yet another Hall of Famer. I had tackled Berry on the sideline early in the game, a legitimate hit, but Weeb thought I was roughing up his man, so he took a poke at me when I got up. He didn't hurt me; he surprised me more than anything and I kind of laughed at him. But it was just one of those things that happened in the heat of battle.

At the time, I don't think any of us realized the impact the game would have. I knew it cost me some money—the Colts' share was $4,674.44 and we got $3,083.27. We had let another opportunity for a championship slip away, and you don't get a lot of those chances in life.

I also knew that I had been involved in one of the toughest, most physically demanding games I'd ever played in. Was it the greatest game ever played? It sure felt like it. But when the 1958 game was over, it was gone forever, and I've always felt a little sad about that because it wasn't just any football game, it was a game for the ages.

7

By the time we arrived in training camp for the start of
the 1959 season, the memory of that championship loss had
faded. After the game most of us scattered around the
country to our homes, and in those days, long before
widespread television and saturation media coverage, you
could go about your business in relative anonymity. You'd
make a couple of appearances at the high-school football
banquet or the Kiwanis Club, but I always found I was
pretty much able to blend into the background when I went
home to West Virginia.

Of course, it was a different story when you got back
to New York, the media capital of America. I suppose
that's one of the reasons we always trained in places like
Winooski. There were just a few reporters who covered the
team on a fairly regular basis, and some of them even
traveled with us during preseason. But because of the
Yankees—and before 1957, the Giants and Dodgers—most
people concentrated on baseball until the World Series, and
we were generally relegated to secondary status on the
sports pages.

Still, in 1959, there were some significant and newswor-
thy changes on the football team. Lombardi had accepted
an offer to coach the struggling Green Bay Packers, a move
that eventually prevented him from returning to coach the
Giants when Jim Lee Howell retired after the 1960 season.

Wellington Mara wanted Lombardi as his head coach, but Vince had signed a contract with the Packers, and in those days, you honored those contracts. So the Giants hired Allie Sherman to replace him as offensive coordinator. Allie had been an offensive assistant with the team before taking a head coaching job in Canada in 1954 and had helped convert Conerly from a college tailback into a T-formation quarterback. I'll give the devil his due. Sherman, the man who traded me to the Redskins in 1964 and not one of my favorite people, was an outstanding assistant coach, a real innovator and one of the first people to put men in motion on offense to get the defense off-balance. Just as he had done with Landry and Lombardi, Jim Lee Howell handed the offense to Sherman and let him do whatever he wanted.

Defensively, there were a few changes, including one at linebacker. Bill Svoboda, our defensive captain, retired after the 1958 season and was replaced in the lineup by Cliff Livingston, a great special teams player who finally got a chance to show what he could do.

Livingston was another one of those screwball characters the coaching staff had to put up with because he was such a talented player. He was from California, and when he first joined the team, some of the guys were convinced he was gay. Crew-cuts were still in vogue then but Cliff had long, blond hair and combed it back over the top of his head. He wore these real tight jeans, his fingernails were always manicured, he had a beach-boy tan, and when he walked, he seemed to strut.

We used to call him "The Living Tongue" and we found out quickly enough that appearances can be deceiving. Cliff was a good-looking guy and he loved women as much as they seemed to love him.

Being from Arkansas, Jim Lee Howell didn't know what to make of Livingston and he was always picking on him. But he put up with him because he performed, and most coaches, even Jim Lee Howell, made allowances. Cliff was one of the first special-team specialists aside from the punter and the placekicker. He was so graceful he probably could have been a ballet dancer. He was fast and quick and gave opposing punters fits because he would sneak in there and block their kicks. I was pretty good at it myself. They never kept statistics on it, but I'll bet I had as many blocked field goals and extra points as anybody who ever played the game. Cliff also played backup linebacker and he saw a lot of action, even though he never started until after the 1958 season.

He saw a lot of action off the field, as well. One time we were playing an exhibition game in Hershey, Pennsylvania, and afterward, we stayed overnight at a local hotel. Generally they didn't make any formal announcement about it, but we all knew that there would be no bed check after a game. So Cliff, as usual, had a date and never bothered to come back to the hotel that night, even though we were supposed to fly to Dallas early the next day to prepare for an exhibition game the following weekend against the Colts.

Early that morning, Cliff called up his roommate, Tom Scott, and told him he was in Reading, Pennsylvania. "Pack my suitcase," he told Scott, "and I'll meet the bus at the Harrisburg airport." When the bus pulled in, Cliff got on and no one said a word. What the hell, we'd won the game the night before, Cliff was a single guy, and as long as he got there in time for the flight, what harm did he do?

Now we were in Dallas practicing for a week and Cliff wasn't able to work out. He'd been hurt in Hershey and they didn't want to risk him for the regular season. The day of the Colt exhibition, we were having our pregame meeting when Howell always gave us last-minute instructions and our postgame itinerary. At the end of his talk he said, "Now, Livingston, you're not going to play tonight, and you better not break curfew and you better not miss that bus."

That's all Cliff had to hear. After the game, Cliff and a few other guys went out on the town and met a couple of stewardesses. They all had drinks together and most of the guys came back to the hotel. Everybody but Cliff, in fact. When we boarded the bus the next morning, Cliff still hadn't shown up, so we took off for the airport. Jim Lee Howell waited for no one.

When we got to Love Field, a gorgeous woman walked up to the bus, knocked on the door, and asked if Tom Scott was on board. "Cliff's out in the car, and he doesn't have any clothes," she told Scott, who had packed Livingston's suitcase again, just as he had done in Hershey the week before.

Word spread through the bus, and now everyone was starting to look for Cliff. Someone yelled, "Heeeeere he comes" and Cliff dashed onto the plane in a bathing suit—and that's it. Who knows what happened to his clothes. I only know he had no shirt, no shoes and socks, no wallet. He was mad as hell because he thought someone had played a practical joke on him. Poor Scottie was just following Howell's orders. Cliff was fined and Jim Lee even made him get up at a meeting and apologize to the team, but no one ever wondered about Cliff's preferences after that.

Gifford, meanwhile, had another preference himself that year. He decided he wanted to play quarterback, even if his best friend and long-time roommate, Charlie Conerly, was still very much the starter. Gifford had played quarterback in high school and for two years at Southern Cal and Lombardi loved to have him run the halfback option because he had a pretty good arm. Frank will always tell you otherwise, but I had a hard time believing he was serious about switching positions. Maybe it was a publicity stunt—Frank definitely knew how to get his name in the paper—but whatever it was, it didn't last all that long. First of all, he was too valuable to the team as a halfback. He was a truly gifted athlete, a nifty running back who was also a great student of the game. Jim Lee let him try it, though, and he played a half against the Lions in preseason. He did all right, but when I watched him at the position, it didn't look like it came naturally to him. He was a little stiff. Anyway, in the second half, somebody got hurt and Frank had to play halfback. That was the end of the experiment.

Frank also picked a bad year to try to become a quarterback. We had a surplus at the position in camp. In addition to Conerly and Heinrich, they had traded to get George Shaw from the Colts. And Wellington Mara's top draft choice that year was another quarterback, Lee Grosscup from Utah. Lee had had a big game against Army, and that was enough for Wellington. Grosscup was a pretty good college quarterback, and he was also a very bright guy, an intellectual type who probably wanted to be a writer more than he did a football player. After he'd been drafted, he wrote a bunch of letters to Murray Olderman of the Newspaper Enterprise Association (NEA) news service, mostly about his college days. Olderman edited them and sold them to *Sports Illustrated,* and the article appeared while Lee was still in the College All-Star camp. It was pretty harmless stuff, but some of it rubbed a few guys on our team the wrong way, especially a line about the Giants being "good drinkers." Maybe so, but who wanted to read it in a national magazine from a kid who had never even been in camp? So when Lee reported to Winooski, he was a marked man. People would hit him in scrimmages as hard as they hit Jim Brown in a game, me included. But I'll give him credit. He was a tough kid and eventually he gained our respect, because he took those licks and always came back for more.

After my own experience as a rookie, I tried to make it a point to help some of those kids out. One day at our camp in Bear Mountain, New York, I saw Lee sitting by himself at dinner and invited him to finish a pizza with us. I won't tell you we were bosom buddies, but I always thought Grosscup was a good guy and deserved better than he got. That year the Giants kept him on the taxi squad, but he never did make it in the pros.

The mention of Bear Mountain always brings back great

memories. When school started at St. Michael's, we'd move camp from Vermont to Bear Mountain for the end of the preseason. Lombardi loved it there because it was close to West Point, where he'd coached before he came to the Giants, and we'd always go up to watch the Army team practice. One year there had been a big cheating scandal at West Point, and as we were watching practice, one of our offensive linemen, Bill Austin, a guy who went on to be a head coach at Pittsburgh and Washington, put his foot in his mouth. The Army team had blown a play in a scrimmage and Austin yelled out, "Whatsa matter, didn't you have your crib sheet out?" Suddenly it got very quiet, and no one was laughing. In fact, I believe it was the last time the Giants were ever allowed to watch Army practice again.

One year we had a little offensive guard in camp named Gerry Huth, a great guy who loved challenges. We got to talking one day about how long it would take someone to climb Bear Mountain, bottom to top. So Huth said he could do it in under a half hour. Well, Svoboda, Chandler, and I started booking bets as to how long it would take him. We had a lot of money riding on it, and Huth ran up that mountain in about seventeen and a half minutes. When he got to the top, he almost couldn't stop he was so pumped up. He was breathing so hard we thought he was close to having a heart attack. Chandler and I had to wrap him in blankets and walk him around like you do a thoroughbred after a horse race.

There was another episode involving Bear Mountain that very well could have cost me my career. One year, we had a preseason game on the Friday night right before the Labor Day weekend, and Jim Lee had told the team that after the game he'd give us time off until the following Monday night at eight. I was always getting homesick in training camp, and after the game, I was planning to head back to West Virginia for a weekend with my family. Then we went out and lost the game, and Jim Lee got angry and changed the rules. Now, instead of Monday at eight, he wanted us back at Bear Mountain by Sunday at eight. I wasn't about to give up a weekend at home, so I made arrangements for Mel Triplett to pick me and a couple of other guys up in Pittsburgh in his car. He was driving back from Toledo, Ohio, and it wasn't that far out of his way. Well, Triplett got a late start going back, and he was scared of Jim Lee Howell, just like the rest of us. He didn't want to be late, so he barreled right through Pittsburgh and never stopped to pick us up. We waited a couple of hours, and when he didn't show, we decided to rent a car and drive back ourselves. Everything would have been fine, until we got lost in the mountains in upstate New York and we got back at about two in the morning, long after Howell's curfew. This was one time he checked beds, and we weren't in ours.

The next day, Jim Lee had his usual prepractice meeting and started talking. "Now some of the boys didn't get back in time last night, so they will be fined seventy-five dollars apiece," he said. That's not even tipping money to some of these players today, but back then, when I was making $9,000 a year, it hurt. And I was furious. Right out there on the practice field I told Jim Lee, "I'll tell you what, I'll hold that seventy-five dollars in my hand, and by God, I want to see you take it away from me."

To challenge a head coach like that, as I look back on it now, was a crazy thing to do, but I was very angry. I didn't want to lose that money, but the fact that he'd taken a day away from us really burned me up. Not to mention that it wasn't really our fault we were late to begin with.

Jim Lee looked me dead in the eye and said, "We'll just see about that."

"Yessir," I shot back, "we'll just see about that because you're not going to be able to take it away from me." Neither one of us was about to back down, and we started practice.

In those days, the Giants had an executive committee among the players. The two captains and one representative from the offensive line, running backs, linebackers, and so on. The committee would hear player gripes about the coaching staff and management and try to settle problems before they got out of hand. So I appeared before the committee that night after practice and everyone sympathized with me. By this time, I had cooled off a little bit, and I also realized I'd made a big mistake challenging Jim Lee's authority. So they asked me if I'd compromise and pay fifty dollars and I agreed to that. Howell went along with it, but he just as easily could have thrown me off that football team.

Of course this was 1959, and by then I was pretty well established. I guess I was dealing from a position of strength, but one thing you soon learned back then was that you were always expendable, and you also knew that you were only one injury away from going home.

I never had a serious injury while I was with the Giants, but I did get knocked out a few times. The first three games I played with the Giants my rookie year the lights went out. I'd go down on all the kickoffs, throw myself into the wedge, hit the big backs—it was just the way I played.

In our last preseason game against the Forty-niners in 1959, it happened again. We were playing in Provo, Utah, at Brigham Young University and a guy caught a pass right in front of me. The whistle blew and as I was getting up, some rookie didn't realize the play was over and kneed me in the side of the head. *Bam,* I was out again.

They carried me off the field on a stretcher and took me to the local hospital, and that's where I woke up. That night, a couple of the Forty-niners showed up to visit me, Y. A. Tittle and some other guys. Nobody from the Giants came by; they didn't even send my clothes over.

By the next morning, the doctors said I could go, so I left the hospital. I know I was still groggy because to this day, I don't remember how I got my clothes or how I got back to the team. In fact, the whole next week I was kind of in a daze. We broke camp in Utah and then flew to

California to play the Rams in the season opener the next week. I practiced all week, had a couple of bloody noses, but still started the game.

The Rams had a hell of a team that year, including two great running backs, Ollie Matson and John Arnette. Chandler told me before the game that for the first time, Howell didn't even bother to tell him where to put the opening kickoff because it didn't matter who got it, either one could take it all the way.

Anyway, early in the game, I tackled Arnette from behind and his heel hit me on the chin. It was like someone had clicked the lights back on. Everything came into focus; I knew where I was and I finished the game.

I guess I had been cleared to play by old Doc Sweeny, but that never meant very much. Doc was a grand old guy who loved to drink beer and talk about Manhattan College basketball. He'd give you the damndest physical examination you ever saw—he'd listen to your heart, take your blood pressure, and check you for a hernia. He'd tell you to cough, and if you coughed, you were okay. End of physical.

There were times during training camp when my weight would go below 220 and he would say, "Well, Sam, you're going to have to come in and drink some beer with me." So I'd go to his room where he had a refrigerator and he'd sit there and tell stories all day.

I'm sure he was a good doctor, but sometimes he did make you wonder. One time Dick Nolan broke his wrist playing and somehow it wasn't set properly at the hospital. So Dick always had his hand at a funny angle on his arm. One day Doc Sweeny asked him how he was doing, and Nolan answered, "Well, Doc, that wrist is still giving me some problems."

"Let me take a look at it," Sweeny said, so Nolan, just fooling around, stuck out his good hand.

"Well, that thing is still bad," Sweeny told him, "we'll have to do something about that." I used to joke with our trainers that if anything ever happened to me out on the field, I hoped they got to me before Doc Sweeny did. One thing about him, though, he did not believe in rushing into surgery, because he knew that could mean an immediate end to a career. So the trainers would tape you back together and try to get you in shape to play.

You always hear a lot of horror stories about athletes taking painkillers like Novocain, and sometimes playing on amphetamines. I never took a painkiller in my life. Some guys liked to get vitamin B-12 shots before a game because they thought it gave them extra energy. Some guys used Benzedrine, the stuff kids use to stay up to study for exams. I used Benzedrine once early in my career and got kicked out of a game. It made me a little crazy, and then I couldn't remember my assignments, so I never used that stuff again. I could always remember to hit people, but I knew how to do that anyway. When you're a middle linebacker, or a quarterback, you have to be able to think clearly, and you can't be so violent that you don't know what's going on.

Back to the 1959 season. We had another good football team that year, and our defense was exceptional. We gave up forty-nine points to the Eagles in the second game after one of our scouts was quoted in the paper as saying Philadelphia wasn't much. That did not sit well with the Eagles, and they really took it out on us. But in our last ten games that year we only allowed a hundred points. Summerall was also having a great year. In fact, that season he accounted for just over thirty percent of our points on offense.

The chants of "Huff, Huff, Huff" were becoming commonplace, and our pictures were appearing in the papers as much as or more than the offense's. Gifford used to walk by while the photographers were posing us and say, "That's okay, guys, you get your face in the paper and I'll make all the money."

We'd go down to Toots Shor's and get treated royally. Toots would come up to us and say "I looooove the defense, I looooove the defense" and he always gave us the best seat in the house.

One day after a game, our locker room was crowded with the usual mix of writers and businessmen. In those days, if you had a friend or a business acquaintance you could always get him in the locker room, or get his kids in for autographs. Most of the writers would talk to the stars of the game, the quarterbacks and the running backs, and for the most part, we all pretty much respected each other. The Giants were generally a friendly bunch of guys and most of the writers never wrote very critically about us, so we got along fine. We all knew the media played a big part in the game, and it never hurt to have your name or your picture in the papers.

Anyway, I was drying off after a game early that season and a fellow came up and introduced himself as a reporter from *Time*. To this day I couldn't tell you his name, but he said, "Sam, we'd like to do a cover story on you."

I thought that was okay, even though I didn't really know much about *Time* magazine. I read the sports pages because that's what interested me. I concentrated on football, not the news of the day, so why read *Time*? Then I asked him how much money they were going to pay me. After all, I'd been getting watches from some of the Giant sponsors for being the game's most valuable player, and I figured if they wanted to put me on the cover, they should pay me.

"So how much?" I asked him.

"Sam," he said, "it's a great honor to be on the cover; we don't pay people. We've had presidents and prime ministers on the cover, and we've never paid anyone."

"Well," I answered, "then I guess you won't be doing a story on me."

"Look," he said, "we're going to have someone paint a portrait of you and I can guarantee you it will be one of the biggest things that ever happens in your lifetime."

That portrait business interested me. I didn't have one of myself playing football, so I told him I'd make a deal with him. If they would give me that portrait, I'd agree to the story. He didn't want to do that either because those portraits were supposed to hang in their boardroom at the Time-Life Building in Manhattan.

"No picture, no story," I told him, and he said he'd get back to me.

A few days later, he called back and said we had a deal. Over the next few weeks, it seemed like they were all over me. People came at me in waves to research this story, and I'd get calls at all hours of the day and night. "We just want to check this out or check that out," they'd say. I was never so happy as when that story finally appeared on the cover.

It was worth it. The portrait was magnificent, and now I tell everyone I've still got my portrait at home and all the rest are at the Smithsonian.

And the guy was right. It really did have a major impact on my life, and I almost blew it. In fact, I still get people sending me copies of that magazine in the mail for an autograph.

I'm sure there was some jealousy among my teammates because of it. I was the first defensive player ever put on the cover, and the article, which appeared on November 30, 1959, under the headline "PRO FOOTBALL, Brawn, Brains & Profits," was extremely complimentary. Here are a few excerpts:

> The four blue-jerseyed men facing him are mountains of muscle. Alert and agile as jungle cats, two linebackers crouch outside the ends. Ranged in an arc behind them are four whippet-fast backs. And a bare two yards away from the quarterback, returning his stare in challenge, waits the key man of the proud New York Giant defense: Middle Linebacker Sam Huff (6 ft. 1 in., 230 lbs.), a confident smiling fighter fired with a devout desire to sink a thick shoulder into every ball carrier in the National Football League.

Or this:

> Sunday after Sunday, pro quarterbacks have learned that whatever play they call, Huff is likely to be in

front of it. Sam Huff is strong enough to flatten a plunging fullback such as the Chicago Bears' Rick Casares (6 ft. 2½ in., 225 lbs.), swift enough to recover from a block in time to nail a halfback sprinting around end, smart enough to diagnose pass patterns and throw an offensive end off stride with an artful shoulder. But Huff is at his rugged best when he knifes through the line and "red-dogs" a quarterback as he fades to pass. The crash of Huff's tackle can stir the Giants bench to bellowing glee, set the rabid fans in Yankee Stadium to rumbling out their own rapid-fire cheer like the chugging of a steam-engine "Huff-Huff-Huff-Huff-Huff." When Sam is on the field, the toughest fans in the U.S.'s toughest sport see what they came to see.

Lombardi was quoted as saying, "It's uncanny the way Huff follows the ball. He ignores all the things you do to take him away from the play and comes after the ball wherever it is thrown or wherever the run goes. Sure, sometimes he goes with the fake. But that's when the ball is there."

And I had a few interesting things to say myself.

"You play as hard and as vicious as you can," I told *Time* magazine. "You've got more chance to get hurt when you're loafin'. . . . You rap that quarterback every chance you get. He's the brains of the outfit. If you knock him out clean and hard on that first play of the game, that's an accomplishment. For that matter, we try to hurt everybody. We hit each other as hard as we can. This is a man's game."

Tough stuff, and nothing but the truth.

8

With Charlie Conerly pitching, Pat Summerall kicking, Alex Webster and Frank Gifford running behind a great offensive line, and our defense just dominating, the 1959 season ended with another Eastern Conference championship.

It also ended with Jim Lee Howell cutting a deal with Wellington Mara that would allow him to retire after the 1960 season. Jim Lee apparently was having more and more difficulty handling the pressure. We all noticed that he was testier than usual over the second half of the season; in fact, some of the players were actually taking bets on precisely what day they were going to put him in a strait-jacket and haul him away. He was always uptight, and down the stretch he was almost unbearable. I'd even heard that his wife had actually gone to the Giants and said her husband was becoming a basket case.

Howell was later quoted as saying, "It got so bad in 1959 that I was sacrificing everything—my life and my family—to football. I'd spend all day at practice, snapping at my players, then take my snarling disposition home with me. I couldn't sleep and I couldn't unwind. It just wasn't worth it anymore. It reached a point where I couldn't stand to lose and I didn't get any kick out of winning." So the Maras made him an offer. They'd keep him in the organization at the same salary, and he would become the team's super personnel scout. They also asked him to stay on for one more season so they could take their time finding a suitable successor.

We clinched a tie for the championship with a 45–14 victory over the Redskins at Yankee Stadium on Charlie Conerly Day. Conerly had taken a pretty good beating all season—hell, he was always taking a beating—but he threw for three touchdowns in the first half and the Redskins were never able to recover. Charlie was showered by gifts from management, and the same crowd that had given him such a hard time earlier in his career gave him several standing ovations. More important to the rest of us, when the Browns were upset by the Forty-niners, we had a piece of the title.

You really couldn't blame our offensive line for Charlie's physical problems. At this point, the guy was pushing forty—none of us ever knew how old he really was—and he was always injury-prone.

The line, in fact, was a real strength of that offensive team. One guard, Jack Stroud, was our enforcer. No one wanted to mess with Stroud. Our center, Ray Wietecha, was a smart savvy guy and a great athlete who could have been a professional baseball player. He was a big, strong slugger and played in the minors as a young man. Maybe he had the same experience with baseball that I'd had; in any case, all of us were happy that he chose football, particularly our kickers. They loved Ray because his snaps always came back to the holder with the laces up, just the way they're supposed to. The guy was uncanny. He never even looked at the holder, but in all the years I played with him, I can hardly remember Wietecha making a bad snap.

Our MVP lineman had to be Roosevelt Brown. He had been a twenty-seventh round draft choice out of Morgan State in 1953, taken by the Giants sight unseen after Wellington spotted his name on a list of black college All-Americans, and he went on to play in nine Pro Bowls and make the Hall of Fame. By today's standards, he wasn't that big, about six-two and 250 pounds. But he was nothing but muscle, a bigger version of Jimmy Brown, and he was all heart. He was so valuable to our football team he even played some defense. Both he and Stroud were so strong, they'd come in on defense in short-yardage and goal-line situations. Rosey also played on all the special teams. He must have had some kind of incentive clause for minutes played, because he always wanted to be out on the field.

He also always seemed to be broke. When I was a rookie, he once asked to borrow ten dollars, and I gave him the money. He was a pretty well-known veteran and as a rookie, I was a little hesitant to ask for it back. Well, late in the year we played the Redskins and had to take the train home from Washington. He came up to me on the train and handed me a ten-dollar bill. "I was hoping you'd get cut and I wouldn't have to pay you back," he said, "but it looks like you might be here awhile."

Rosey loved to play the game, and in later years, he really paid the price for all those trips on the kickoff squad. At one point, they had to give him an artificial knee, and he had real problems with that. A lot of the guys I played with still have severe physical problems from football. In a sense, we were guinea pigs. There was no such thing as arthroscopic surgery, where they put you under for an hour, fix the damage and clean out the joint and get you back on the practice field in a matter of days. I'm certain much of today's sports medicine is a direct result of experimenting with new techniques on the athletes of my era.

Back then when you had a knee operation, you might as well just have called it a career. They'd cut you open from one end of your knee to the other and really do a number on you. A lot of guys wanted no part of surgery, so you played in considerable pain to avoid it. Rosey Brown was the perfect example.

My dear friend and roommmate, Don Chandler, probably became a punter because of surgery. He grew up in Oklahoma and was a tremendous baseball player. But he hurt his arm and they had to operate on his shoulder. After that he was never the same. He could have been a great running back, too, but every time he'd raise his arm, that shoulder would pop out. So he learned how to kick the ball.

Chandler was a lot like Conerly, kind of a grump. He'd sit there in the morning, smoking cigarettes and drinking coffee, and bitch about everything—the weather, the food, the fact that he wasn't back home in Oklahoma. But what a kicker. He was another great weapon for our defense because he would put an opposing offense deep in their own territory.

He was not a picture-perfect punter. He'd almost kick it off the side of his foot, soccer-style. But I've seen him kick the ball 90 to 100 yards in the air, and that is no exaggeration. In Dallas once, I saw him kick the ball from his own end zone and land it out of bounds on the two.

In 1959, Chandler averaged 46.6 yards a punt, a Giant record that still stands. Even so, it seemed like Landry was always trying to get him to change his technique. Landry was a methodical man, and he loved the way Yale Lary of the Detroit Lions kicked the ball. Classic form. So Landry would start working with Chandler, trying to get him to kick through the ball instead of having it go off the side of his foot. It never worked. Don would try it and take 20 to 30 yards off his kick, so he'd go back to the way he knew best.

Most coaches don't like to work with guys who can't play because they don't want to waste their time. But take a great player who doesn't really need much help, and that's who they want to coach. In 1969, my last year with the Redskins, we had a rookie back named Larry Brown, the very same Larry Brown who went on to lead the team to the Super Bowl in 1972 and become the NFL's MVP that year. The first time Vince Lombardi saw Brown carry the ball, he knew he had something special. So he told his backfield coach, a terrific guy named George Dickson, to "leave that little son of a gun alone. He's a football player.

You coach all the rest of them dumb backs, but just hand the ball to Brown and he'll show you what to do with it.'' That was Lombardi's way. If a guy could do it, don't mess with him, even if it's not classic form. That's probably why Lombardi loved Chandler so much. He got the job done. In our next-to-last game against the Browns in 1959, we got the job done, too.

After we'd clinched a tie for the conference title, Cleveland came to town the following week and we had more than 68,000 people in the stadium. It was no contest. Conerly completed 14 of 21 passes for 271 yards and three touchdowns, and Jim Brown was held to 50 yards in 15 carries. Our fans were so ecstatic that in the final minutes, thousands streamed onto the field and Cleveland's coach, Paul Brown, fearing for the safety of his players, and maybe even his own, took his team to the dressing room while they tried to restore order. It could have been a dangerous situation. The public address announcer, Bob Sheppard, even announced that the game would be forfeited if the fans didn't leave, and that was enough incentive to clear the field and finish the game. I ran to the dressing room myself when the people started coming out. You never know when someone might try to do something crazy, and I figured that was the safest place to be until the crowd calmed down.

The next week we beat the Redskins, 24–10, in the season finale, and now it was time for a return engagement with our friends from Baltimore, who had won the Western Conference title. But I had other concerns away from the football team.

Late that season, Mary was due to have another baby. She wanted to stay in West Virginia, but I made her come to New York. We rented a house in Flushing, and I wanted her in the big city because I thought the medical care would be a lot better than back home.

When Mary gave birth to Cathy in 1957, she'd had some bleeding problems that she never really told anyone about. When her doctor in New York found out, he decided the best thing would be to induce labor. With me at practice all day and traveling on weekends, he didn't want to take any chances. So we got her scheduled for the procedure.

While we were getting ready for the championship game, I took Mary to the hospital one morning to have the baby. I figured I could go to practice and get back in time to be with her when it was over. Back then, they didn't allow fathers in the operating room, and even if they had, I'm not sure I would have gone in. I had a hard time giving blood, let alone watching surgery. In fact, Mary always used to joke that they had to get me a hospital room just to give me an inoculation.

The fact that I made it a point to concentrate on football sounds a little cold now, but that was the mentality of the game at the time. There was no such thing as taking a few days off from practice; you were expected to be there every day, no excuses. The Rams actually traded Robustelli to the Giants because he wanted to spend time with his wife and new baby instead of reporting to training camp.

Anyway, they induced labor, but after the baby was born, Mary's uterus burst, and she almost bled to death. They didn't even have time to call me. They performed an emergency hysterectomy and had to give her five pints of blood. When I came home from practice that day at three, the lady who was watching the kids told me to call the hospital right away.

I was told to get there immediately and when I met the doctor, he was almost hysterical himself. He told me she was alive, but just barely. The baby was fine, but Mary was in bad shape. It took her a long time to recover from that, and as it turned out, the decision to have her come to New York to give birth probably saved her life. If she had stayed in West Virginia, where they take childbirth almost for granted, I don't think she would have made it. Over the next couple of weeks, nurses would actually come into the room and shake their heads. They couldn't believe she was alive.

That's how my son J.D. came into the world, with a

real bang. He was named Joseph after my best friend in college, Joe Marconi, and the D. was in honor of three of my best friends in New York—Don Chandler, Don Smith, the Giants' publicity director, and Dick Voyce, who lived near us in Flushing and became a great friend of our family.

Dick worked in the textile business and he and Smith were buddies. That's how I got to know him. While Mary was in the hospital, Dick would be over there almost every day while I was at practice, keeping her company. I'd go from practice to the hospital, then go home and try to catch a few winks at night. It was a heck of a way to prepare for a championship game, but I never missed a minute of practice, never missed a meeting—that's just the way I was.

We went into that game against the Colts feeling pretty confident. Conerly had led the NFL in passing and was the league's Most Valuable Player. Summerall finished second in the scoring race and our defense was also rated number one in the league. I was voted defensive MVP.

Landry, of course, was concerned about containing John Unitas, Raymond Berry, and Lenny Moore, the same group that had beaten us the year before. He also decided that he was going to single-cover Moore and double-up on Berry and their tight end, Jim Mutscheller. "We decided to concede a touchdown to Lenny Moore and cover him with only one man," Landry said at the time, according to Barry Gottehrer, the author of *The Giants of New York*. "This way we'd be giving them their strength, hoping to cut off everything else. If our defense worked, I thought we might win, 17–14 or 21–17."

So poor Lindon Crow, a cornerback, got the assignment of covering Moore. Landry was so stubborn, he'd hardly ever change his defense to help anybody. He'd always say, "You're a professional, you play against the best and you're supposed to be the best, so you've got to figure out a way to cover." Well, Lindon got burned all day, and eventually it cost us the game.

We started off real well—in fact, we led at the half,

9–7, on three Summerall field goals and maintained that lead through the third quarter. Late in that quarter, we got a little momentum going and started driving. We had a first down at the Colt thirty-eight, then came up with another one of those fourth-and-one situations at their twenty-nine. Unlike the previous year in the championship game when Gifford was stopped short and the Colts managed to rally and send the game into overtime, Howell gambled this time and decided to go for the first down. Conerly handed off to Alex Webster, and for one of the few times in his career, Alex was stopped short by a small mob of Colt defenders. Even though we still had the lead at that point, it was the beginning of the end.

The Colts went on to score twenty-four points in the fourth quarter. Jimmy Patton had been knocked out with a foot injury and early in the fourth, Lindon Crow got kneed in the face by Moore on a 36-yard pass play and was knocked silly. He stayed in the game, but it was obvious our secondary could not stop Unitas.

The great Colt quarterback scored on a 5-yard run early in the period for a 14–9 lead. The game turned on the next series. Backed up on our ten with third and eight to go, Conerly called a pass but was intercepted by Andy Nelson at the thirty-one. After a 17-yard runback, the Colts had the ball at our fourteen. Unitas threw for a touchdown to a rookie receiver, Jerry Richardson, and a few minutes later, Johnny Sample, who would later be my teammate in Washington, picked off another pass and returned it 42 yards for a touchdown.

The final score: Colts 31, Giants 16, and in truth, I believe the better team won that day. Our defense was probably a little better than theirs, but there was no comparison with their offense. Unitas could get you from anywhere on the field. That year he set an NFL record with thirty-two touchdown passes. Once we got behind, we did not have the kind of blazing speed on the ends or in the backfield that could have gotten us back into the game.

Conerly was a grind-it-out, precise-passing-attack kind of guy, so there was no way. I can remember it was an awfully gloomy train ride back to New York. We had lost another championship, and word had gotten around that Landry would be the head coach of the expansion Dallas Cowboys the following year. First you lose a Lombardi, then you lose a Tom Landry, and you have to figure your football team is going to suffer.

Right after the game, we wasted little time going back to West Virginia and that was a mistake on my part. Mary was still not a hundred percent from the operation, but when she got out of the hospital, I loaded the family in the car and we drove home. I didn't realize she was still that weak from having J.D. and I figured she'd do better back home. Our lease in Flushing also was up and I wanted to get home for the holidays, so we made the trip. We drove through a snowstorm on the Pennsylvania Turnpike and the drive was a traumatic experience.

In the off-season that year I also worked full-time for the Philip Morris Tobacco Company. They picked five of us from the Giants—myself, Modzelewski, Patton, Chandler, and Crow, and we covered the areas we lived in.

They gave us a company car and an expense account and paid us $250 a week to drive around and meet with wholesalers and retailers. We'd also give speeches at the local Kiwanis and Rotary clubs, hand out free samples and that kind of thing. You'd go into a town, meet the company's local representative, and they would have your agenda all laid out for you. I also made some commercials for them, and the heck of it was, I didn't even smoke. I never did as a kid, and never have, but they didn't care.

I worked for a guy named Jack Landry, the finest marketing man I've ever been associated with. He got Philip Morris to become one of the NFL's first big television sponsors and to this day he and Pete Rozelle are good friends. It was a job that helped me learn the business world inside out. It gave me wholesale experience, detail experience, helped me develop confidence as a public speaker, and paid good money.

Of course one of the worst trips I ever took in my life resulted from that job. Somebody decided it would be a great idea to take that little guy in the Philip Morris ads— you know, the bellhop who'd scream "Call for Philip Morris"—on a promotional boat trip down the intracoastal waterway, New York to Florida. He got on the boat but after a couple of days, he became seasick. So another genius had the bright idea to subsitute a Giant for a midget, and I was their man. I met the boat and got on board. The captain was an ex-admiral and maybe the meanest son of a bitch I'd ever met. I didn't know a damned thing about boats, but here I was stuck on board with this guy, and he's treating me like I'm a deckhand. It seemed like all I saw for ten days was cattle and alligators. When we got to Florida, we'd stop and have lunch with the local dignitaries at a yacht club or somebody's fancy house. But we slept on board and this crazy captain would have everybody up at five in the morning to work on the boat. Finally, we got to the end of the line, and we were supposed to take the boat back up north. No way. I got off that boat as fast as I could, hopped a flight to New York, and never looked back.

As long as we're talking about boats, I had a couple more nautical adventures.

The next time I got on a boat was in 1964. I'd been traded to the Redskins and a local boat company asked me to make an appearance for them at the Washington Boat Show. In exchange, they promised me the use of a yacht for a year. That sounded like a pretty good arrangement, and I accepted the offer, even though I didn't know a gybe from a jab. To be honest I wasn't much of a sailor. It would take me twenty-five tries just to park the thing at the dock. So I started hiring a captain whenever I wanted to take the family out. One summer day, we went out on Chesapeake Bay. It was hot, and Sam Jr. asked if we could tie up and go swimming. I wasn't crazy about the idea, but this captain I'd hired said he knew a great place. So he took the boat out and dropped anchor under the Bay Bridge near Annapolis. The captain shut off the engine and he and Sam Jr. dove into the water and started swimming away from the boat. In reality, they were being pulled farther and farther away by the current, which can be very treacherous at that particular location. As they got farther away from the boat, the captain started hollering that he was in trouble. Our friends, the Murrays from West Virginia, were with us that day, and Max Murray started running around the boat looking for a line to throw. He ran down into the galley, hit his head going down the steps and almost knocked himself out. Meanwhile, Sam Jr., who was a pretty strong swimmer, managed to get back to the boat and I grabbed him and pulled him on board. The captain was another story.

Finally, I found a line and I took that safety ring and with one throw—maybe the greatest throw in the history of rescue operations at sea—I put that ring damned near right around his head. He grabbed the line and we reeled him back in. I don't think we ever swam in the Bay again.

In the early 1970s, Mary and I started to go to some of the Super Bowls with a group from Bristol-Myers. They'd put together a package deal for their best customers and would make a big weekend out of it. One year, the game was in Miami, so they decided to lease this huge yacht and take everyone on a cruise up the waterway, dock at a fancy restaurant, and have a big party. After my previous experiences with boats, I tried to talk them into just letting the yacht stay at the dock and have the party on board, but they didn't want to hear that, so off we went.

Well, there was the usual spread of food and drink on board, and the captain they'd hired liked to have a few drinks himself. We were all playing cards and having a grand old time when suddenly, we heard a tremendous *bang* that seemed to shake the whole boat. At this point, our captain was feeling no pain and had allowed the ship to run into a buoy. There was another problem. We were out in the ocean. I ran up to find the captain. He was dead drunk, couldn't even stand up, and had no idea where we were or what had happened.

We managed to stop the boat and I thought I knew where we were. The buoy we hit was marked number two, so I got on the radio and raised the Coast Guard.

"Where are you?" they asked.

"Buoy number two," I said.

"Which buoy number two?" they asked.

"I have no idea."

They said unless I could be more precise, there was no way they could possibly help us. They suggested I get on the radio and see if there were any other boats in the vicinity who could give us a better line on our position. So I got on the radio again and started asking if anybody could see our lights. We got lucky, because some guy in a fishing boat was out there at two in the morning and heard the call.

"How'd you like to make an easy hundred," I said. "Where are you?"

"Oh, about two hundred yards away," he answered.

"Well, drop your fish and come on over here," I said. He was there in a couple of minutes, and despite my reputation of being tight with a buck, I'm here to tell you that was one hundred-dollar bill I did not mind parting with. He came over and guided us back to port.

One last boat story.

The Redskins were in the Super Bowl in 1972, and the Marriott Corporation asked me to see if George Allen, the Redskin coach, would agree to go on a Caribbean cruise with a group from the company a few days after the game. They also wanted me to go along, but after all my previous disasters, I told them no way. In addition to the fact that I hated boats, just the thought of being stuck out in the ocean talking football with George Allen for ten days was not my idea of a good time.

"Tell you what I'm going to do," I told them. "I'll get

George, I'll fly with him to Miami and get him and his wife on that boat, but I'll wave good-bye from the pier, thank you.''

That's exactly what I did. And every day I checked on that boat, and it was not a happy cruise. Poor George got stuck in some of the foulest weather ever to hit the Caribbean. Even worse the boat's stabilizers weren't working very well, and everybody on board was seasick for a week. So keep me away from boats. Canoes, rowboats, sailboats, catamarans, luxury yachts—it doesn't matter. You want to see the violent world of Sam Huff, meet me at the marina. Better yet, don't bother.

9

"Today you will play pro football, riding on Sam Huff's broad back. We've wired him for sound with a tiny transistorized radio transmitter. It's not allowed in regular league play and it's the first time it has been done on television. The transmitter is embedded in his pads, the microphone goes in front. You're on the receiving end, and you're going to be closer to pro football than you've ever been before. This is our story: The Violent World of Sam Huff."

Those words, spoken by Walter Cronkite on network television on the evening of October 30, 1960, served as the introduction to a program many people believe helped bring professional football out of the dark ages and into the light. I'll let the historians be the judge of that, but that show, "The Violent World of Sam Huff," certainly was a milestone in my career and brought me more recognition—good and bad—than I ever dreamed possible.

The idea for the show began with Burton Benjamin, a CBS producer. Riding to work in New York City on a commuter train every day, he said he'd been hearing a lot of talk about the Giants in general and me in particular, and he wanted to put together a documentary on professional football. "I wanted to get the series away from history awhile and do something on a contemporary figure people were talking about," Benjamin wrote in *The New York*

Times a few years ago. "The question was: how to give a film on Huff a dimension that would lift it out of the routine football profile."

When they first approached me in the off-season, I was immediately interested. After all, they were going to pay me $500 and agreed to rent me a car while they filmed during training camp. The car was very important. Nowadays, you look in a professional football team's parking lot and you see brand-new Mercedes, Jaguars, Cadillacs, and Oldsmobiles. Back then, none of us drove to camp because we had only one car, and the wife and kids needed it. I was about the only guy in camp with a car that year, and I was a very popular man.

Then the CBS people started negotiating with the Giants and the league about wiring me for sound. That was Benjamin's special angle. His idea was to give his audience a real feel for pro football, and he wanted to do it in an actual game. At first there was some resistance from the higher-ups, but they eventually gave him the go-ahead in an exhibition game.

There were three sequences in the film, which was shown on "The Twentieth Century" program, a weekly thirty-minute show you could say was the early version of "60 Minutes." In the first segment, they filmed me back home in West Virginia, walking on the old high-school field, then talking in front of the mine where my dad had worked.

"Any time that you play football," I said, "there is no place for nice guys. I mean you have to be tough, you have to go all out. I always feel real good when I hit someone . . . you feel that you've accomplished something, you've made a beautiful tackle, and when we're out on that field we have to shake 'em up. It's either kill or be killed."

Standing in front of the mine—the same one that blew up and killed seventy-eight men a few years later—I said, "As a kid, I was raised in a coal-mining camp. Coal mining is all I've ever known, ever since I was a youngster. It's a very dangerous occupation and I'd rather take my chances on a football field. As long as I can play football, I'm going to stay out of there.''

The other segments were filmed during practice, with Jim Lee Howell actually looking like a real nice guy, fooling around with the players, cracking a joke here and there. They interviewed Mary and there was a cute scene we staged in a room at training camp with Modzelewski singing a Polish folk song, Rosey Grier strumming his guitar, and all the guys joining in. Another scene showed a few minutes of action in a training-camp classroom, with Harland Svare, our new defensive coach, diagraming plays and asking questions of me, Jimmy Patton, and Cliff Livingston.

And all the while, Cronkite talked about professional football.

"Pro football is really a collection of specialized trades,'' he said at one point. "There are passing specialists, like Charlie Conerly; pass-catching experts; men who only punt, men who only place-kick. Perhaps the middle linebackers like Sam Huff capture the imagination because they are rovers, masters of the red dog and the blitz, able to dart backward to cover the short pass zone, able to move in to fill a gap in the line.''

It was pretty basic stuff, but to a nation getting its first inside look at pro football, it was all new, especially the meat-and-potatoes of the show—the last segment featuring the game itself with me wired for sound.

Cronkite again: "Finally, the end of the day. The hot shower will sting a dozen places where the skin is scraped away. There's a meal ahead and you may not be able to swallow, a two-hour conference and twenty-two plays to learn by morning. Yet this is only the beginning, a prelude to the big games to come when the leather really begins to thud. That's when the world of Sam Huff becomes most violent, and that's the world we have wired for sound.''

They put the mike and a little transmitter in my shoulder pads and we went through three or four of them in practice. They did wire me up in one practice game in New

Jersey, but all they got was static and they couldn't use it in the show. All of the game action in the actual program was taken in a preseason game against the Chicago Bears in Toronto.

There was a lot of talk about it in the newspapers the week of the game; some of the writers were trying to drum up a little controversy by saying they had wired the wrong guy—it should have been Bill George of the Bears because he was the better linebacker. That tactic didn't help sell many tickets to the game: there were only about 5,000 people in the stands, but that didn't make much difference to the show. The CBS people were much more concerned with the action on the field than in the crowd, and we gave it to them.

Early in the game, a Chicago receiver, Harlon Hill, came up and belted me long after the whistle had blown. I got up and said to him, "Harlon, for godsake you never hit anyone in your life, what the hell did you do that for?"

"Aw, Sam," he said, a little sheepishly, "I was just trying to get on TV."

I later found out that the Bears were all talking about the show. "Hit Huff, get on TV," they were telling each other.

Harlon's late hit didn't make it off the cutting room floor, but another incident did. The Bears had a receiver named Bill Dewveall, and on one play, he came right up the line and clobbered me under the face mask with his forearm. The Bears always played like that, rough and tumble, that's why they were always called "The Midway Maulers." Well, I called him and his mother a lot of names that never made it on the air, either. This did:

"Whaddya do that for, eighty-eight?" I screamed. "You do that one more time, eighty-eight, and I'm gonna sock you one. You do that again, you'll get a broken nose; don't hit me on the chin with your elbow . . . Hey, eighty-eight, I'm not gonna warn you no more now."

To this day people still come up and ask me exactly

what it was that number eighty-eight did to me and whether I ever did sock him in the nose. No, I didn't. I do remember that during that game I did get pretty hyper. The Bears really were coming after me and I didn't like it. In fact, on one play, I was so ticked off I hit some poor rookie on my own team in a pileup near the sidelines and broke three of his ribs.

To tell you the truth, I wasn't too crazy about the show's title, but that wasn't my decision. I knew it was catchy, but I didn't like the word "violent." I still don't. I don't consider myself a violent person, even though football really is a violent game. When I asked Kyle Rote about it, he shrugged his shoulders and said the same thing: "It's a violent game, Sam, you might as well face it."

My final lines in the show emphasized that point.

"I usually feel real good after a ball game for about two or three hours," I said. "Then your blood starts to circulate and you start to feel those bruises. And the next day it's not a very good feeling and sometimes you have to call your wife to help you out of bed. It's a rough game. It's for the men, not the boys. But I've got no complaints. Pro football has been real good to me."

After the show aired, I don't think any of us were prepared for the reaction. Everybody in the media was talking about it or writing about it, and I got hundreds of letters from around the country.

It also had a tremendous impact on professional football. Here was the greatest television newsman of all time narrating this film about a football player, and for the first time the average person knew what it was like to be a National Football League player. They got taken into training camp, they got taken into the huddle, they heard me call signals while I was gasping for air. They saw how we practiced, they realized there was classroom work involved, that you really didn't just throw the ball out in the middle of the field and choose up sides like a pickup game. Then they heard what pro football sounded like through that microphone in my shoulder pads. You could hear the thud, the pounding, the grunts, the hits, and then I had my little talk with number eighty-eight. The whole thing was perfect. It was beautifully written, Cronkite was Cronkite, and it came at a time when pro football was just beginning to attract a lot of attention. The 1958 title game was part of that, and so was the *Time* cover.

Of course there was also a flip side to all this attention. There was a lot of jealousy toward me—not so much from my own teammates, but from around the league. It wasn't my fault that they singled me out for all this coverage. I played middle linebacker for the New York Giants in the media capital of America in front of the NFL's most fanatical fans. But that didn't play too well in other parts of the country. As my friend Dave Kindred wrote a few years ago in *The Washington Post,* "Some may have thought the extraordinarily graphic film—never had we seen this war up close and personal—raised Huff's fame to heights disproportionate to his ability."

Even to this day, you hear people say I was a media creation, that every time Chris Schenkel called the play-by-play when our defense was out on the field, he would invariably say, "Huff makes the tackle." Let me tell you something. I made a lot of tackles, because that's the way our defense was designed by Tom Landry. Am I supposed to apologize? Hell, you could go back and look at the films and see who was making the tackles. But it was all done as part of a team concept, and my teammates accepted that.

A lot of times around the league, I was portrayed as the villain. I became a sort of lightning rod. The Giants would come into town and you'd read stories in the local papers about how overrated I was and wasn't it a shame they didn't do the violent world of Bill George, or Joe Schmidt or Ray Nitschke. I was like the villain in professional wrestling. I'm still not convinced that the reason it took me so long to get into the Hall of Fame wasn't directly related to all the attention I had received in New York. The guy voting in Green Bay couldn't like me because I was always beating up on Jim Taylor. The guy in Cleveland wasn't going to vote for me because I was always taking on Jimmy Brown.

I'll tell you something else. In 1959, I was named defensive MVP of the NFL. In 1960, after "The Violent World of Sam Huff," I didn't even make All Pro, and I had a better year in 1960 than I'd had in 1959. There's just no question that there was a lot of resentment for all the attention I was getting, and in later years it really hurt me.

The show had another kind of repercussion. I'd walk into a restaurant or bar and sooner or later somebody would feel it was necessary to get in my face to challenge me. A guy would come into a place with his girl friend and try to impress her by going after me.

One time I was sitting in a bar on Third Avenue and a guy came over, pulled up a stool, and said, "You're Sam Huff, aren't you? Well, you don't look so tough to me, I think I can take you."

This was not the first time I'd been confronted, and by now, I'd had it. I looked him right in the eye and said, "You might be able to take me, but I'll tell you this, you better make a commitment, because if you can't take me out, you're a dead man. I'll kill you. I'll take your head right off your shoulders."

Now he backed off. "I was just kidding," he said.

"Well, I'm not. You want to challenge me, you're on."

That guy was out of there like a shot. It also taught me a very valuable lesson. If you don't want to be challenged like that, don't go to those kinds of places; you'll only get yourself in trouble. That's all part of playing professional football.

Overall, though, I'd have to say I'm still very proud of that show. I also like to remember what Artie Donovan, the old Colt tackle, told me in Baltimore a few years ago. "Sam," he said, "every defensive player who ever played this game owes you a debt of gratitude." That was my reward for "The Violent World of Sam Huff."

There weren't very many rewards the rest of that year.

The 1960 season started off with three straight wins, but our injuries started catching up with us. Webster got hurt in an exhibition game. He was trying to squeeze out a couple more yards when he got hit in the knee and missed most of the season. Conerly missed our early games with an elbow problem but came back halfway through the season to help us beat the Cleveland Browns, 17–13, at Municipal Stadium.

The game was memorable for two reasons: we held Jimmy Brown and his offense to a net of 6 yards on the ground, including 29 yards in 11 carries for Brown, and my buddy Little Mo demonstrated how violent our world really was.

Early in the game, Mo got his hand stepped on and a cleat had opened up a real deep gash. Most football players are chicken when it comes to blood—particularly their own blood. They don't mind seeing someone else bleed, but when it's dripping out of your body, look out.

So Mo held up his wounded hand and started screaming at me. "Call time-out, Sam, call time-out."

No way.

In those days, if you had a player hurt on the field and the doctor and trainer came out to help him, they'd call time-out against you. You only got three a half, so if a guy was injured, unless it was real serious, we'd literally pick him up, drag him to the sideline, and throw him off the field. We were coached not to call time-out on defense because the offense would need those precious time-outs for the final two minutes.

So I walked up to Mo, grabbed his fingers and squeezed them together to try to stop the bleeding. "I'm not calling time-out, Mo. We're gonna stop 'em right here and we'll get you out of here." He just looked at me like I was crazy, shook his head, and said, "Man, I've seen some cold-blooded people in this game, but you are the worst." Then he pulled his hand away, walked back to the line, and played the next couple of downs. We stopped them and finally got off the field. They put eight stitches in that hand,

and to this day, Mo probably hasn't forgiven me. But that's the way it was; that was the mentality of the game.

By the time we reached the halfway point of the season, we were 5–1–1 and the Philadelphia Eagles were 6–1. The race would be decided in the next two weeks because, through a scheduling quirk, we faced Philadelphia in back-to-back games, the first at Yankee Stadium, then in Philly.

To this day, every time I think about the Philadelphia Eagles, I think about Frank Gifford. And every time I see Frank Gifford, I wonder why he'd not dead.

The Eagles had a pretty good football team that year because they had some outstanding individual talent—players like Norm Van Brocklin, Pete Retzlaff and Tommy McDonald, and Chuck Bednarik. I always thought we had more overall talent, especially on our defense, but everything seemed to click for them that season, just like everything clicked for the Redskins in the '88 Super Bowl. They may not have been the best team in the league—I thought San Francisco was—but they did what they had to do and just kept winning.

In that first game at the Stadium, we took a 10–0 lead, then fumbled it away. Late in the fourth quarter, we were down, 17–10, with only a couple of minutes left to play. We also had the ball at the Eagle thirty and were driving toward a tying score when Frank took the worst shot I have ever seen on a football field.

Conerly was playing quarterback, and he circled Frank out of the backfield and brought him across the middle, right in front of the Eagles' veteran middle linebacker Chuck Bednarik, the last of the two-way players. Bednarik was all football player, the toughest guy you'd ever want to run into on either side of the line. He was thirty-five years old, a veteran of twelve years, and had decided to play one more season because he sensed the Eagles might make a run at a championship. He also needed the money to buy a new house, and that year, playing center and middle linebacker, he earned every penny of it.

Frank really shouldn't have been running that route. He

was trying to come underneath the linebackers, which you always want to try to avoid, especially against a guy like Bednarik. You didn't want to catch the ball in front of him because he'd close in on you from behind and try to kill you.

Frank caught the ball and was trying to get across the field when Bednarik nailed him. Chuck weighed about 240 and he hung Frank out on his arm, just clotheslined him and smacked him on the chin. Frank did a complete somersault in midair, and finally landed on the back of his head on the infield dirt at Yankee Stadium. He was out cold and fumbled the ball, and the Eagles recovered.

After the play, Frank was lying there and Chuck was slamming his fist in his hand, jumping up and down and celebrating the fumble recovery. You see that kind of stuff all the time today, guys doing dumb little dances, high-fiving or spiking the ball. But back then it was frowned upon. People would kill you if you did some of the stuff these guys get away with now. But Chuck got real excited because it was a big play that had forced a turnover. Now all they had to do was run out the clock.

Meanwhile, Frank was just lying there, and the crowd was as quiet as I've ever heard it. When the defense went onto the field, I walked past Frank as they were working on him. His face was bedsheet-white and his body was trembling, just shaking all over. Then they took him to the locker room on a stretcher, and I remember going into our defensive huddle and everybody saying, "It's all over for Frank, no way he can survive a hit like that."

We were all shaken up, but we finished the game. The Eagles didn't give us another shot at the ball and we lost, but that wasn't our biggest concern. As we walked toward the locker room, a couple of medical people were wheeling out a body on a stretcher from the training room. It was covered with a sheet, and now everybody was really shaking.

"Oh my God," somebody said. "It's Frank."

Thank God it wasn't. We found out a little later that one of the security guards had been listening to the game on a transistor radio and got so excited, he had a heart attack. They took him into the training room and tried to revive him, but he died right there. That was the body they were wheeling out. What a shock.

After the game, there was quite a bit of controversy about the play. Frank had suffered a really bad concussion that put him in the hospital the rest of the week, sidelined him the rest of the year, and forced him to sit out the entire 1961 season.

Bednarik took a lot of heat because of his little celebration. One story goes that he got a call at home from a woman who asked him, "Why'd you do that to Frank Gifford?"

"I did nothing except tackle him fairly," Bednarik told her.

"The poor man," she said. "He's got a family and children and has to spend Thanksgiving in the hospital."

"I'm a family man with children, too," Bednarik said, then hung up.

Gifford, to his credit, never held Chuck responsible for the hit. "He was just doing his job," Gifford told an interviewer at the time. "I ran into him later and we sat down and had a beer. The thing never came up. We talked about his kids."

I never believed Chuck was happy that Frank was out cold. It was in the heat of the moment, he'd just made a great play that won them a very critical football game. In fact, the Eagles went on to win the conference and the championship, too. It was the greatest shot I have ever seen, and I hold no grudges against Chuck Bednarik. The only thing I'm sorry about is that I didn't get that hit on somebody. As a linebacker, you lie awake at night dreaming about hits like that. This was a shot you could hear all over New York.

And I'll tell you this. Nobody on our team said afterward, "Let's get Bednarik." No way. Hey, Bednarik was a tough guy doing what he was paid to do. Nobody to my knowledge ever went after him because of that hit.

When you play a game like this, people get hurt. It's part of the business. It is a game of contact, a violent game. When Jack Tatum hit Darryl Stingley a few years ago and put him in a wheelchair, that was a shame, a terrible tragedy. But anyone who has ever played this game knows that's the risk you take. You accept it, or you don't play. I don't blame Tatum. I blame the guy who sent Stingley out on a post pattern over the middle right into the hardest hitter in professional football. Tatum was doing his job, and so was Chuck Bednarik, and that's the unfortunate part of this game.

Anyway, the next week we lost to the Eagles again, even after we'd opened up a 17--0 lead. Van Brocklin brought the Eagles back and beat us, 31–23. The following week, the expansion Cowboys tied us, 31–31, after they had lost ten straight games, and two weeks later, Jim Lee Howell's final season concluded in a dismal 48–34 loss to the Cleveland Browns.

The Howell era had ended with a 6–4–2 record. In his seven seasons, the Giants had won three conference titles and a world championship, but the best was yet to come. And the worst, as well.

10

●●●●●●

Allie Sherman was never one of my favorite people, but as long as he left our defense alone, I thought we'd still be a dominant football team.

Make no mistake, Sherman really was an excellent offensive coach. He'd been a T-formation quarterback at Brooklyn College and had always been a great student of the game. He had good ideas, interesting game plans, used a number of different sets, and was one of the first people to put men in motion. In addition, he had a pretty good eye for offensive talent.

He also had absolutely nothing to do with our defense. Harland Svare, my old linebacker teammate, was now an assistant coach assigned to the defense, but for all intents and purposes, the defense coached itself. Sherman almost regarded us as strangers. He hardly ever came into our meeting room and, over the next few years, we basically were on our own, which was fine by me. We were still using the same basic Tom Landry defenses, and Sherman, at least in his first year, was far more interested in revamping his offense.

The Giants of 1960 had been a slow, plodding offensive team. Our running back and receivers had virtually no speed and our quarterback, Charlie Conerly, was pushing forty. And Frank Gifford, a big-play back and one of the team's most valuable players, was advised not to play after

Chuck Bednarik turned out his lights at the end of the 1960 season.

When we came to training camp at Fairfield University in Connecticut for the 1961 season, right away we knew something was going to happen. In fact, one day Wellington Mara came to a defensive meeting and asked us what we all thought of a guy named Y. A. Tittle, a veteran quarterback with the San Francisco Forty-niners. Wellington told us there might be a good chance of getting him and and he wanted some input from the guys who had to play defense against him. That's a little unusual for an owner, but we'd been together for a long time, and he was as close to his players back then as any owner could be. Well, he got yes votes from every one of us. Y. A. was one of the game's great passers; Sonny Jurgensen was the best I've ever seen, but Y. A. was right up there with him. He drove defenses crazy. He had an excellent feel for the game, ran the bootleg with the best of them, and might have been the finest screen passer in the history of professional football.

At the time, the Forty-niners coach, Red Hickey, was planning to install his new offense, the shotgun, to take advantage of three younger quarterbacks with fresh legs—Billy Kilmer, Bob Waters, and John Brodie. Washington fans will recall that Kilmer could barely hobble onto the field when he played for George Allen in the 1970s, but back then he was one hell of a runner, and Hickey wanted to take advantage of it. Y. A., who was thirty-four, was still a talent, but Hickey's shotgun was not designed for a balding, nearsighted signal-caller who had taken a pounding from twelve NFL seasons, so Yat became expendable.

Still, when we broke camp for our annual West Coast exhibition swing, the trade had not been officially made. We were in Portland, Oregon, and coincidentally, we had a game against these very same Forty-niners. By now, the word had gotten out that something was brewing, and we were even told that if Y. A. got in the game, not to rough him up, he was valuable property—and almost *our* property. The Forty-niners opened up with their shotgun, which was a dumb offense to use all the time in professional football, especially if you value the health of your quarterback. We were beating up on them pretty good when old Yat came into the game in the fourth quarter and almost pulled out the win. After all, we didn't rush him that hard and we certainly weren't about to hit him because he was probably going to wind up being our starting quarterback.

When the game was over, the Forty-niners finally told him he had been traded to the Giants for Lou Cordileone, an offensive guard who had been our first-round draft choice the year before.

When informed he'd be heading west, Cordileone wanted to know what the Giants got in exchange for him.

Y. A. Tittle, he was told.

"Is that all?" he asked.

It was more than enough. In fact, it was one of the great heists of our time. Over the next few years, Yat became one of the most successful and popular players in the history of the Giant franchise, but in the beginning, his offensive teammates did not exactly go out of their way to make him feel at home. Right away, we had an instant quarterback controversy. Conerly had somewhat reluctantly come back for one more year, and we still had Don Heinrich and Lee Grosscup on the roster. So there was a little bit of tension in the offensive unit. The defense was different. We put our arms around the guy and treated him like one of our own. We knew Y. A. was going to put points on the board, and that's all we wanted.

Yat hung around with the defensive guys—we were all veterans and he knew we appreciated having him. The man loved to play cards, especially a game he introduced us to called Boo Ray. Don't ask me to explain it because I still don't know the rules. It was an old Louisiana betting game and we called Y. A. the Boo Ray King because he was always winning. We weren't really allowed to gamble, so we used matchsticks instead of chips. No one ever got taken to the cleaners; the most you'd ever lose was a few bucks a day, and Yat was always right in the middle of the action, wheeling and dealing and having a grand old time.

Still, when he first came to the Giants, he had some reservations about the football team. In the first place, he'd done real well in business in the Bay area and wasn't exactly thrilled about moving his family across the country. He also took a look at the Giant offense and didn't exactly like what he saw. In San Francisco, he had great talent on offense, people like Joe Perry, Hugh McElhenny, Billy Wilson, and R. C. Owens. In New York, he had a flanker with a bum knee, Kyle Rote, and a banged-up fullback, Alex Webster.

We were still in training camp in Portland after the Forty-niner game and Y. A. and I went out to dinner one night. We were sitting there and Y. A. kept shaking his head.

"We can't win here," he said.

"What are you talking about?" I asked him.

"Well," he answered, "Kyle can't run anymore, Gifford is out, Webster's beat up, I got Phil King in the backfield and he's slow. We've got no speed whatsoever."

I looked him dead in the eye.

"Let me tell you something, Yat, we win here," I told him. "It's great to have you because you're going to score a lot of points for us. But we can win with you or without you; it won't make any difference to us because this team wins with defense, always has and always will, and don't ever forget it. All you need to do is get us ahead by three, and we'll take care of the rest."

I think that got Yat over the hump. He told me later he really appreciated me telling him that, because he'd never looked at it quite that way. It was also the beginning of a great friendship. We respected the hell out of each other, even though he used to kid me all the time about hitting him late when I played against him. One time when he was with the Forty-niners, I sacked him and he was on the bottom of the pile. I'm lying there and somebody's pinching my stomach. It was Y. A. He told me that was the only thing he could grab hold of. He was ticked off about getting sacked, so he pinched me. That's the kind of competitor he was.

As it turned out, his concerns about the offense were a little premature. A few days after the Tittle trade was announced, the Giants made all the right moves to get him a swift receiver. My great friend Don Smith, the Giants' public relations director, was in Los Angeles to advance a game against the Rams and had lunch one day with Elroy Hirsch, their general manager. The Rams wanted to take Roman Gabriel, a quarterback from North Carolina State, as the first pick of the draft. But the Giants owned the number-one choice after trading George Shaw to the Minnesota Vikings, an expansion team that year. Hirsch asked Smith what he thought the Giants might want in trade for that number-one pick. I've never known an NFL PR man who had the authority to make a trade, and Smitty was no exception. But he threw out a couple of names off the top of his head, and Del Shofner was one of them. Shofner was coming off a bad year. He'd been hurt and there was some question as to whether he could come back. Some people in the Ram organization were even questioning Shofner's desire. Anyway, Smitty called Wellington and told him the Rams might be interested in trading Shofner. Tittle had played with Del in a Pro Bowl game and told Wellington he was one of the best receivers in the league and to make the trade if he could. The next week, Shofner was ours, and Y. A. never complained about his offense again.

Del was a tall, skinny guy, about six-three and 180 pounds. We called him "Slim" or "Blade" and when I think of Del, I think of Clint Eastwood. Lean and mean out on that field, great speed and better moves, with legs strong enough to break tackles and leap into the air. We also became great friends. He loved to play golf, he loved the horses, and he loved money. He always said the girl he was going to marry would have lots of money, and damned if she didn't. Chandler, Shofner, Tittle, Joe Morrison, and I always hung out together. Every night before a game in New York, we'd all go out to dinner and we always flipped a coin to see who would pay. We found out that Tittle couldn't see without his glasses, and he didn't like wearing them in public. So Y. A. usually lost the coin flip. What the hell, he was a quarterback and could afford it.

In addition to Shofner, the Giants made several other great trades that year. We got Joe Walton, a little tight end, from the Redskins. Joe played at about 180 pounds, and he was small for the position. But he had good hands and he was a devastating blocker. He never said much, but even then, you knew he studied the game like a coach, and he went on to be an outstanding offensive coordinator under George Allen and, later, head coach of the New York Jets. The addition of Shofner allowed Sherman to move Rote to flanker permanently. They traded Mel Triplett to the Vikings, and Webster worked like a crazy man to get himself into shape to play fullback. He even got Mara to write an incentive clause into his contract that would pay him a bonus if he was one of the league's top ten rushers. By the time the season started, he was literally a new man, going from 235 at the start of camp to 215 on opening day.

The defense wasn't ignored, either. We got Erich Barnes, a quick defensive back, from the Chicago Bears, and that really helped our secondary. Barnes was tall and lean and he had a little mean streak in him. If you caught a ball in front of Erich Barnes, he would make you pay for it. And when you caught something near the sideline, you'd better get way out of bounds because Erich would come after you. He'd take you a *long* way out of bounds.

So now all the pieces seemed to be in place, with one exception. In our exhibition game against the Rams, Yat got hurt on his first play as a New York Giant. He bobbled the center exchange, fell on the ball, and then had two Rams fall on him. The diagnosis: two fractured transverse processes in his back, with a five-week recovery period. So much for the new, improved Giants.

When we started the season, Yat was just about healed, but Sherman decided to go with Conerly. He'd been playing throughout the exhibition season and it seemed like the logical choice. The controversy hadn't really started yet because of Y. A.'s injury, and both guys knew it was a ticklish situation. Charlie had been The Man for so many years, but he also was a team guy. So was Yat. They were both very competitive but they also realized that they were in this thing together. It was a lot like the situation with Sonny Jurgensen and Billy Kilmer in Washington in the early 1970s. They were good friends off the field, but they fought like hell for the job on the field. They helped each other out, and they respected each other's ability.

In our first game of the regular season against St. Louis at Yankee Stadium, Charlie didn't get much help from anyone and we lost to the Cardinals, 21–10. Three turnovers led to all three Cardinal scores and Charlie had a dreadful day passing, with only 9 completions for 75 yards. Y. A. probably could have played that day, but Sherman decided not to use him.

Charlie started the second game, too, against the Steelers, but this time, when he began to struggle, Sherman sent Tittle in. Y. A. completed his first 8 passes as a Giant and finished 10 of 12 for 123 yards. Shofner caught seven passes and Webster helped the cause with a 59-yard run in a 17–14 victory.

The next week, Allie decided to give Charlie one more shot. Maybe he felt he owed it to the man who had sacrificed so much for this football team over the years. But Allie also was hedging his bets. Y. A. was warming up on the sidelines in the first quarter, and when Charlie threw an interception early in the game, Y. A. replaced him.

Charlie wasn't happy about it—in fact, he told Sherman he didn't appreciate being yanked like that, and you could hardly blame him. But Y. A. made the most of the opportunity, completing 24 passes for 315 yards and we rallied to beat the Redskins, 24–21. Clearly, this game marked the changing of the guard and that's all anybody in New York was talking about. All of a sudden, the Giants had an offense, and it didn't matter that the guy running it looked like a balding, nearsighted college professor.

Y. A. started the next two games, wins over the Cardinals and the Cowboys, and had us up, 7–0, against the Rams. Then Y. A. started to struggle, and Allie never flinched. He switched again when the Rams opened a 10–7 lead in the third quarter. Now it was Charlie's turn to take advantage of an opportunity. He threw a touchdown pass to Rote for a 14–10 lead, then threw 37 yards to Shofner for another score and we won, 24–14. Conerly was a hero again, but Y. A. kept the starting job, even though we lost to the Cowboys the next week, 17–16.

We were getting ready to play the Redskins again, but Y. A. was having some arm problems. In fact, he hardly practiced all week. At our pregame meal, I was sitting next to him and he told me, "Sam, I don't know what you're going to do today, because I don't think I can play. My arm's killing me, I haven't practiced all week, I haven't even thrown a ball."

He showed me his right arm, and it was the color of a piece of fresh liver. He was so bruised I couldn't believe it. This was four hours before the kickoff, and I don't know what he did, but Y. A. started that game, and he was magnificent. Battered arm and all, he passed for three touchdowns and we barely squeaked by, 53–0. I still don't know how he did it, whether he took a shot or what. I never asked. But it did teach me a lesson.

Any time you hear a quarterback has a sore arm and he's listed as doubtful, look out. If they can't throw it deep, they do all the fundamental stuff. They don't try to over-extend themselves, and as a result, they can just pick you apart. A hurt quarterback will normally play better than a strong quarterback. Look at the 1988 Super Bowl. Doug

Williams twisted his knee, had to be helped from the field, and then put 35 points on the board in the second quarter. When it's over, the guy's on crutches, but he's got a smile on his face.

The next week, the Giants and all our fans were smiling, too, because our clubhouse man, Pete Previte, came up with a play that caught everyone by surprise. Previte worked as a locker-room attendant for the Yankees and he used baseball logic to pose an interesting question. When a baseball team needs a stolen base or wants speed on the basepaths, they put in a quick pinch-runner to get the job done. So why not try it in football? We were sitting around one day and Pete went to the blackboard. He began drawing all these X's and O's, and we started teasing him. "Get us another Coke, Pete," that sort of thing. But when he got finished, a lot of guys were paying attention. He knew that the only speed we had on offense was Shofner, so he drew up a play that included Erich Barnes and Jimmy Patton, two of our fastest defensive backs, with the offense. He put those two and Shofner on the field at the same time and the idea was to send those three deep and a flanker and a running back out in patterns as well. Actually, it was probably the first time anyone had ever drawn up a "trips," or triple formation. We practiced a lot of trick stuff and hardly ever used it, so no one gave it much thought. No one except Sherman.

In the first half against the Eagles, Allie decided to use it. With the ball in our own thirty-eight, Patton and Barnes came into the game and lined up on opposite sides. The Eagles didn't know what to do. They wound up having a linebacker, Maxie Baughan, covering Barnes, and it was no contest. Erich just streaked down the field on a fly pattern and Y. A., operating out of the shotgun to give him a little more time to see the defense, hit him in full stride for a 62-yard touchdown that will forever be known as the "Pete Previte Special." Y. A. threw three touchdown passes that day and we won, 38–21, and I have to give Sherman credit.

He saw something he liked and he wasn't afraid to use it. After that, Allie would get all kinds of plays sent to him in the mail. We used to laugh at some of them, especially the plays with thirteen men on offense and only eleven on defense.

A few weeks later, we had to face the Eagles again in the next-to-last game of the season. We were tied for the conference lead and the winner of this game would probably win the title. For some reason, Y. A. could not get us moving, and once again, Sherman decided to switch back to Conerly. After the game, he said he only intended to take Y. A. out long enough for him to study the Eagle defenses, but Conerly immediately got hot and Y. A. never went back in. On his first series, Charlie drove the team 50 yards for a touchdown, and later on, he hit Shofner for two more touchdown passes.

But the unsung hero of that game was my old buddy Chandler. Early in the fourth quarter, with the Giants leading, 21–17, Don came in to punt. He always had the habit of keeping his kicking leg high in the air on his follow-through, and in this game, he left it up there long enough to draw a roughing the kicker call against a Philadelphia linebacker, John Nocera. The official who called the play was a fellow named Ronnie Gibbs, and he had a reputation for calling that penalty. Like I said, we had a book on the officials, and Chandler knew it. The Eagles screamed bloody murder over that call—they all insisted that Don had never been touched and was faking all the way. Sonny Jurgensen, the Eagle quarterback that day, still shakes his head when we talk about it. Whether Chandler was acting or not, he allowed us to keep the ball and we drove for the clinching touchdown in a game we had to win.

The next week against the Browns, all we had to do was tie for a return ticket to the championship game, and that's all we could manage, 7–7 against the Browns. It wasn't pretty, but who cared? We won the conference, Sherman was voted Coach of the Year, Y. A. finished the season as the Most Valuable Player, Shofner caught a team record 68 passes, 11 for touchdowns, and old, banged-up Webster finished with 928 yards rushing, third best in the league. He got his bonus, and we had another shot at a title.

At least we thought we had another shot, until we stepped off the airplane in Green Bay. It was about five degrees below zero and there were 5,000 people at the airport, all of them there to boo us. I don't want all those good people in Green Bay to get offended, but that never was my favorite city. They didn't exactly welcome me with open arms, mostly because of my rivalry with Jim Taylor, as ornery a fullback as you'll ever see. We had some dandy run-ins over the years, especially in the 1962 title game, and I was not a candidate for a key to the city in Green Bay.

Maybe it sounds paranoid now, but I had two big fears once I'd gotten established in the league, and especially after all the publicity I got on the "Violent World" show. I was always concerned about having one of my children kidnapped, and I was really worried about some crazy person taking a shot at me with a gun. I used to get all kinds of hate mail, and you just never knew if some nut was out there, not just in Green Bay, but anywhere around the country. When you think about all the barroom brawls—and even an occasional shooting—that break out over sports, it really was not that farfetched.

Whenever I was on the road, I never took any chances. I spent most of my time in Green Bay in my room at the Northland Hotel. Hell, it was too cold to go outside anyway. I'm not trying to make excuses, but this was definitely Packer weather. Lombardi would tell his team that the cold was only a state of mind. They wouldn't even wear gloves in practice; Vince wouldn't allow it.

It had been a typical Green Bay winter, and the day of the game the field was frozen. It had warmed up to about fifteen degrees and the wind was blowing at ten to fifteen miles an hour. We definitely were not happy about the weather conditions; in fact, we'd brought sneakers and practiced in them, but we wore regular cleats during the game. We could have worn ballet slippers that day and it wouldn't have made much difference.

The Packers were awesome. That's the only way I can describe it. The fact that they were playing Lombardi's old team didn't help. Nor did it help when Kyle Rote lost a potential Tittle touchdown pass in the sun in the first quarter, or when our rookie running back, Bobby Gaiters, overthrew Kyle in the end zone on a halfback option play.

The first quarter ended in a scoreless tie, but from then on, it was all Green Bay. They opened a 24–0 lead at the half and our offense was held to six first downs for the game. Y. A. had four of his passes intercepted, with only 6 completions in 20 attempts. Conerly came in at the end, but he didn't do much better.

Meanwhile, the Packers, with Paul Hornung and Jimmy Taylor, ran all over us. They gained 183 yards rushing, while we managed only 31 after Alex sprained his ankle early in the game and couldn't play in the second half. Hornung finished with 89 yards in 20 carries, caught three passes, and set a record by scoring nineteen points—a touchdown, three field goals, and four extra points.

Because of injuries, we had to start Joe Morrison, normally a running back, on defense at safety. He'd played some defense late in the season, but poor Joe had to cover their great tight end, Ron Kramer, and that didn't help the cause either. Kramer was a brutal blocker and he hurt us badly that day, with four catches, two for touchdowns. But all the Packers were at the top of their game and Lombardi started smiling long before it was over.

There was no question that the two best teams in football were playing that day, but the conditions definitely favored the Packers. Again, this is not sour grapes, but you wonder what would have happened if the game had been played at a neutral site, the way the Super Bowl is now. Maybe the Packers still would have won. Like the Colts of

1958 and 1959, they were an excellent football team. When you look at the rosters of the Colts and Packers, you say to yourself they may have been two of the best teams ever to play the game. In 1961, the Packers had a balanced attack, a brilliant, precise quarterback in Bart Starr, and a brutal running game. Our offense was pass-oriented, and when it's that cold, a running attack will always be more effective.

So, for the New York Giants it was more of the same sad story—a wonderful regular season and another bitter loss in a championship game. Unfortunately, it was a pattern we never did manage to break.

11

After the 1961 season, I finally decided it was time to make New York our permanent base of operations. The kids were getting older, we wanted them to have some kind of continuity in school, and it had become very obvious to me that there would be many more opportunities to succeed away from the football field in the big city.

That off-season, I was still working for Philip Morris, and I wanted to join the company full-time, not just for the six months before the start of training camp. But they weren't especially interested; they were getting their money's worth out of us as part-time employees, and they really didn't want to change their method of operation. I stayed with them, giving speeches and making appearances around the country during the week, but I wasn't sure how much of a future I'd have when I decided to stop playing and start a career.

One day, I got a call from a fellow in Memphis asking me to come down to give a speech on a weekend. I didn't really want to—I was traveling all the time and the weekends were my only chance to be with my family—but he offered me $500 and all expenses paid. So I accepted, made the speech, and thought nothing of it. My mistake. Apparently, a Philip Morris sales representative was in the audience, and he told the guy who'd originally contacted me the group could have gotten me a lot cheaper if they'd gone through the company. The sales rep also called a marketing executive in New York and told him I'd been down there. Well, this executive called me into his office that Monday morning and bawled me out. "You're not supposed to be doing things like that," he said. "We're paying you to work for us and on your day off you're charging people for a speech. That's like stealing as far as I'm concerned."

Stealing? On my own time? On my day off? I started to get hot, especially when I heard the word *stealing*. I may be a lot of things, but that was uncalled for. I took out my company credit card, threw it in his face, and told him never to accuse me of stealing. I told him I worked five days a week for the company, ten to twelve hours a day, and the way I spent my day off was nobody's business but my own. I was so angry I was ready to throw the guy out the window. I guess I was yelling pretty loud because my friend, Jack Landry, came running into the room and got between us. I told them I was quitting on the spot, but Jack got me out of there and calmed me down. They had scheduled a bunch of appearances for me over the next three months, and I agreed to honor those commitments, only because of my friendship with Jack. But that was the end of my relationship with the Philip Morris Company.

During training camp prior to the 1962 season, another opportunity came along, and it was the beginning of a long and prosperous relationship that eventually allowed me to make my mark in the business world. We were working out one day at Fordham University when a couple of marketing guys from J. P. Stevens, a huge textile company based in New York City, talked to me about doing some commercials for their company. My friend, Don Smith, the Giants' publicity director, was always looking out for me and he had told them I might be interested.

They were promoting a new kind of slack fabric, "Consort" they called it, seventy percent orlon and thirty percent wool, and they wanted me to help them with their advertising campaign. One day, I think I made twenty-eight different commercials, one for Macy's, one for Gimbel's, one for Sears, and on and on and on. I talked so much they were giving me lemon juice to help get my voice back.

I was dealing with two of J. P. Stevens' top marketing people, Bud Treacy and Charlie Kelly, both of whom became my good friends and colleagues. I asked them if there was any possibility of going to work year-round for J. P. Stevens. They told me they were looking for someone to serve as a spokesman for the company and to work with customers when they came to New York. The next day, they took me to dinner with Whitney Stevens, the son of the owner R. T. Stevens, and Arthur Sobel, the vice-president of sales and marketing. They told me they'd try me in the job for six months and if I liked them and they liked me, I'd join the company on a full-time basis.

So I started right away, even though the football season was about to begin. It sounds crazy now, but I'd go into their office at Forty-first and Broadway every Monday, still hurting from the game on Sunday. But I'd meet with the customers, go out to lunch with clients, and tried to learn the textile business. I guess I must have been doing something right because about two months later, Arthur Sobel knocked on my door, shook my hand, and said, "Sam, as far as we're concerned, you have a job here for as long as you want it."

I stayed with that company for seven years and it was a great experience. I learned the textile business, I learned sales, and I learned marketing. Treacy, Kelly, and I traveled all over the country promoting their products; we were like the Three Musketeers, and we always had a good time together, enjoyed each other's company.

Of course football was still the main priority in my life. I was in the prime years of my career, and the Giants still were my main focus from July to December.

In 1962, there were several significant changes on the football team. Charlie Conerly finally retired after fourteen seasons as a Giant quarterback. Kyle Rote, who had played on nothing more than a big heart and lots of guts, also decided it was time to rest those banged-up knees permanently. Pat Summerall, who, like Kyle, had been working part-time in the broadcasting business the past few years, also retired to devote all his time to it, leaving Chandler to handle place-kicking and punting.

Frank Gifford, meanwhile, had spent a lot of time in the broadcast booth during his year off, but he still had the urge to play. "Everyone thinks I have some secret motive for coming back," he said, "and I guess I do. I like to play football and I missed the game and the life last year . . . I wouldn't be here if I didn't think I could help the team."

With Rote now on Sherman's staff as a backfield coach, Gifford was shifted to flanker and three different guys, Joe Morrison, Phil King, and Paul Dudley, alternated at halfback, with Webster playing fullback. On defense, Sherman traded away Cliff Livingston to the Vikings and replaced him with a rookie, Bill Winter from St. Olaf's College in Minnesota.

At the time, other than losing a guy who had been a real character, we didn't think the trade of Cliff was that big a deal. But when you look at that year's draft, Winter was the only defensive player who had much of an impact, and that was a pattern with Sherman. When you study his drafts and his major moves in those early years, you see that he always concentrated on beefing up the offensive team, his pride and joy and the unit he spent almost every waking moment with. Eventually, ignoring the defense would cost him plenty.

That year, Andy Robustelli and Jimmy Patton were player-coaches for our defensive team, meaning that once again we were virtually coaching ourselves, and that was fine with me. Andy was a great Hall of Fame player, but in the beginning, he didn't know the defense that well. As a defensive end, he had always been mostly concerned with the guy who played in front of him on offense. He didn't really have a feel for the coordination involved with the line, the linebackers, and the secondary. I had to know it all because I was the man in the middle of everything, with my head up. So Andy would come over to J. P. Stevens every Monday and I'd review the defenses with him so he'd know what was going on.

During training camp, Allie wanted to make some changes, though we fully expected to keep using the basic Tom Landry inside-outside 4–3. Under that system, I'd take my key and flow toward the ball. Allie changed that. He always wanted me to go to the strong-side gap—the side the tight end was on—to plug the hole between the center and the guard. Now if the play went to the other side, I'd be caught in traffic and couldn't get through to make the plays. Unless the play came right at me, I was not much of a factor. Well, we practiced this silly defense in training camp, and I kept my mouth shut, thinking that the coaches would all be watching the film, see that it wasn't as efficient as the old system, and eventually scrap it or just use it occasionally to cross up the opposition. I was taught to respect coaching decisions and, for the most part, I did.

Late in the exhibition season, it was becoming fairly obvious to me that we weren't going back to the Landry 4–3. So I went to Andy and told him I didn't think I could play this way all the time. It was all right as a change, to give a quarterback a different look and confuse him now and then, but all the time? That was ridiculous. He said, "Sam, I agree with you, but this is the defense Allie wants you to play, and you're just going to have to do it."

That wasn't good enough for me. So right before the start of the season, I went to see Sherman. I went into his office and said, "Allie, please explain your philosophy on this defense, because I can't play it all the time. I can't make tackles from sideline to sideline the way I'm used to doing. I'm just taking one gap and I can't go out in pursuit, and that's going to kill this football team."

Sherman answered, "You know, Sam, you're always bitching. Why don't you just play the defense the way it's designed? That's the way I want it and that's the way you'll play it. If you're going to play on this team, you're going to play my defense."

I told him I would, but I left there shaking my head, prepared to make the best of what I considered a bad situation. Fortunately, our offense scored so many points, the team didn't have to rely on the defense as much as in the past. The defense gave up more points and yards, but our offense with Y. A., Shofner, and Gifford was just incredible. After a 3–2 start, we wound up winning our last nine games, including a 49–34 victory over a Redskin team that was challenging us for the conference lead halfway through the year. Tittle completed 27 of 39 passes in that game, including 12 straight, and threw for seven touchdowns, tying the league record.

After the game, Y. A. was asked why he didn't try for an eighth touchdown pass, and his answer showed why the man was so loved by anyone who followed our football team, and so respected by his peers around the National Football League. "It would have been bad taste," he told *The New York Times*. "If you're leading by so much, it just doesn't sit right with me to fill the air with footballs. I'm the quarterback, it would be showing off."

Our defense never had a chance to show off that year, and in a game against the Cardinals, their running back, John David Crow, was just killing us in the first half. In my opinion, Crow was very nearly the equal of Jim Brown. He was big, strong, and loved to run over people. We were still playing Allie's dumb defense and John David Crow was coming through holes like you've never seen. They were using a simple trap play, Rosey Grier was getting blocked from all sides, and I couldn't get to the hole because I was going to the strong side and couldn't get back.

In the locker room at halftime, I was steaming, though I bit my tongue and tried not to get in trouble. But I couldn't help myself. When we got into our defensive huddle at the start of the second half, I looked at Robustelli and said,

"Goddammit, Andy, you're gonna let that little son of a bitch Sherman ruin us. Well, not me. I've had it. We're getting murdered by Crow—why don't you stand up to Sherman and tell him what we've got to do?"

Andy looked at me and said, "Okay, let's play the inside-outside but we won't tell anybody. We'll just do it and worry about it later." For the first time all season, I played with a smile on my face. We hadn't practiced the defense all year, but we were a veteran team, and we could play that system in our sleep.

The Cardinals had a big lead at the half, but the second half was another story. We shut them down and they couldn't move. I remember that our coaches had three reels of film of the Cardinal offense from the first half, but they only had about half a reel from the second. When it was over and we had rallied for the victory, no one said anything in the locker room. Hell, we had won—we had come back from being way down and we were ecstatic. But when we reported to practice on Tuesday, Allie Sherman was not happy at all.

For one of the few times I can remember, he came into our defensive meeting room, and he jumped all over us. "Let me tell you something," he snarled, and now the veins in his neck were popping out. "When I put up a defense, you will play that defense. Do I make myself understood? And you will go back to playing that defense, the way it is designed to be played. Do you understand?" Yes, we did, so we went back to the defense for the rest of the season. The offense was going crazy every week, and it didn't matter that much until the championship game against the Packers.

We had clinched the title in the twelfth week of the season when Chandler kicked four field goals in a 26–24 victory over the Bears, and when the regular season ended, Tittle led the league with a record 33 touchdown passes, Shofner averaged 21 yards a catch and had 12 touchdown receptions, and Gifford averaged just over 20 yards a catch in a great comeback season, while Chandler broke a team scoring record with 104 points. Sherman also was voted Coach of the Year for the second straight season, but I can guarantee you none of our defensive players were asked their opinion.

In fact, in that championship game, we mostly ignored Allie's defense again. We had to. We were playing the Green Bay Packers with Bart Starr running that precision Lombardi offense and Jimmy Taylor and Paul Hornung coming at us almost every down. This wasn't Sherman's money, this was *our* money, and the only chance we had to beat those guys was to play our old defense. And even that didn't help.

Once again, the conditions were absolutely brutal. It was Green Bay weather, except the game was played in New York. The temperature at kickoff in Yankee Stadium was twenty degrees and falling, and the wind was blowing at thirty-five miles an hour. I'm no expert on wind-chill factors, but I can tell you that was the worst weather I ever played in. In fact, a lot of the Packers who were in that game and the famous minus-sixteen "Ice Bowl" in Green Bay against the Cowboys in 1967 said it was colder in Yankee Stadium in 1962. A couple of players actually had frostbite when it was over.

The buildup before the game, as usual, involved me and Jimmy Taylor. We had a pretty fierce rivalry, and Taylor was always being quoted as saying things like "I love to sting people" or "I like to find people and just run over them." Well, those are fighting words to a linebacker, and that got my juices going.

Taylor was a maniacal competitor; even to this day he'll do whatever it takes to win on a golf course or a tennis court. As a football player, he'd swear at you on the field. He'd kick you, gouge you, spit at you, whatever it took. It was a street fight. He ran hard and he loved to kick you in the head with those knees; I loved playing against him because I never had to go far to find him. He'd try to find you so he could run over you. And he was always shooting his mouth off on the field. You'd knock him down and he'd say something like, "I only got four this time, next time I'm going to get more."

I'd yell back, "Oh yeah, let's see you come in here and get it." Even his own teammates would tell him to shut up because they knew the more he talked, the angrier the defense would get. Taylor was also a great option runner. He'd get a handoff and head off tackle following his blocking, and he had the choice of going outside or cutting in. And if he came inside, he knew I'd be there to meet him. On one play in that 1962 title game, he decided to take it outside and I went with the flow. It was right in front of the Giant bench and I can remember thinking to myself, *Okay, it's live or die right now.* I went into him with every ounce of energy I could muster and I truly don't remember getting up. But when I did regain my senses, I noticed there was a dent in my helmet from where his knee had hit me. Neither of us went out, and that banged-up helmet is now in the Pro Football Hall of Fame. That's how the man ran, low to the ground so that all you ever saw of Jimmy Taylor was knees, shoulder pads, and helmet.

Taylor spent most of that game bitching every time he was hit. In the years since, he's insisted that I actually bit him during the game. Not true. I couldn't bite him; I had my face mask on, and if I did bite him, it was only because he had his hand under my mask. It shouldn't have been there in the first place. But honestly, I don't remember biting him, though I suppose I would have if I'd had the chance.

Because of the conditions and the opponent, this was definitely the toughest game I ever played in, and I know Jimmy said the same thing when it was over. He gained 85 yards in 30 carries, and he said afterward, "I got more bruises in this game than I got in five or six others."

The weather was again very much in the Packers' favor. As usual, we were relying on a passing attack, and with the wind blowing so strong that our bench actually flew onto the field at halftime, Y. A. just couldn't get it done. He'd throw a ball and you could see the wind just take it and knock it down. He completed only 18 of 41 passes and the Packers' middle linebacker, Ray Nitschke, was on him all day, blitzing almost at will.

Green Bay opened a 10–0 lead at the half, though we got back into the game when Erich Barnes blocked a Max McGee punt and our reserve end, Jim Collier, recovered for a touchdown in the end zone. But when Sam Horner dropped a Packer punt a few minutes later, Nitschke recovered. Five plays later, Jerry Kramer kicked the second of his three field goals for a 13–7 lead.

Unable to throw deep, Y. A. finally got the offense moving from our own twenty to the Green Bay eighteen, using shorter play-action passes. But two holding calls pushed the ball back to the forty and the drive stalled. Finally, with Taylor grinding out the yards despite our best efforts to stop him, the Packers kept the ball for five minutes and finished us off with Kramer's third field goal for a 16–7 lead with 1:50 to play.

I was pretty upset about that game. I really felt our defense had done the job. We held Taylor to less than three yards a carry and if the wind hadn't been blowing, who knows what might have happened? I was also pretty ticked off about Taylor and his big mouth. After the game, he accused me of cheap shots, piling on, biting, general all-around dirty play.

"The man is the dirtiest player in the league," Taylor charged. "He tried to cripple me. He used his elbows and his knees when I was on the ground.

"I was just beginning to get up when somebody piled on me and I bit my tongue. I was spitting blood for the rest of the game. I think Huff hit me with his elbow in the first period. Sam Huff is a great one for piling on. He always has done it. Sam likes being there on top of the pile. Somebody was in there twisting my head, and someone was in there digging a shoulder or an elbow into me. I had a few words with Huff about it.

"I can't remember what I said, but I would have to say he was piling on, and I wanted that to stop. I never heard so many people criticizing a player as Huff has been criticized. I'm sure all his critics weren't just Green Bay or Jim Taylor fans."

Those kinds of comments kept the heat on long after the final whistle. Over the next few weeks, I got all kinds of weird phone calls and vicious hate mail, and Jimmy was right about one thing, it didn't just come from Green Bay.

But in my mind, our tactics that day were not dirty. Jimmy Taylor would do anything he could to get an extra couple of inches—crawl on his hands and knees if he had to. And in pro football, you are not down until the whistle blows. If he's squirming around down there fighting for those inches, you can be damned sure we were fighting just as hard to keep him from getting them.

Jimmy was certainly entitled to his opinion, and I'm not going to deny our main objective was to knock him down and knock him down hard. But in my mind, we were not playing dirty football that day. This was a world championship game, and players on both sides were going at it. We'd been humiliated by this very same Packer team the year before in the title game, and we were not about to let that happen again.

What also aggravated me was that Allie Sherman never once opened his mouth and defended me. I always took great pride in the way I played, and the fact that Allie never stuck up for me bothered me almost as much as what Jimmy had to say.

So I took matters into my own hands. I asked Don Smith to get a group of writers together and show them the game films and let them determine if I was a dirty player. I wasn't going to be there to plead my case, I told him. Let them decide for themselves. If I'm a dirty football player, I want it written like that; and if I'm clean, I want it written like that. You know what? They saw the film and the general consensus was that Nitschke was the dirtiest guy on the field, a hell of a lot worse than me. On one play, Phil King was four yards out of bounds and Ray just plowed into him for no reason. But nobody on our team complained about Mr. Nitschke. The writers saw that for themselves, and after that film session, some of them came out and defended me.

I'm not going to deny that we didn't go into this game with blood in our eyes. And I'm not going to deny that we wanted to let Jimmy Taylor know he was going to get hit, and hit hard, and hit often. But I never in my life went into a game trying to hurt anyone; that's the ticket to a very short career in the National Football League because players have very long memories. If you're a cheap-shot artist, somebody's going to come back at you sooner or later; and when they do, look out, you're talking about serious hospital time, and maybe even the end of a career.

After that game, Jimmy Taylor did check into the hospital, and I felt like I probably should have, too. In addition to my Hall of Fame helmet, I had a slight concussion as a souvenir, and a few weeks later, I got another memento in the mail.

Someone sent me a picture that showed the referee setting the football down long after the whistle had blown, and I've still got Jimmy Taylor in a headlock. That's just the way we played the game.

12

●●●●●●

As long as I live, I will never forgive Allie Sherman for trading me to the Washington Redskins in 1964.

I know that sounds irrational, especially when you consider that almost twenty-five years have passed, but I can never forget it, nor can I ever forgive him.

But let's back up a little. There is no question in my mind that Sherman deliberately set out to destroy what may have been the finest defensive team in the history of the National Football League. Why? Only Sherman can answer that. My own theory is that his ego got in the way of football logic. We used Tom Landry's defense. It had been built around our individual talents, and it had been adjusted whenever necessary to cope with opponents' defenses or new personnel. But it was not Allie Sherman's defense, and he systematically broke it up.

The trade of Cliff Livingston in 1962 was the first indication. The failure to use prime draft choices to pick outstanding college players for the defensive team was another sign. And before the 1963 season, a major blow was struck when Sherman decided to trade Rosey Grier to the Los Angeles Rams in exchange for John LoVetere, a six-foot-four, 275-pound defensive tackle who moved into the starting lineup, but took a long time to get used to our system.

In my last two seasons with the Giants, I played next to three different strongside linebackers after Sherman traded Livingston. Bill Winter played the position as a rookie in 1962, then got hurt, so we replaced him with another young guy, Bob Simms, who had been drafted as a receiver. He, in turn, was replaced by our top pick in 1962, Jerry Hillebrand, an All-American tight end at Colorado who spent the 1962 season on the taxi squad learning how to play linebacker.

There were whispers that our defense was getting too old, but that was ridiculous. Yes, Robustelli was getting up there, but most of us were in the prime of our careers when Sherman started to mess around, and we still overpowered most of the teams we played.

The trade of Rosey Grier made no sense to me. He was a lovable guy, one of the more popular players on the team. Sure, he had a weight problem, no question about it. His weight was always out of control when he showed up in training camp after a big off-season of eating. He was over 300 pounds and probably would have been the greatest defensive lineman of all time if he'd been closer to 275. But he was usually able to get himself into playing shape, and when he wanted to play, no one was better. If it had been up to me, I would have kept Rosey in New York in the off-season and put him on a year-round program. But in those days, no one ever really thought about doing that. The hell of it is, Rosey went to the Rams, realized that he better get himself in shape or find a new line of work, and had some very productive years on the West Coast. Meanwhile, LoVetere hurt his knee in 1964 and eventually had to quit the game. He was a good guy, worked hard and tried even harder, but that was another trade that didn't work out.

In 1963, Hillebrand played on my left side and Tom Scott was on the right. Hillebrand was not a very physical player, but he was smart and a good athlete, and he always listened to whatever I told him. I spent most of that year coaching him, and he did everything I asked him to do.

Scott was a guy with raw talent, and he definitely had a mean streak. He'd just beat guys up. He wore a large hockey pad on his elbow and liked to clobber people with it. He warmed up for games by beating on his locker, just pounding on it with his elbows. He looked like he was frothing at the mouth because he had this strange, wild look on his face. He even got into a fight with Jim Brown once, and it might have been the only time Jim ever got thrown out of a game. It's funny, too, because I see Tom every once in a while now. He's involved in the Heisman Trophy voting and he's always in a pinstripe suit, very Ivy League. Back then, I thought he was just a little bit crazy.

There were a few other changes on the team. Our veteran center, Ray Wietecha, retired and was replaced by Greg Larson, and we also traded to get Hugh McElhenny, who had played eleven seasons in San Francisco as a running back. We needed another offensive weapon like a hole in the head, but with Allie Sherman running that offense, nothing surprised us. Well, almost nothing.

In 1963, we started off with a 37–28 victory over a good Baltimore Colt team. Y. A. threw 3 touchdown passes, but late in the game as he was scoring a touchdown, Y. A. got clobbered so hard, he had to be helped off the field.

That week it became apparent that he was too banged up to play. The year before we had acquired Ralph Guglielmi, a Notre Dame guy, from the Redskins, and he prepared to start our second game against Pittsburgh. In the locker room that Sunday, Allie gave the worst pregame talk I've ever heard from a head coach. He got up there and said, "We'll probably lose this game today, but I'm not going to risk the whole season by playing Y. A. We'll just go out there and play without him." Imagine that, a head coach telling his team they had no hope. With that kind of inspiration, we went out and got drilled, 31–0.

After the game, Allie walked into the locker room and was so furious he tried to rip out the wires for the post game radio show on WNEW, and he couldn't do it. I had to laugh, because Allie was so angry he was literally swinging from the cables. I guess he was still mad the next week, because he blamed Ralph for that loss and wasted no time trading him to Philadelphia. Poor Ralph; he goes to Philadelphia and the next week we play the Eagles. In practice that week before the Eagle game, we talked about what we were going to do if Ralph got in. And there was a very good chance that was going to happen.

Their starter, Sonny Jurgensen, was hurt and he wasn't supposed to play, so they started King Hill. Early in the game, we blitzed and I got a good clean shot on King and knocked him out of the game. Now it was Ralph's turn. He came in and on the first play, Robustelli busted through all alone and broke three of Ralph's ribs. Now Jurgensen had to come in and play. He was hurting, and we intercepted three of his passes and beat them bad, 37–14.

In the locker room, Katcavage made me laugh talking about Ralph.

"I never liked the guy when he was here," Kat said.

In truth, we'd all been pretty upset about that trade because Sherman had told us the day the final cuts were made that this was the team he was going to stick with to win a championship. Then we got blown out by the Steelers and suddenly Ralph was the scapegoat. Hell, it wasn't all his fault. In football, when you lose, there are twenty-two guys who can be blamed. Sherman lost a lot of credibility when he shipped Ralph off to Philadelphia, and that was probably another trade that never should have been made.

Later, when Y. A. got hurt in the championship game against the Bears, Sherman had to go with a rookie, Glynn Griffing, against the best defense in the league, and Y. A. had to hobble back on for the second half because he knew we had no shot if he didn't play. I'm not saying Ralph would have won that football game for us, but we certainly would have had a better chance with a veteran quarterback as a backup than a rookie.

Anyway, we started off the 1963 season 3–2, but then got hot, winning eight of our last nine games, including a 33–6 win at Cleveland when we shut down Jim Brown again, holding him to 40 yards in 9 carries.

Later in the season, football didn't seem to matter so much when President John F. Kennedy was shot in Dallas. I considered myself a lucky man because I had gotten to be friends with him, even campaigned for him in West Virginia in 1960. But Pete Rozelle decided that the games would go on as scheduled that weekend and that was a big mistake. I was devastated when I heard the news of the assassination. Don Chandler and I were driving across the Triboro Bridge in Manhattan when we heard the news bulletin on the radio, and like everyone else, we were just stunned. Nobody was thinking about football and to this day I don't know why Pete didn't cancel. I guess they had all those tickets sold and with that kind of investment they felt they had to play. So we faced the Cardinals that week, and I can't remember one thing about that game other than we lost, but that seemed very insignificant at the time. Neither team was into it, and it was probably the worst game of football I've ever been involved in.

It was our only loss down the stretch, but we went into our final game against the Steelers having to win to get into the title game. We opened up a 16–0 lead before Pittsburgh came back to 16–10. Then we broke it open in the second half after Gifford kept alive a drive with a stunning one-handed catch on third and eight from deep in our own territory. We won the game, 33–17, for our third straight conference title, and once again, Y. A. was the toast of the town. He set another NFL record with 36 touchdown passes and completed sixty percent of his throws, a team record, with only 14 interceptions. Shofner had 64 receptions, giving him 185 over a three-year stretch, and Gifford came back with 42 catches, including 7 for touchdowns. Our offense was incredible, scoring 448 points in fourteen games. In ten of these games, we scored 33 or more points. Our defense played well, too, though not quite as well as our opponents' defense in the title game.

With George Allen running it, the Chicago Bears defense had allowed only 144 points for the season. Using a double zone in the secondary, they led the league in defending against the pass and also had the most interceptions: 36. It seemed like a classic matchup, a great offensive team against the best defense, and we were ten-point favorites going in, even if we were playing at Wrigley Field. Once again, the conditions were brutal. Nine degrees at kickoff and a field frozen solid, and once again, we were in trouble.

I was especially concerned about Chicago's tight end, Mike Ditka. I'd been watching films of him, and I noticed that if he saw you were just standing around, he'd stick out an elbow and cheap-shot you. Back then, long before he took over as head coach of the Bears, he was known as "Iron Mike," and it's no coincidence that in January 1988, he became the first tight end ever voted into the Hall of Fame.

I wanted that elbow business to stop right away. Before the game, I told Jerry Hillebrand that we were going to make sure Mr. Ditka got a special-delivery message on the subject of unnecessarily rough play. I told Jerry to get over Ditka's outside shoulder and when he came off the ball, nail him right in the face mask and knock him back toward me in the middle because I was going to knock him back toward Jerry. We did that on the first series, and Mike started shouting: "What are you guys trying to do to me?"

"Mike," I said, "I've been watching the films, and I've seen what you've been doing to some people. I happen to play by the rules of the game, and that's how I'd like this game to be played. Why don't you try it?"

Needless to say, we did not have a problem with Mike Ditka for the rest of the afternoon; he only caught one pass and he'd been the leading pass receiver among tight ends in the NFL that year. But I wish that had been our only problem.

You knew things weren't going right when Shofner had a certain touchdown drop out of his hands early in the game after we had opened a 7–0 lead on a 14-yard Tittle pass to Gifford.

On the play after Del's drop, the Bears' Larry Morris

intercepted a pass and returned it to the Giant five. Two plays later, Billy Wade, a mediocre journeyman quarterback his entire career, ran the ball in to tie the game at 7–7. We had a chance to go up by a touchdown in the second quarter when we had second and goal at the Bears' two-yard line. The offensive players said later they wanted to bust a wedge play over the middle but Allie had insisted on calling a sweep. Joe Morrison was tackled for a loss on second down as he tried to go left, then was tackled again on third down on another sweep to the right. We had to settle for a Chandler field goal and a 10–7 lead that would come back to haunt us.

Neither team could score again in the half, but disaster struck for the Giants in the second quarter when Morris blitzed and slammed into Tittle's left knee. Y. A. had to hobble off the field, and Griffing, the rookie, replaced him. In the locker room at halftime, God knows what Y. A. had to do to that knee. I don't know if he took any shots, but they wrapped that thing up as best they could and he said he wanted to play, even though he could barely walk.

I tried to talk him out of it. I went up to him before the start of the second half and said, "Yat, stay out, we'll win it for you with the defense. Remember that conversation we had back in Portland when I told you all we needed was three? You got us the three, now let us get you that title. They can't move the ball on us, just stay the hell out and we'll take care of it."

"Sam," he said, "this is my last chance to win a championship, I've got to play. I want to wear that ring."

So he played on a knee that probably should have kept him out for a month. He had screwed up the ligaments and couldn't move back there, and now it was the Bears' turn to play a little defense.

Y. A. hobbled back to throw a screen pass, and Ed O'Bradovich picked it off and went 62 yards down to our fourteen. Two plays later, Wade snuck the ball over for a 14–10 lead, and that's how the game ended. We had one last desperation shot in the final ten seconds. Tittle threw deep to Shofner, a combination that had worked so much magic all season. But on this day the ball was just over-thrown, and Chicago safety Richie Petitbon intercepted—the fifth of the day against Y. A.—and the Bears and their fans began to celebrate what I have always considered a fluke victory.

While you could understand—if not accept—losing to the Colts or the Packers, two of the greatest football teams that ever played the game, the Bears were not in their class. Yes, their defense was outstanding, but their offense wasn't much. Our defense had dominated them. They only gained 93 yards rushing in the championship game, 129 passing, and both their touchdowns were set up by long interceptions. But the final score is all that counts, and we came up short again for the third straight year.

There was a lot of talk in the papers about what went wrong, who was to blame, the usual kind of stuff when you lose. But anyone with half a brain had to know that if Y. A. Tittle hadn't hurt his knee, there was no question about who the best team was and who would have been wearing those rings.

But Allie Sherman obviously had other ideas. While I went off to work for J. P. Stevens, Sherman went to work dismantling the team.

The first step was trading Dick Modzelewski to the Cleveland Browns in March. That stunned me. Mo had a good year and he was a guy who kept the football team loose, a real leader who gave his blood and guts for that team week after week. So a couple of days after that trade, I went over to the Giants office on Columbus Circle and spoke to Wellington Mara. "What's going on?" I asked him. "Why in the world would you trade Mo?"

"Sam," he said, "I can't tell you everything because we're putting a lot of pieces together here and we think we have to make some changes."

I told him, "You've traded Livingston, you've traded

Rosey, and now it's Mo. What about me, am I next?''

"Nothing's going to happen to you," he answered.

I told him I appreciated that. I told him I was doing well in New York. I had a good job, my family was settled, I loved New York and I loved the Giants. "You don't ever have to worry," he said to me. "You're one of the family. We'll never trade you."

"Well," I said, "your word is good enough for me."

He also asked me that day to sign my contract for the next season. I think I was making $17,000 at that point and they were going to give me $19,000. But I didn't go there to talk about money and I told him I wanted to think about it. "No problem," he said, "and as long as you're here, why don't you say hello to Allie before you leave."

So I went down the hall and talked to Sherman for a minute. Despite our differences, I had a passable relationship with him. He was the coach, I was a player, and it never got to the point where we couldn't communicate with each other. So I told him I was a little concerned about Mo getting traded to Cleveland and he said, "Don't worry about that, it's no problem." So I left, and I didn't think too much more about it, other than that training camp was going to be awfully dull without all those Polish folk songs.

A couple of weeks later, I had to go to Cleveland for J. P. Stevens to speak at a manufacturers' sales meeting. In the Cleveland airport, I bumped into Don Smith. We made some small talk about Mo's trade and I jokingly told Smitty that if they ever traded me, I'd want to take him with me. We laughed and went our separate ways.

That night I went out to dinner at Ed Modzelewski's restaurant in Cleveland. I was sitting there with Big Ed, Dick's older brother, and a girl came over to the table and said there was a phone call for him. He left the table and came back and said it was Mary, she was looking for me.

That shook me up. I thought something terrible had happened, maybe one of the kids had been hurt.

"Sam," she said, and it was obvious she'd been crying,

"Allie Sherman just called. You've been traded to the Washington Redskins."

I couldn't believe it.

"Who'd they get for me?" I asked.

She told me I had been traded for Dickie James, a little halfback and kick-return specialist, and Andy Stynchula, a defensive end. Now I was really shocked. Only a few hours earlier I had seen one of my best friends in the airport, a Giant executive, no less, and he hadn't given me any indication of what was going on. So I called Smitty.

"You son of a bitch," I yelled into the phone, "why didn't you tell me I was getting traded?"

"What are you talking about, Sam, the Giants wouldn't ever trade you," he answered, thinking I was pulling his leg. But this was no joke.

They hadn't even told Don Smith about the trade, their own PR man, but he said he would try to find out what was going on. He called Wellington, and finally he was told the truth, and he was probably more upset than I was. By the next day, the Giants still hadn't announced it. At my sales meeting, I got up and told the people in the room I had played my last game for the New York Giants. I was very emotional, I had tears in my eyes, hell, I still get choked up just thinking about it now, twenty-five years later.

That day I also picked up the telephone and called Art Modell, the owner of the Cleveland Browns, and asked him if there was any way he could work out a deal with the Redskins that would get me to Cleveland. "Let me play for you," I told him. "I'd love to get a shot at the Giants." I knew the Redskins weren't going to be very good and I also knew the Browns would be my best chance at a payback. But Art said there was nothing he could do, so I went home.

When I got back to the house in Flushing, it was a wild scene. Reporters were everywhere. Hell, they told me news of the trade had stopped the ticker on Wall Street. I had a stack of phone messages up to the ceiling, and I called every one of those people back that night.

Later on, a New York City policeman knocked on the door and handed me a note with a message to call Bob Stevens. I didn't know anyone by that name, but I figured it must be important if the cop had to deliver the message. I got on the phone and it was R. T. Stevens, the chairman of the board of J. P. Stevens. "You know," he said, "I've been reading about this trade in the newspaper and I just want you to know something. You've been with us for a while and you've been a great employee. I'll put this in writing if you want. I'll be your ace in the hole. If you want to go to the Redskins and continue to work for us, we'll work that out. If you don't want to play anymore, you have a job with us as long as you want it." I appreciated that, and at that point, I needed that kind of support.

And there was more of the same from a very unlikely source. One night that week, there was another knock on the door. I looked out the window and a long black limousine was parked in front and a chauffeur was standing outside. "I'm Mr. Sonny Werblin's driver," he said, "and Mr. Werblin and his wife are in the car. They wonder if they might come in for a second."

Sonny Werblin? I had never met the man, but I knew he owned the New York Jets of the old American Football League. Now he wanted to come into my house. When he sat down, he shook his head and said, "They just did me the biggest favor anybody could ever do by getting you out of New York. I wish you could come play for me, but I don't want to get in a contract war with the NFL."

He went on to say that he'd been over at Shea Stadium watching the Mets and had started thinking about the trade. He couldn't believe it either, and he just wanted to come by to say hello. He also invited me to come with him the next day to Monmouth Park, a race track he owned in New Jersey. I went with him, and Sonny Werblin, a perfect stranger, became a good friend.

After the trade was announced, I went to work at J. P.

Stevens and I was still in a daze. Bud Treacy saw me and told me to get out of there, just take a little vacation, because I was in no shape to do anything. But before I left, I also got a phone call from Wellington Mara.

"I've got to talk to you," he said. "How about meeting me at the New York Athletic Club in an hour?"

"Fine," I said, "I'll be there." It was all I could do to keep a civil tongue.

That afternoon we met on the third floor, and Wellington couldn't look me in the eye. As he talked, he stared out the window. "I don't know what to say," he began. "I lied to you."

"Yes, you did. Well," I answered. "You hurt me and you hurt me bad. You know, when I started playing for you, we once argued over five hundred dollars on a contract. You got so mad you threw papers all over the room. You threatened me and you told me you'd trade me so fast I wouldn't even know where I had landed. I signed the contract that day and you, sir, you had my respect. But now, you will never have it again, because you lied to me." He didn't say anything else, and I stormed out of the room.

I felt very bad about that meeting, and over the years, Wellington and I have settled our differences. I will never believe he wanted to get rid of me, but he had a head coach who had convinced him that he had to make changes. Over the years, Wellington and his wife Ann have always been extremely gracious, and I still love and admire them both.

Years later, Well was asked by Gerald Eskenazi in his book, *There Were Giants in Those Days,* about the breakup of our football team.

"It's easy now to look back," Mara said. "Allie believed the team was never going to be good enough to win the whole championship. He said we'd never be better than second best. I think he felt that maybe they were jaded or had gone as far as they were going to go.

"Obviously I did [agree with the trades after 1963]

because I could have stopped any of those deals. But I didn't sense the era was ending."

But for the New York Giants, the greatest era in the team's history was over. The next year was a disaster. The Giants went 2–10–2. In 1965 they were 7–7; in 1966, 1–12–1; in 1967, 7–7 and in 1968, 7–7 again, including four straight losses at the end of the season that finally got Sherman fired.

But in 1964, that was little consolation for me. Here I was twenty-nine years old, playing middle linebacker for a great football team. And now, just like that I was gone, traded by a coach who had allowed his ego to get in the way of sound football judgment. Ever since the trade, Sherman has always told people I was slipping, that I was slowing up, that he had talked to me about adjusting my game to his system but that I had refused, that the defense was getting old and he had to do something about it. None of that was true. Too old? Hell, I played five more years in the league, and long enough to get my revenge.

It also bothers me that Sherman never had the decency to call me into his office and tell me face to face about the trade or that he wanted to make changes. As far as I'm concerned, he can burn in hell. He destroyed a great football team, and in the process, he hurt a lot of great people.

He also came very close to being destroyed by me on one occasion.

A few weeks after the trade, I got a call from Wellington's brother Jack, a sweet man and a very dear friend. He wanted me to play in the Giants annual golf tournament in Westchester. He told me he always would consider me a member of the Giants family, and it would mean a lot to him if I could join my old teammates. He also asked for another favor.

"The one thing I don't want is a confrontation with Allie," he said.

I told him I would be there, and I promised I would

avoid Sherman. But of course, after the round, as I was drying off from a shower, here comes Allie. He walked right up to me and said, "Maybe you think I need to explain to you why I traded you. Well, I don't think so."

"Get away from me, Allie," I said. "I gave Jack Mara my word or you'd be a dead man right now."

At that point, Alex Webster and another guy got between us and Alex got Allie away from there. If he hadn't, I don't know what I would have done. If I hadn't given my word to Jack Mara, Allie Sherman would not be alive today.

And to this day, when people ask him about the trade, he lies, or just clams up. Len Shapiro even gave him the opportunity to explain the trade for this book. Here's what he said:

"After that season, we reevaluated our ball club. That was not a young team, and we felt we had to rebuild. . . . Now Sam never laid down on us, but we felt we weren't going to get enough from him. It was a football decision, and that's all I really want to say about it. I didn't know Wellington said that [that I would not be traded]. I talked over all my moves with management. But I don't want to get into a debate about it. I'll pick my own venue. I'm not going to go pro and con with you."

If you can figure out what that means, please let me know. All I can say is that trade hurt me so badly, after all I'd given, after all I'd done. It never should have happened. I know it, the football fans of New York know it, Wellington Mara knows it, and surely Allie Sherman knows it.

And that is why I'll never forget, nor will I ever forgive him.

13

●●●●●●

There never was any doubt that I was going to play for the Washington Redskins, though I admit I was not exactly overjoyed at the prospect of heading south.

Neither was Mary. In fact, she wanted me to retire after the trade. Not so much because she was worried I might be getting too old or too slow to play. No, she was just as angry at the Giants as I was, and she also thought that if I didn't play, the trade would be nullified and New York would get nothing for me. *She* wanted revenge, too.

But not playing didn't make much sense to me. I still hadn't gotten football out of my system. What did make sense was to make the Redskins pay for my services. I still loved the game, but more than ever, I realized how much of a business football really was. I was no longer a naive kid from West Virginia. I'd been in the big city for seven years, and I knew exactly what I wanted and what the Redskins were going to have to give me to play in Washington.

My first contact with the Redskins was with their coach, Bill McPeak. He came over to the house in Flushing about a week after the trade. Mary was sick in bed with strep throat, which was a good thing, because she probably would have yelled at McPeak about the trade. Fortunately, she couldn't even talk.

Anyway, McPeak never discussed a contract. He was a football guy, an excellent coach with an outstanding eye for personnel. In 1963, he had been elevated to general manager and been given virtual carte blanche to improve the team. He had already traded to get Sonny Jurgensen from the Eagles to run the offense, and now he told me that he was going to build his defense around me. He was shaking up the whole football team, with Jurgensen and me as the nucleus. We met several more times, and finally the big question came up: "How much will it take, Sam?" I would have been making about $19,000 in New York, and I told him I wouldn't come to Washington for anything less than $35,000.

He didn't exactly fall out of his chair, but he did tell me he couldn't authorize that kind of salary. He wanted me to talk to Edward Bennett Williams, the famous Washington attorney who was taking over the team from the family of the original owner, George Preston Marshall, who had given up control the year before.

So I went to Washington to talk to Williams, and I was scared to death. Here was a guy who had represented some big-time people, Jimmy Hoffa, the Andrews Sisters, many other celebrities, and now I had to talk money with him. Even back in the mid-sixties, very few players had agents or lawyers, and I was definitely going to be at a disadvantage.

But Ed started off trying to put me at ease. He told me how much the team wanted me and needed me, he told me they wanted me to wear number seventy, which was still very important to me, and he told me they would continue to add good players to turn the Redskins into a contender.

He was pressing all the right buttons, but he also knew I wanted $35,000. "You know, Sam, that's a lot of money, and that's a lot more than we pay any of our linebackers," he said at one point. Then he started talking about the team's salary structure and how unfair it would be to pay one guy twice as much as any of the people he'd be playing with. "It's the principle," he said, and that set me off.

"Screw principle," I snapped. "I've been hearing that same damned principle crap from Wellington Mara for eight years. So don't talk to me about principle. It doesn't mean anything to me because the same guy who told me he wasn't ever going to trade me just traded me to you. How's that for principle?

"Mr. Williams," I finally told him. "If you want me to play for the Washington Redskins, it's going to cost you thirty-five thousand, and not one penny less."

EBW got the message right away. Like I said, he's a very smart man. "Sam," he said, "I understand your position, so here's what we'll do. I'll give you a thirty-thousand-dollar player contract and we'll write it in that for another five thousand, you'll also do some scouting for us in the off-season. Bottom line, it's thirty-five thousand dollars."

I told him he had a deal, but I didn't want to sign a contract that day because I wanted to talk it over with Mary first. So I went back to New York, figuring it would take a while for all the paper work to get done. Well, a few weeks passed, and now it was late May, early June, not too far from the start of training camp, and I still hadn't signed, even though we had agreed on the basic terms.

I was still working for J. P. Stevens and going into the New York office every day with two of my friends, Don Smith and Dick Voyce. We car-pooled it from Flushing. Smith was my pal, had been ever since he covered the Giants for the old *Long Island Press* in the 1950s. He was a fine reporter back then, and kind of feisty, too.

After a loss against the Redskins one year, I remember he just took us apart in a column, talked about my baby fat, said Little Mo looked like a damned ballerina. But the one thing that caught everybody's eye was the story's headline: "Giants Quit." Now you can say a lot of things to a football player, but don't ever tell him he's a quitter. The front office was so upset about it, they wanted to bar

Don from the weekly Tuesday press conference with the head coach. Smitty went anyway, but as soon as he got there, he was asked to leave. So he walked out one door and came back through another. Anything to get a story.

Finally, Jack Mara, Wellington's brother and a compassionate guy, pulled Smitty aside and told him why the team was upset. "We don't want to control the media," Jack told him, "but let me tell you something. Don't you ever say my football team quits. We may not play very well. We may come out flat. We may do a lot of things, but the New York Giants will never quit."

Anyway, they straightened it out, and Smitty and I became best friends. One night, he invited Chandler and me over to his house in Flushing for dinner. This was when I was still living in a hotel. Dick Voyce was there, too. Smitty's wife, Theresa, cooked a huge roast, and she asked Don to slice it up. Smitty was kind of grumpy, and not what you'd call the world's greatest host. "Nah," he said, "I don't cut real well, you do it, Sam." So I looked around the room, saw there were five people for dinner, and with that West Virginia math I've always been famous for, cut the roast five ways and put a huge slab of meat on everyone's plate. That was the beginning of a great friendship.

Now, a lot of years later, we were riding into work and Smitty, still a loyal Giant employee, started agitating me about signing my contract with the Redskins. The Giants were a little worried that I might not do it, and if I decided not to play, they'd lose Dickie James and Andy Stynchula. In my mind, that was no great loss, but I was in no big hurry to sign the contract.

"How much you asking for, Sam?" Don Smith said one day.

I told him I wanted $35,000.

"Are you crazy, no linebacker in football makes that much money."

I'd already talked with Edward Bennett Williams and I knew I was going to get it. I just hadn't signed. But Smith and Voyce didn't know that, so I had a proposition for them.

"I'll bet you guys a thousand right now that I get the thirty-five thousand."

"You're on," said Smith.

"And I'll take half of that action," Voyce chimed in.

A few weeks later, I finally went down to Washington and signed, but my friends didn't know it. We were riding into work one day and Smith started getting on me again. "Hey, Fatso [he always called me Fatso], when you gonna sign that damned thing?"

"We still have a bet, right?" I asked him.

"Yes."

"Well, boys, read it and weep," I said, pulling out the signed contract from my briefcase. You should have seen their faces. It was like they had been hit with a sledgehammer. Then they read the contract, and they said the bet was off because I was getting $5,000 extra to scout, not play. Well, I never did get paid off and to tell you the truth, I was going to let them off the hook anyway. They were my best friends, and Smitty and I still laugh about it twenty-five years later.

A few weeks after that, I reported to training camp in Carlisle, Pennsylvania. I had decided that I was going to go in and try not to make any waves. I was new there, I'd played against a lot of these guys, and I had to come in and make friends with people I'd been competing against and didn't like very much. I also figured they didn't care for me, either. I had played on the same team that had beaten them, 53–0, in 1961; in fact, the Giants had a twelve-game unbeaten streak against the Redskins going all the way back to 1957, and I had played in every one of those games. I also decided not to take a car to camp. Hardly any of the Giants ever drove to training camp; in 1960, when they filmed "The Violent World of Sam Huff," I had the only car because CBS rented it for me as part of the deal.

When I got to Carlisle, I counted seven Cadillacs in the

players' parking lot. Not only were they driving big cars, these guys had refrigerators in their dormitory rooms stocked with beer. It seemed like a country club. The Redskins even paid for the players' laundry and dry cleaning. Some guys would drive to Washington on an off-day, load up all their family's wash and dry cleaning, and haul it back to camp because the Redskins would pay for everything. I also found out the Redskins weren't exactly welcomed with open arms in Carlisle, a quiet little college town about two hours from D.C. The year before, a couple of guys had torn up a few bars, and the people at Dickinson College where we stayed weren't happy either. Players would buy a newspaper, read it, and throw it on the floor. Nothing ever got thrown in a waste basket or a laundry bag. What the hell, there were maids to clean up your room, locker-room guys to sweep up after you, college kids to take away your food trays at the cafeteria.

In New York, the players minded their manners a little bit better. And they also took up collections for the maids and the kids who served us food in the dormitories. The Redskins never did that until I started the tradition that summer. I also helped set up an executive players committee, just like we had in New York, and of course, McPeak wanted me to help install Landry's 4–3 defense. That's all we practiced in camp.

It was an interesting group of football players. The Redskins were never known as a disciplined team. The whole operation was disorganized. George Preston Marshall, the team's founder, had always operated the club on a tight budget, and the front office was in total disarray. The publicity man, Dave Slattery, actually negotiated contracts with some of the players. The front office was virtually nonexistent; hell, we didn't even have a coach for the receivers. Bobby Mitchell eventually made the Hall of Fame, but for the most part in his early years with the Redskins, he never even had a receivers coach working with him on his pass patterns. He basically coached himself, ran whatever routes he and the quarterbacks worked out.

We did have some characters on that team. Johnny Sample, the cornerback best remembered for his days with the Colts and Jets, was on that roster. He was indicted and convicted of cashing stolen government checks a few years ago. He liked to gamble, gave the coaches fits, and always flouted the rules. At our team dormitory on the Dickinson campus, there was a circular drive in front of the building, and McPeak specifically told the players they were not allowed to park there, those spaces were for the coaching staff. He had no more gotten the words out of his mouth when Sample's car, a big green Cadillac, was parked in that driveway, right next to the front door.

We had a guy named John Paluck who played defensive end. "Mean John," we called him. He played tough. In fact, he's one of the few guys I played with I actually was scared of. No one ever messed with Mean John.

In addition to getting Jurgensen and me, McPeak also made a lot of other trades that year. From Chicago, we got a receiver named Angelo Coia and Fat Fred Williams, a defensive tackle. From the Colts he traded for kicker Jim Martin and fullback J. W. Lockett. From the Steelers came receiver Preston Carpenter and linebacker John Reger; from the Eagles defensive back Jim Carr; and from the Browns, another defensive back, Jim Shorter.

The draft also provided help. McPeak and Bucko Kilroy, our chief scout, took Charley Taylor, a phenomenal athlete from Arizona State, with the first pick, and also drafted two more future All-Pros—center Len Hauss of Georgia and defensive back Paul Krause of Iowa. Like I said, McPeak had a great eye for talent. Taylor had been a running back in college and that's where McPeak used him. Charley didn't move out to wide receiver until Otto Graham showed up in 1966, and he was good enough to make Rookie of the Year. Sonny also had the services of Mitchell, who was still in the prime of his career after joining the

Redskins in 1961 as the first black player in the history of the franchise.

But for the most part, the offense was awful. We probably had the worst offensive line I'd ever seen in all my years in football; Sonny was lucky to escape with his life that first year. Our defense wasn't much better. It was really just a ragtag bunch, totally undisciplined, and basically, they just chased the ball. There was no real system, until we started working the 4–3 into their heads. Our defensive coach was my old Giant teammate, Ed Hughes, but we never really got along that well in New York. The friction grew worse in Washington.

One time we got beat when a tight end went over the middle and caught a deep pass late in the game. I had taken my key and stayed with the running back and somebody blew the coverage behind me, but Ed blamed me for it, even criticized me in the papers. I didn't appreciate it, and I let him know it. He also knew I knew the defense better than he did, and I guess he didn't appreciate me, either.

We both grew to appreciate Krause. Paul showed up late in camp that first year after the College All-Star game, but right away we knew we had something special. It seemed like Paul was always around the football. All he did was lead the NFL with twelve interceptions his rookie year, with two more nullified by penalties. He was so fluid in his movements, and he played back there like Mickey Mantle in centerfield. I spent a lot of time teaching him the defense, and late in the year, I also tried to teach him a little about discipline.

At this point, he probably had nine or ten interceptions. The defense was coming onto the field and I was always the first guy in the huddle because I had to call signals. Well, I was just about to call out a defense when I looked up and saw Krause nonchalantly moseying into the game. "Let me tell you something, Krause," I yelled at him. "I've been playing this game a hell of a lot longer than you and I've never been the last guy in the huddle. That better be the last time for you. I don't care how many interceptions you've got, start acting like you want to hit somebody and play."

To his credit, Paul didn't take offense; in fact, I think I shook him up a little. He went on to become an All-Pro, and we became great friends. I also tried to use all his skills. That year we blitzed quite a bit. That was a part of the game I loved, trying to outthink the quarterback. That first year playing against the Giants, I called a safety blitz with Krause coming in on the quarterback and Y. A. was so rattled he threw up an interception. Yat was furious and I laughed all the way to the sidelines.

One time, though, I got myself into trouble with another one of our defensive coaches, Chuck Cherondolo, a former All-Pro who had coached in Pittsburgh and Philadelphia. Chuck was a great guy, and a fine coach, too, but I crossed him up once and I've regretted it ever since.

I was playing the usual chess game with the quarterback and sent Krause in on a safety blitz. Well, on the very next play, Cherondolo sent in another blitz. I figured that's exactly what the quarterback was expecting, so I wanted Krause to stay deep and hope the guy would just throw it up for grabs. I ignored the defense sent in from the bench and kept Krause back. Sure enough, the quarterback threw it downfield and Paul intercepted. When we got to the sidelines, Chuck came over to me. He never made a scene, which I always appreciated, but he was not happy, and I could hardly blame him.

"Sam," he said, "you know more football than I'll ever know in my lifetime, but please, don't ever do that to me again. When I send in a defense, please use it."

"Chuck," I said, "I was dead wrong. It was just the timing. I had it all set up. I knew what I wanted to do and when you sent in that blitz, I was in a real bind. But you're exactly right, it will never happen again. I promise you." And it never did.

We started off the 1964 season with four straight losses.

None of them were really humiliating, and you could tell that given time, this team might just come together. But Jurgensen was getting booed unmercifully, though I must say he silenced his critics in the fifth game. In his first head-to-head duel with Norm Snead, the guy the Redskins traded for him, Sonny clearly came out on top. He completed 22 of 31 passes for 361 yards and we beat the Eagles, 35–20, breaking a seven-game losing streak. In fact, we went on to win five of our last seven games, including big wins over the Giants and Cowboys.

Our first game against the Giants that year was a very emotional experience for me. It was the third game of the year, the Giants home opener at Yankee Stadium, and I wanted to win it more than anything in my whole life. I was introduced before the game, and the crowd gave me a long standing ovation. After the game, I visited the Giant locker room and Pete Sheehy, the legendary clubhouse man who had also worked for the Yankees since the 1920s, paid me a great compliment. "I've been here since the days of Ruth and Gehrig," he said. "and that ovation was equal to anything I ever heard for any of the Yankees." That touched me, and helped ease some of the pain from a loss that never should have happened.

We were ahead of the Giants, 10–6, late in the football game. Y. A. had broken his ribs the week before against the Steelers and wasn't even supposed to play. Gary Wood, a kid quarterback from Cornell, started instead and was zero for ten passing against us in the first half. We had that 4-point lead late in the game and we were trying to run off some time when disaster hit. Charley Taylor fumbled the ball deep in our territory and the Giants recovered. They drove down to the goal line, and now it was fourth and one with the game on the line. I knew damned well they were going to give the ball to Alex Webster, and they tried. Except Wood blew the handoff. I keyed on Alex and tackled him short of the goal line, but after he missed Alex with the handoff, Wood had no choice but to keep the ball.

So he bootlegged it in for the score. A broken play, and we lost the game, 13–10. After it was over, I was beside myself. Maybe that's why as we ran off the field I locked my eyes on Allie Sherman and gave him a shot from the side. I didn't knock him down, didn't hurt him, and probably surprised him more than anything. I guess I couldn't help myself—it was a dumb thing to do, something I'm not very proud of. But that's how emotional and how frustrating that game was for me.

At the end of the season, I did take some pride in the fact that our defense had finished third overall in the National Football League. Even more important, we had taken a unit of eleven individual ball players and started playing a coordinated kind of game. We still didn't have a lot of talent on defense—certainly nothing comparable to the Giant teams I had played on—but I was very optimistic about the future, and so was the team's management. Despite a 6–8 record, at one point we had been 5–5 and very nearly pulled off the team's first winning season since 1955.

I also took a little bit of satisfaction from the Giants' dismal season. Though I felt bad for all of my friends still on the team, the fact that New York finished 2–10–2 warmed my heart. Allie Sherman took a lot of heat, and he deserved it. Y. A. was so banged up that season, he decided to retire. The famous picture of Yat on both knees, with blood streaming down his face was taken in the Pittsburgh game that season, and the agony on his face told you everything you had to know about the 1964 New York Giants.

Back in Washington, McPeak was given a contract renewal, and when we reported to training camp for the 1965 season, I honestly thought we would be a contending football team. McPeak had made no blockbuster trades, but we did add some talent. We got Rick Casares, a hard-running veteran fullback from the Bears, Darrell Dess, a guard from the Giants, and defensive end Bill Quinlan from the Lions. In the draft, McPeak picked some winners who played a major role on the Redskins for years to come— tight end Jerry Smith from Arizona State, offensive tackle Jim Snowden from Notre Dame, defensive back Rickie Harris from Arizona, and, in the eighteenth round, linebacker Chris Hanburger from North Carolina.

Chris became the surprise of that camp. He wasn't that big and had played mostly center at Carolina, not linebacker. But as soon as you saw him in the drills, you knew McPeak's reputation for spotting talent was absolutely justified. Ed Hughes fell in love with Chris and worked with him quite a bit. With me playing inside and Chris playing outside linebacker, we made a great team. He went sideline to sideline as well as any linebacker I ever played with. The only flaw in his game was tackling. His technique was awful, and I always used to get on him about it. He'd never drive a shoulder into a ball-carrier, he was always using his hands and pulling people down. Later on, though, he'd jump right back at me. The last couple of years of my career, I got knocked out quite a few times and Chris would always remind me of it. "If you're such a great tackler," he said, "how come I'm always scraping you off the field?"

We opened the season with great expectations, only to fall flat on our rear ends. Things got so bad that in our third game, after losing the first two, it was decided that Dick Shiner, a second-year quarterback from Maryland, would start ahead of Jurgensen. Sonny was not happy about it, and when the Cardinals jumped all over us and we were way behind, McPeak told Jurgensen to go in late in the game. Sonny flat-out refused. "You wanted to go with Shiner, you made your choice," he said. "I'm not going in." And you could hardly blame him.

After our losing streak hit five, Edward Bennett Williams decided to call a team meeting. Up until that point, the only time you ever saw EBW was when you won. He'd come into the locker room, shake hands with the players and chat a bit, but that was about it. One day before practice, he came out to RFK Stadium and asked the coaches to leave the room. "We've lost five straight and we've spent a lot of money on this football team," he told us. "We've got a lot of great players out there and I'd like to know what's going on. I want to lay it all on the table and find out what's wrong here."

One of the first guys to speak up was Quinlan, the guy we had just gotten from Detroit. He had also spent three years with the Packers from 1959 to 1962, and he didn't like losing any more than the rest of us. "Mr. Williams," he said, "when I was with Green Bay, we partied a lot, we drank a lot, and we won a lot. The trouble with this team is we don't drink enough around here."

Holy cow! For a guy to come out and say something like that to the president of the club in a crisis situation absolutely floored me. But there was more. Now Mean John Paluck, a guy who hardly ever talked, got up. "What Quinlan says here isn't exactly true," Paluck said. "I've been here a lot of years, and I can tell you we've drunk enough and partied enough to be world champions."

Williams couldn't help but laugh. What the hell, we were already 0–5 and the season was pretty much shot. But that talk went a long way toward clearing the air, and we actually started to play better.

We won the next game, 24–20, over the Cardinals and after Sonny threw three touchdown passes, he presented Williams with the game ball. We won four of the next five games, then had a home game against a much-improved Dallas Cowboy team at RFK that went a long way toward finally silencing Sonny's critics.

It didn't start off so well. We were trailing, 21–0, early in the second quarter, and I heard later that the Cowboys' owner, Clint Murchison, left the stadium at halftime to fly back to Texas. His mistake.

We scored late in the first half, added another touchdown in the third and still another early in the fourth. Now we were trailing, 24–20, but the Cowboys intercepted

Sonny right after that and Don Meredith threw 35 yards to Frank Clarke for a touchdown and a 31–20 lead.

But now it was Sonny's turn. Boom, boom, boom, and we were in the end zone with a touchdown pass to Bobby Mitchell. We got the ball back with about four minutes to play, and boom, boom, boom, we scored again, this time on a 5-yard pass from Jurgy to Angelo Coia with 1:12 to play. I always kidded Sonny about scoring too soon, because the Cowboys had one last shot. Meredith began moving the Cowboys up the field. Finally, we stopped them and Danny Villanueva came on to kick a 44-yard field goal. But he never got it off. Fat Fred Williams and I opened a hole in the line and Lonnie Sanders came through to block the kick. We won, 34–31. Sonny had completed 26 of 42 passes for 411 yards, and he owned the town.

Unfortunately, it didn't last. We lost our next two games, and even a 35–14 victory over the Steelers in the last game couldn't save McPeak's job. We had finished 6–8, the ninth straight losing season for the franchise, and Edward Bennett Williams was about to get very much involved. A few weeks after the season, he fired McPeak, and I've always felt that was a great mistake. Over the previous two years, when the purse strings suddenly had gotten looser, Bill had gone out and added a lot of talent to that team. The offense was almost unstoppable, and the defense, with a few more trades and draft picks, could have been more than respectable. I also thought Sonny and I had started to turn the team's attitude around. When I first got there, these guys went into every game thinking they had almost no shot. By the end of the 1965 season, all that had changed, especially after they saw what Sonny could do on offense. But McPeak never got the chance to get the team over the hump.

Edward Bennett Williams, a man who loved to put on a show in a courtroom, was changing his venue but not his tactics. After a long search for a head coach—with some of the top names in football being bandied about—on January 25, 1966, he settled on Otto Graham, the Hall of Fame quarterback of the Cleveland Browns, as his new head coach and general manager.

This was one time when the brilliant attorney should have been overruled.

A West Virginia boy: sixteen years old, standing in my parents' yard.

High school sweethearts: Mary and I.

My mother and father, Catherine and Orly Huff.

The 1951 Farmington High School team. I'm number 22, in the middle of the second row. Coach Ray Kelly is at the extreme right.

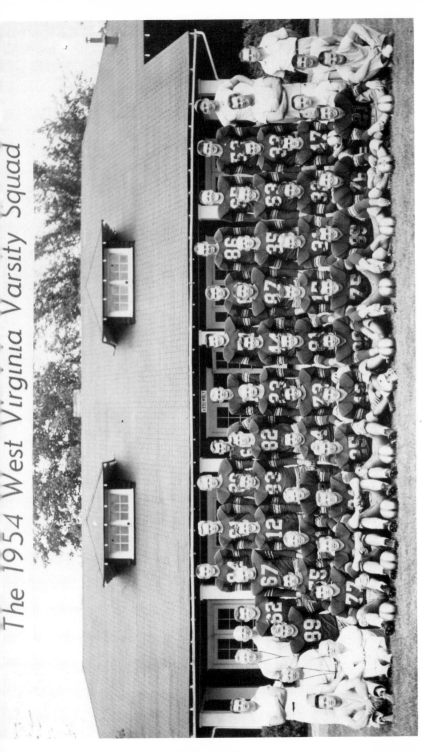

The 1954 West Virginia Varsity Squad

The 1954 West Virginia University team, with me—number 75—in the front row.

Here I am with my coach at West
Virginia, Art "Pappy" Lewis.

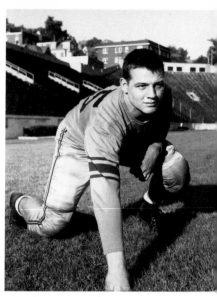

Ready to go at Mountaineer Stadium,
West Virginia University.

With Giants' Coach Jim Lee Howell.

My rookie year with the New York Giants, 1956. Notice the ripped pants
ourtesy of Wellington Mara.

The 1962 Giants with me in the third row, second from left. Four other future Hall of Famers are in this picture: Y. A. Tittle (14), Rosey Brown (79), Frank Gifford (16) third row, third from right, and Andy Robustelli (81) last row, first from left. Future New York Jets coach, Joe Walton (80) is in the second row; Coach Allie Sherman in the middle of the fourth row.

A handful of running back: me stopping Jim Brown.

Going in to block a Lou Michaels field goal in a game against the Colts.

Rosey Grier and I waiting for action.

As the referee spots the ball in the background, Jim Taylor and I are still going at it in the 1962 championship game against the Packers. I've got Jimmy in a headlock. *(Vernon J. Biever Photo)*

The Huff family the day of The Trade, April 10, 1964. From left to right: Mary, my son J.D., me, my daughter Cathy, and Sam, Jr. We're smiling here but needless to say it was not a happy day. *(AP Wirephoto)*

Now a Washington Redskin, running back an interception against the Pittsburgh Steelers. *(Paul Fine Photo)*

Collaring Johnny Roland of the St. Louis Cardinals with Chris Hanburger (55).

Hollering at a long-suffering official.

Taking a breather on the bench at Robert F. Kennedy Stadium. *(Nate Fine Photo)*

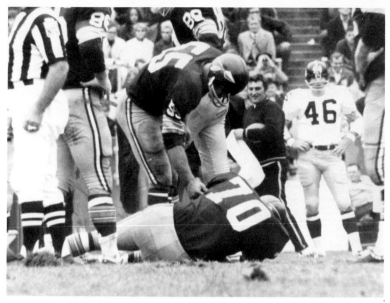

Who turned out the lights? Chris Hanburger tries to help. *(Paul Fine Photo)*

Retired, traveling in Phu Bon Province, Vietnam in 1968. This trip was one of the most moving experiences of my life. The man walking behind me was killed in action two weeks later.

Back in training camp in Carlisle, Pennsylvania, in 1969, after sitting out a year. *(AP Wirephoto)*

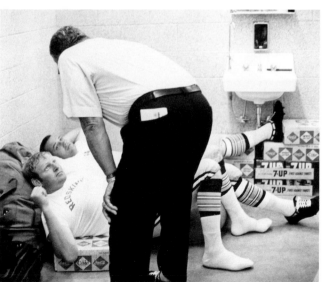

Sonny Jurgensen and I get an earful from Vince Lombardi. *(Paul Fine Photo)*

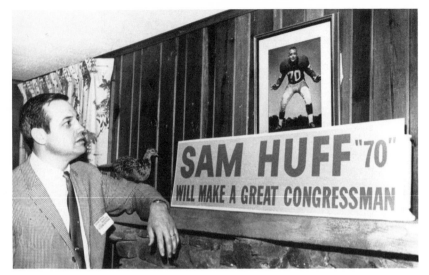

Life after football: running for a West Virginia congressional seat in 1970.
(AP Wirephoto)

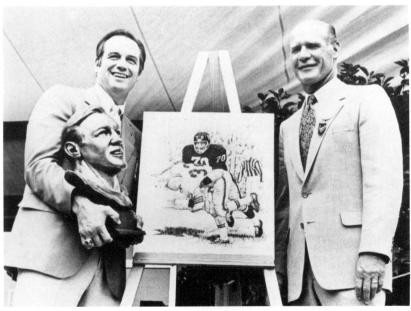

With Tom Landry, who presented me for induction to the Pro Football Hall of Fame in 1982.

Reunion for what some call the greatest game ever played, the 1958 championship game between the New York Giants and the Baltimore Colts. Hall of Fame quarterback John Unitas is on the right.

Linebackers past and present: with New York Giants' star Lawrence Taylor. *(Ray DeAragon)*

Redskin owner Jack Kent Cooke, Coach Joe Gibbs, and I. *(Nate Fine Photo)*

Three men in the booth: I'm on the left, Frank Herzog is in the center, and Sonny Jurgensen is on the right.

14

●●●●●●

A few weeks before Otto Graham's hiring was announced, I got a telephone call from Edward Bennett Williams. My heart jumped. Had I been traded again, cut from the team?

"I've got good news for you, Sam," he said. "The Defense Department has arranged for you to take a two-week trip to Vietnam."

I'd be lying if I said I was overjoyed at the prospect of winging off to Southeast Asia. The war was escalating there daily and I had never even been outside the United States, other than my trip to Canada the year they shot "The Violent World." Now they wanted me to go to a war zone.

Still, the more I thought about it, the more eager I was to go. They had asked me, Frank Gifford, John Unitas, and Willie Davis to spend two weeks touring the country, visiting the troops out in the fields and spending a lot of time at our bases and hospitals. It was a great honor to be selected, but Mary couldn't help but kid me about it.

"It sounds like you won a contest called 'The Linebacker We'd Most Like to Send to War,' " she said. "Who nominated you, Jim Brown or Jimmy Taylor?"

Truthfully, I was flattered to have been asked, and a few weeks later, we were on a Pan American flight heading for Saigon. It took twenty-three hours to get there, and when we arrived, some of the brass met us at the plane and drove us straight to our hotel. The Grand Concourse in the Bronx was never like this. The whole place was surrounded by a barbed-wire fence, and Marine guards were stationed behind sandbags on the sidewalk in front of the hotel. That first afternoon, we were briefed, given a couple pairs of fatigues and an identification badge with the word "noncombatant" written on the front. Willie Davis looked at it and said, "Hell, man, this badge is no damned good. It's in English. How are those VC going to know what it means?"

"Don't worry, Willie," he was told. "If they get that close to you, they won't give you time to get your badge out of your pocket." That was the first time the reality of the situation hit home. We were definitely in a war zone. Davis even asked if he could be issued a gun and was told, "They'll shoot you faster if you've got a weapon."

That day we were taken on a tour of Saigon, and I've never seen anything quite like it. I've never seen traffic jams like that and I've also never seen that kind of poverty. People were living on the streets, there were beggars everywhere, and garbage and raw sewage flowed freely in the streets. The sights, the sounds, and the smells were almost beyond belief.

At one point, I asked one of the soldiers assigned to us how you knew who the enemy was. Our guys were all in uniform, how could you tell who the bad guys were? "Any one of 'em could be the enemy," he said. "See that guy over there. Well, if he walks up here and shakes your hand, he's a friend of yours. If he walks up here and shoots you, then he's the enemy."

The next day we made our first of many visits to a field hospital. This one was at Tan Son Nhut airport outside Saigon, the last stop for the wounded before they were flown out of the country. On the way over, we passed three truckloads of South Korean soldiers, and we were told they were some of the fiercest fighters you'd ever see. After they passed us, someone threw a firecracker at one truck, and all hell broke loose. Those Koreans jumped out of their trucks and just opened fire on everything—trees, buildings, stray dogs. I heard later that luckily, no one was hurt, but it shook us all up.

As it was, I was already a little queasy about going to the hospital. I get a knot in my stomach just thinking about getting a flu shot, and now we were getting ready to walk through a field hospital with all these kids wounded, crippled, and maimed. It was the worst thing I had ever experienced, seeing these young men, some of them only a couple of years older than my son, Sam Jr., with arms gone, legs gone, just shot to hell.

But these were also the bravest people I've ever met. I talked to a sergeant, a fourteen-year veteran, who had stepped on a land mine. He was lying in bed, bandaged from head to toe and half his face had been blown away. "Sarge," I told him, "I hate to see you like this, it's a privilege to meet you. You don't have to say anything, just hang in there."

"Hell," he said through the bandages, "I can still talk. Just got messed up a little."

With so much misery and suffering all around me, I had a change of attitude real quick. We were here for a purpose, to cheer up the troops—our kids, your brother, my brother. I said to myself, "If you don't have the guts or the nerve or whatever it takes to go through a hospital, well, you've got to be a bigger person than that." It became a mission for me, and I was able to handle it. It was never easy, and Gifford was having a hard time dealing with it, too. He was pretty shaken up. Hell, we all were.

Over the next two weeks, no one ever shot at us as far as I could tell, though I found out a few months later that a couple of days after we left, one of our Vietnamese guides was picked off by a sniper. Still, there were some pretty scary experiences. Landing on an aircraft carrier puts your heart in your mouth every time, and I never did get used to it. Assault landings weren't much fun either. One morning, we went to a place called Quang Ngai, a base of operations out in the field for our Special Forces. Assault landings were designed to evade enemy gunfire. You came into the area at a height that was out of rifle range, then all of a sudden you just about nose-dived to the ground. As we came in, Willie Davis said I was gripping his leg so tight, I almost broke it. I turned around and looked at Gifford, and his face was crimson. We spent a lot of time on that trip kidding Frank. He'd once appeared in a World War II movie, *Darby's Rangers*. We kept telling him that Warner Brothers wasn't filming this war and you didn't break for lunch between firefights.

We went to twenty-two different places in twelve days, and it was the most fascinating and frightening tour I'd ever taken. People make a big deal about football players, how tough we must be to play the sport. Well, let me tell you something, it's nothing compared to what these kids went through over there, not even close. It also made me think long and hard about what we were doing in Vietnam in the first place. When I ran for Congress in 1970, I was very much in favor of withdrawing our troops. It was such a futile exercise, such a tragic effort. And it's a place I'll never forget.

It took me a long time to get Vietnam out of my mind. All of a sudden, football wasn't all that important to me. Maybe that's why training camp at the start of the 1966 season seemed to last forever.

We had a new coach, Otto Graham, a very nice fellow who I've always felt was just a little too laid-back to be a successful head coach in the National Football League. There was no question he had a fine football mind, he'd been a great quarterback for the Cleveland Browns for a lot of years. But I always had the sneaking suspicion that Otto didn't really like what he was doing. Out on the practice field, he seemed kind of disorganized. As you might expect, he spent most of his time with the offense, and he turned his defense over to Ed Hughes.

I remember the early practices were long and boring, and for the first time, I really began to dislike training camp. In the past, I had always looked forward to it. Now, I couldn't wait to get out of there.

I also was starting to get concerned about how Otto prepared a team to play. We were getting ready to face the Baltimore Colts in our first preseason game at RFK Stadium, but during the week of practice, no one ever mentioned our opponent. We had no scouting report, nothing. So I went to Otto in the middle of the week and asked him what was going on. We were about to play against John Unitas, in front of our fans, and we knew nothing about the Colts. Somebody ought to speak up real soon, I told him.

"Sam, I'm probably a little different kind of coach than you're used to," he said in the understatement of the year. "I don't think you can keep ball players motivated for a full season, so what I want to do is play a lot of people in this first game. You're not going to play much. Neither is Sonny. I know what you guys can do and I want to see some of the younger guys. When I cut a man, I want to make sure he gets a fair shake."

The plan was for me and Sonny to play the first quarter, and that was it. Nobody had ever played me in only one quarter in my life, and now I was being asked to sit and watch, against a great football team that we knew nothing about.

The result was predictable. The Colts slaughtered us, 35–0. Sonny and I played two series and that was it. Otto played everybody but the security guy. He was definitely a different kind of coach. Of course, we had gotten an inkling of that in the college draft that year when the Redskins selected Charlie Gogolak, a soccer-style kicker from Princeton, as their first-round pick. Edward Bennett Williams justified the move by saying he was sick and tired of every extra point being an adventure, but it was not a good move. No one in the history of football had ever used a number one on a kicker, and there was good reason for it. Most kickers are flakey and you'd be taking a hell of a chance wasting that pick.

What made it worse was that nobody liked Charlie

much. He was a very bright guy who I always believed never really wanted to play football. I think Williams liked him because Charlie talked about going to law school, and the Redskins certainly helped pay his way. They gave him bonuses, a big salary, and the little guy hardly even practiced. He'd kick for five or ten minutes a day, and that was about it. He was not very popular and he usually went his own way. I think he knew most of us were not happy that the Redskins had used their top pick to get him. Hell, we needed offensive and defensive linemen and linebackers. We needed real players, not sidewinder kickers.

The draft didn't provide much help, but we did get a couple of decent players in trade and off the waiver wire. Otto sent safety Jim Steffen, a popular player with the fans and an excellent safety, to the Cowboys for defensive back Brig Owens, offensive tackle Mitch Johnson, and offensive guard Jake Kupp. After the season started, we got linebacker Jim Carroll and running back Steve Thurlow from the Giants. But the most intriguing move of the year as far as I was concerned came when they acquired Joe Don Looney, the very appropriately named running back.

New York had made Looney the number-one pick the year I was traded, and I knew all about him from my old roomate, Don Chandler. Looney had gone to Oklahoma, so the Giants decided to room him with Chandler, who was from Tulsa.

We were going to play an exhibition game at Cornell against the Giants that year, and when we got to Ithaca, I went over to see my friend Chandler. Right away, he started talking about Looney. "Sam, he's crazy," he said. "You've never met anyone like him. I just can't figure him out."

No sooner had he said it than Joe Don walked into the room. He looked like a movie star, a big Burt Reynolds. He was wearing a T-shirt, blue jeans, and a pair of sandals, with muscles everywhere, a regular piece of the rock. We started talking and I told him that he was lucky to be in a great organization playing in a great city. "Great?" he said. "I hate this place. These coaches don't know what they're doing. I'm hurt, and they make me come up here to this game. Shofner's back in New York. He's hurt, he didn't have to make this trip. I got a sore leg. I can't play. I can't run. I ought to be back in the city."

Very strange.

After that, I kept hearing other stories. Y. A. Tittle told me that Looney didn't want to come out to practice, so the coaches asked Yat to go talk to the kid, figuring he'd have a little respect for a veteran quarterback. Yat went to his room, and sat down to talk to Looney. The stereo was blaring and Yat was trying to talk seriously with him, and all Looney did was laugh. He just laughed at Y. A. Tittle. Never stopped until Yat got so ticked off, he left.

I'd also heard that Wellington Mara went over to his room and tried to get him to come out. Joe Don refused. So Wellington slipped a note under his door and told him he'd be fined $200 if he didn't come to practice. Looney slipped another note back under the door. It said, "Make it $250."

The Giants eventually traded him to Baltimore, and the Colts sent him to Detroit. One day, Otto called Sonny and me into his office and told us he was thinking about bringing Joe Don Looney into camp. We needed a big strong running back to complement Charley Taylor and A. D. Whitfield, a tough little guy but hardly a superstar. I flashed back to my visit with Looney at Cornell and started shaking my head. First of all, I told Otto, three of the best organizations in football wanted no part of this guy, why did we think we could change him? "We got enough guys on this team who are a little weird," I said, "why do we need another one?" Sonny agreed. But it was apparent this was already a decision that had been made, and I sensed that Edward Bennett Williams was behind it. Joe Don Looney was another big name, a number-one draft choice, and we could get him cheap. So Looney reported to the Redskins.

A few days later, Otto called me in again. He needed someone to look after Joe Don, baby-sit him on the road. He asked me if I'd mind rooming with him.

Yes, I would, I told him. I was rooming with Sonny, we got along real well, and I was in no mood to change. "Sam, we'll make it worth your while," he said. "If you room with him and keep him out of trouble, we'll give you a fifteen-hundred-dollar bonus." Now that got my attention, and the next week, I had myself a new roommate, and a new headache, as well.

This was not an easy job. As good-looking as this guy was, he always attracted women. Before home games, they used to put us up at the Mayflower Hotel in downtown Washington. One night, Joe Don had gone down to the coffee shop for a hamburger before curfew and I was lying in bed watching "Gunsmoke" when I heard a knock on the door.

A very pretty girl was standing outside. She was looking for Joe Don and she wanted to come in. I told her Joe Don wasn't there, but she said she'd wait. She said she'd come all the way from Delaware and she'd heard a lot about Joe Don. She almost floored me when she just came right out and said: "I want to spend the night with him."

I told her she had definitely picked the right guy, but I still wasn't going to let her in. By this time, Joe Don had come back upstairs, and he let her in the room and wanted her to stick around. I was still in bed, lying there with no clothes on, and Joe Don got so angry with me he pulled the sheets off. "Just give me ten minutes," he said.

No way. I mean, I could just see that $1,500 floating out of my wallet, and I wanted that girl out of there before the coaches started their bed checks. Finally, she left, and my bonus was still alive.

But I always had problems with the guy. Joe Don wasn't a real good sleeper, and if he didn't sleep, I didn't sleep because I didn't want him sneaking out on me. We were back at the Mayflower, and one night he got up at three in the morning and opened the window. I wasn't sleeping that soundly anyway—with Joe Don I always kept one eye open and one ear cocked—and when I heard the venetian blinds go up, I honestly thought he was getting ready to jump, that's how wacky this guy was. I bolted out of bed and started yelling, "Don't jump, Joe Don, don't jump."

"What are you talking about, Sam? I'm just trying to get a little fresh air," he said, looking at me as if *I* were the cuckoo in the room.

I managed to survive with him that first year, but this was not a match made in heaven. The next year, we were practicing out at RFK for the opener against the Eagles. We were in full gear and it was a typically humid September day in the nation's capital. We were hot and tired but Otto kept us out there all day. We were in a drill where the offense was running Eagle plays for the defense. It was supposed to be run at half-speed, with no hitting. A back would run through the hole, you'd get in position and basically just touch him and let him go. Joe Don was playing fullback, and they called a play for him called "thirty-nine toss." He got a pitchout, then cut back inside and hit the hole. So I pursued the play, got myself in position to make the tackle and just stopped, like you're supposed to do in a half-speed drill. But Joe Don didn't stop. He lowered his shoulder and ran over me—hit me in the chest with his shoulder pads and sent me flying five yards backward on my butt. I was lying there, kind of dazed, and he walked up to me, stuck the football in my face, and said, "How'd you like that, big boy? I knocked the crap out of you."

I was furious. "Psycho," I said, "you just picked on the wrong guy."

On the next play, I knew what was coming. They had called a trap play, and Joe Don was going to get the ball again and come right up the middle. Our center, my friend Len Hauss, knew I was steaming so he just got out of the way and didn't even try to block me.

Right before the ball was snapped, Joe Don stood back

there with his hands on his hips, looked over my way, and said, "Here I come again, big boy, let's see what you got."

He got the ball, came right through the hole, and let me tell you, I was there to meet him. I came off the ground and hit him with everything I had, right on the button. You could have heard the pads popping in Richmond. The ball flew one way, his headgear flew another, and Joe Don came after me. Oh, we had one lovely little fight out there. We were slugging it out and Otto didn't know what to do. They couldn't get us apart, and Joe Don was screaming and yelling: "I'll kill you, I'll bomb your house!" I mean to tell you, it was a brawl to beat all brawls, because I was a complete maniac myself.

Needless to say, Joe Don Looney and I never roomed together again. For one of the few times in my life, I can honestly say I couldn't have cared less about that $1,500. It wasn't worth the aggravation.

Jurgensen and I never had any problems like that, and I also want to set the record straight on Sonny's reputation. In Philadelphia, he was always regarded as a playboy; hell, when he was traded to Washington he always used to joke that the bartenders in Philadelphia started wearing black arm bands when he left. But he was a grossly overrated partier. The problem was, Sonny just wasn't a good sleeper, so in training camp, he'd get restless after curfew and go out to a bar to have a beer and play the pinball machines. Now I'm not going to tell you he didn't like to have a drink, but a lot of that stuff was exaggerated.

He also was the coolest quarterback in a huddle I ever saw, and he was pretty cool off the field, too. That became very apparent to me shortly after we started rooming together. Sonny had been through a divorce in Philadelphia, and one night we were lying in our hotel room before a game when he got a phone call from an old girl friend back in Philadelphia. This was no ordinary phone call, however. She told Sonny she'd just swallowed a bottle of sleeping pills. Sonny jumped out of bed and said something like, "Oh my God, this girl says she's trying to kill herself."

I thought he was joking. "Forget it, Sonny, let it go, we got a game tomorrow." But she wasn't joking. He got on the phone and started calling some friends in Philadelphia and they managed to break down the girl's door and save her life. Sonny played the next day, and it was like it'd never happened.

We had other guys who liked to skip out at night, too. We had a receiver named Preston Carpenter, a guy we had gotten from Pittsburgh, and he broke curfew one night before a home game. Washington at that time was really sort of a small town, and somebody had seen Preston in a bar and called the team to report it. We were playing the Browns, and early in the game, with us still very much in it, Sonny called a play for Carpenter, threw him a perfect pass, and he dropped it in the end zone.

We lost the game, and Otto was very upset. He called me and Sonny in and asked us how much we thought he ought to fine Preston. I recommended $500. Sonny said $250. Otto finally decided on $1,000, and then he looked both of us in the eye. "If it had been either one of you guys," he said, "it would have been five thousand apiece."

"Don't worry, Otto," I said, "you'll never get that kind of money out of me. No beer after eleven o'clock is worth five thousand dollars."

Still, Otto wasn't much of a disciplinarian. He was sort of the absentminded-professor type. At training camp, he loved to play tennis, which might tell you something. Can you imagine Vince Lombardi playing tennis? George Allen? Joe Gibbs?

After a while, we used to make fun of him. He always had on a porkpie hat, and his clothes hardly ever matched. He never wore a tie, just liked to wear a polo shirt and golf pants, white socks and hush puppies. At practice, he'd slap his clipboard constantly. The players used to bet on how many times he'd do it walking from the locker room to the practice field.

Personally, I liked the guy, but I always felt he just didn't like the pro game. He'd been at the Coast Guard

Academy as head coach and athletic director the previous seven years, and the lifestyle in Washington was a hell of a lot different, with a lot more pressure.

One day, he really did get under my skin. He called me into his office and told me that on the field I was a great captain, "but off the field, I don't think you're much."

"What are you talking about?" I asked. I always prided myself on living a decent, quiet life.

"I'm talking about after practice," he said. "When I say practice is over, you and John Reger [another linebacker] are always the first guys off the field. I don't think that's right and if it happens again, I'm going to fine you."

"Wait a minute, Otto, you mean that when you say practice is over, you mean practice is *not* over?"

"That's right," he said. "Jerry Smith and a lot of other guys stay out there and work on their pass patterns. So I want you guys there, too. Don't be heading for the barn."

So from then on, when Gogolak came out to practice his five minutes of kicking, Reger would shag the ball, throw it to me, and I'd throw it to the center. A real waste of time, but anything to make Otto happy.

The Graham era started off badly. We got drubbed by the Browns, with President Lyndon Johnson in attendance up in Ed Williams' private box. Otto made no friends in the White House when he said, "Maybe the President will stay home next time." He also had the fans grumbling the next week when we lost to the Cardinals, 23–7. Still, by midseason, we were 5–3, and by then, Otto had made one of the great moves in NFL history.

In the seventh game, he switched Charley Taylor from running back to wide receiver. Taylor bitched about it at the time, but there's no question it saved his legs and prolonged his career. When he retired in 1977, he had caught more passes than any receiver in the history of the NFL.

Part of the reason for the switch was our offensive line. Taylor was so quick, he made most of his yards on his own because he couldn't wait for his blockers. Our guards were not the fastest in the world, and when they pulled out on a sweep, before they could hit their men, Charley was running in front of them.

Otto was very offense-minded—hell, he had to be. Our defense wasn't very good; we hardly had a pass rush and teams had little trouble moving the ball on us. Sonny would always ask me how many points I thought we needed to win. I'd usually say 30 and we had a shot. It was embarrassing.

Late in the season, we finally played a team that had a worse defense than the Redskins. It was time to meet the New York Giants, and they were giving up more points than any team in the history of the game. In fact, the 1966 Giants under Allie Sherman may have been the worst excuse for a professional football team I have ever seen. Before the game, Sonny asked me how many points we needed. "Sonny," I said, "you'll score sixty."

He thought I was out of my head, but I had seen the films. They'd played the Rams two weeks earlier and had given up 55 points; it was like men against boys. There was no doubt in my mind that Sonny was going to light it up, though I have to admit I wasn't exactly confident that our defense could stop the Giants.

On the field before the game, Kyle Rote interviewed me for his pregame radio show. "What do you think about the game?" he asked. "We'll score sixty," I said into the microphone for all my friends back in New York.

As we were doing our calisthenics, Otto asked me what I thought. "Otto," I told him, "we're gonna kill 'em." Now I had never in my life said any such thing to a head coach. But I was a believer. "And Otto, I want to ask you one more thing: show no mercy. Show no mercy to that little son of a bitch across the field, because this is our day."

I was right about the offense, but the damned defense wasn't doing anything. At one point, we were up, 49–41.

Sonny had just led us to a score and as he came off the field he passed me and said, "Jesus, Sam, how many do I have to score?"

"Don't let up," I said. "Just don't let up."

At that point, our defense did stiffen a bit, and Sonny got the lead up to 69–41. In the final seconds, we were just trying to kill the clock. We had a fourth down at the Giant twenty-two and a time-out was called with seven seconds left. While Otto was talking to Sonny, I took it upon myself to yell for the field-goal team to get out there, and before anyone knew what was happening, Gogolak had kicked a 29-yard field goal for a final score of 72–41.

After the game, Otto took a lot of heat for kicking the field goal and rubbing it in. When the writers asked him why he didn't just kill the clock, he said, "Gogolak needed the practice." But it wasn't Otto's decision to kick that field goal, it was all mine. The 72 points we scored were for a lot of people: me, Mo, Livingston, Rosey, and all the old Giants. That was a day of judgment, and in my mind, justice was finally done.

The next week, we gave the fans another thrill. This time we went at it with the Cowboys, and once again we lit up the scoreboard. Late in the game, it was 31–31, and A. D. Whitfield returned a Cowboy punt 30 yards to the Dallas twenty-four. For one of the few times I can ever remember, Sonny couldn't get us any closer and we actually lost 5 yards on three plays. Meanwhile, the clock kept ticking toward zero and no one was calling time-out. When it got under ten seconds, fans were on their feet screaming, and so were the players, but Sonny never lost his cool. He walked away from the huddle and started talking to an official. Finally, when it was under five seconds, he told the referee, "Well, it's about that time. I'll take that time-out now." With three seconds left, Gogolak came on and kicked a field goal to win the game.

The last game of the season was almost an anticlimax, and we played that way, losing 37–28 to the Eagles and finishing a disappointing 7–7. And in 1967, it got worse, especially for me.

The offense kept scoring points at a record pace. Sonny finished the year with over 4,000 yards passing. After all, he was throwing to two future Hall of Famers, Charley Taylor and Bobby Mitchell, and a great tight end, Jerry Smith. Taylor and Smith finished one-two in the league in catches and Mitchell was number four, an all-time NFL first, and Charley led the league despite missing three games with an injury.

This was also my season to get hurt. In all my years of playing professional football, I'd never been injured badly enough to miss a game, until 1967. We were 2–2–1 and playing the Rams in Los Angeles. George Allen was the coach and Roman Gabriel was his quarterback. Gabe was a big man, six-three and probably 225, and the hardest tackle to make is to bring down a big quarterback who doesn't really know how to run, or where he's going to run. Early in the game, Gabriel scrambled up the field and tried to dodge me. He got me a little off-balance, and then Spain Musgrove, our big defensive tackle, came into the play and hit Gabe from behind. My foot got bent backward underneath Spain, and it was like two tons of bricks had landed on me. I don't know how he didn't break my leg, but it ripped all the tendons around my right ankle. The team doctor, George Resta, and our trainer, Joe Kuczo, said it was the worst ankle injury they'd ever seen.

I wound up missing five games. They kept giving me cortisone shots, heat treatments, anything to get me back on my feet. With me, our defense wasn't all that good. Without me, it was awful. But I couldn't even walk without limping. I wanted to play in the worst way, but Ed Hughes saw me hobbling around and wouldn't let me. I finally got back in against the Eagles. They had moved down toward our goal line in the third quarter and Hughes sent me in, figuring that I wouldn't have to move very far. When I trotted into the huddle, the crowd gave me a standing ovation and that was a great thrill. That we came back and tied the Eagles, 35–35, after I got back in there helped ease the pain, too.

But I played with a lot of pain the rest of that year. In fact, it took about six months for me to be able to walk right on that ankle. The worst days were Tuesdays, when Dr. Resta came to practice. When I saw his car pull up, my heart always skipped a beat. I'd go into the training room so the players wouldn't hear me scream when he'd come at me with a needle that looked a foot long and jab that thing right into the joint. Oh, that was painful.

By the end of the season, I was pretty depressed. Otto was getting to me, the team was going badly—we finished 5–6–3—I was banged up and could hardly walk. Everywhere I went, people were telling me that maybe it was time to give it up. A lot of them were my friends. and they meant well. I was always hearing things like, "We don't want to see you get hurt," or "You've been a great player; don't just hang on for the paycheck." Before too long, I started to feel that way myself.

Finally, before the last game of the season, I told Joe Blair, the Redskin publicity man, to call a press conference. He had all the media waiting for me, camera crews from all over town, the networks, and a couple from New York, too. I came in after practice to our dressing room, and I sat down in front of my locker, the one right next to Jurgy, and my whole career flashed in front of me. I looked up at those pads, and the head gear and the equipment I wore all the time, and it suddenly hit me that I wouldn't be doing this anymore. So I just sat there and started crying, right in front of the whole team.

Most of the guys didn't know what to do. One of the players went in and told Otto I was sitting there bawling. He came in, sat down next to me, and put his hand on my shoulder.

"Sam," he said, "everybody gets old."

Thanks, Otto.

Anyway, I composed myself long enough to meet the press, and I broke down again.

Dave Brady wrote in *The Washington Post,* "Tears flowed like champagne at a championship celebration as the Redskins inched up and gave Sam Huff an understanding squeeze on the shoulder. Elbows on thighs and head bowed, he gave unintelligible answers to uncomprehended murmurings as the full import to retire gave him a wrench."

But the full import really hit home the next year. My decision to retire after the 1967 season may have been the biggest mistake of my life.

15

● ● ● ● ● ● ●

Until Vince Lombardi rescued me from my premature retirement as a player, I would have to say that my time away from football was one of the most miserable experiences of my life.

I moved the whole family from Alexandria, Virginia, back to the New York area. We bought a beautiful house in Franklin Lakes, New Jersey, in Bergen County, and I joined the ranks of the commuter, driving in every day to my office at J. P. Stevens. I enjoyed my work, but something kept gnawing at me. I was still relatively young, only thirty-three years old, and I just didn't feel like a retired football player. And the closer it got to training camp, the worse I felt. Then one day, all of those feelings were put on hold and reality set in.

I'd been playing in a pickup softball game one night after work at a field near the house. My youngest son, J. D., had ridden over on his bicycle to watch with a friend, and when it started to get a little dark, I told him to start heading for home.

A few minutes after J. D. left, the game ended and I got in the car and started home, too. A couple of blocks from my house, a lot of cars were backed up, and I was stuck in traffic. While I was sitting there, Scott Thompson, J. D.'s friend, rode up to the car on his bicycle and said, "Mr.

Huff, you better come quick. J. D.'s been hit by a car and he's in bad shape."

I jumped out of the car and ran up the street. J. D. was lying on the pavement and was already being cared for by Dr. Carmine Diorio, who happened to live right up the street. J. D. was a mess. He had a broken leg, his head was all scraped and cut, and he had a shoulder wound that was bleeding badly. It seemed to take forever for an ambulance to get there, but Dr. Diorio had called ahead to the hospital and had a neurosurgeon waiting for us. To this day, I'm convinced that J. D. would not be alive if he hadn't gotten such great emergency treatment at the scene of the accident and at the hospital.

In the beginning he was in bad shape. J. D. was in a coma, and stayed that way for eight days. But because he'd gotten immediate medical attention, he had survived the initial trauma, and now it was just a matter of time. Mary spent every waking hour she could at the hospital; I was there a lot, but it really did get to me, seeing that little guy just lying there. After about a week, he'd start yawning every once in a while, almost to let you know that he was going to come out of it. Even after he regained consciousness, he had to spend a total of forty-eight days in the hospital, getting all kinds of physical therapy. He also was having some difficulty talking. He had suffered a little brain damage and it was affecting his speech. I happened to mention that to one of my neighbors, and he said he had a friend who was a speech therapist. I called her and that day, she went over to the hospital and within ten minutes, she had him talking. It was amazing.

J. D. made a full recovery, but it took a long time to get him right. He was probably the best athlete of the three kids, but after that injury, he had some coordination problems and never did play sports seriously. Sam Jr. played some football in high school. We sent him to Fork Union Military Academy in Virginia, and I went to see him play one day. He was a wide receiver, and afterward I kidded him about not hitting anyone. "Sam, you can't play football and not hit people," I told him.

"Dad," he said, "that's the way you play, I don't play it that way." After that, I let him decide for himself whether he wanted to keep playing. I never encouraged my kids to play football, because it's a tough game, and if you're not born to it, if you don't want it, and if you don't really like it, you ought to try something else.

That was my problem. I still loved the game, but I had no one to play with. And then, I got very lucky; I got one more chance to stay in the game.

After the 1968 season, Otto Graham was history. Incredibly, he had traded Paul Krause to the Minnesota Vikings for a reserve tight end, Marlin McKeever, who later became a linebacker under my tutelage, and the team at one point lost seven of eight games and finished 5–9. The fans were grumbling and Edward Bennett Williams was at it again, looking for a big name—the biggest name of all, in fact.

Williams had always been enamored of Vince Lombardi and I've been told he tried several times to get him to come to Washington. When McPeak was fired in 1965, Lombardi's name had come up before they settled on Graham. By now, Lombardi had relinquished the coaching duties in Green Bay and was the team's general manager. But Vince didn't belong up in the owner's box, and he was bored with it. When Williams also offered him a small percentage of Redskin stock, that sealed it, and on February 7, 1969, Lombardi was named coach and general manager of the Washington Redskins. "I can't walk across the Potomac," he said at a press conference that day, but no one in the room believed him.

A few weeks before he got the job, I was flying on a business trip from New York and Vince and his wife Marie just happened to be on the same flight. A total coincidence. Knowing how friendly we'd been since his days with the Giants, Marie asked me if I'd like to take her seat next to Vince. So I sat down and we started talking.

"I hear you're talking to the Redskins about coaching the team," I said. The word was out on the grapevine, and I still had some pretty good sources of information.

"There's a real good chance of it," he answered. "We're trying to put the deal together now."

"Coach," I said, "if you ever do get the job, I would really love to coach for you." At that point, I was seriously thinking about ditching the business world and getting back into football, with the goal of eventually becoming the head coach of an NFL team. Vince said he'd keep that in mind.

A few days after he got the job in Washington, he called me in New Jersey. "I was thinking about our conversation on the airplane," he said, "and I've had some second thoughts about it. I've got somebody else in mind to coach the defense. He's got a little more coaching experience than you do."

He was talking about my old teammate, Harland Svare. I told him I thought Harland would be a good choice, and then I made him another proposal. "How about letting me work with the linebackers under Harland, and I'll be a player-coach."

That really intrigued him. "You think you can play another year?" he asked.

"Yes sir, I know I can."

"Well," he said, "I need to buy some time with this team. If you can give me one year, we can develop some guys behind you, and that just might work out. Why don't you come down to Washington and we'll talk about it."

Meanwhile, the people at J. P. Stevens were trying to talk me out of it. It's funny, because one of the things that had gotten me thinking about playing football again was a film I had seen in a company sales meeting. Lombardi had done a film called *Second Effort,* the greatest motivational movie I'd ever seen. That really started me thinking that I could still play.

At about the same time, I had been passed over for a promotion. The company had come up with a new fabric, Spandomatic, that we thought was going to be "the thing" .

in men's wear. It was a fabric that stretched and gave a real comfortable fit, and we thought it would be a big seller. I had wanted to run my own department and I thought this was the perfect opportunity, but they promoted someone else. So with some reluctance, and the knowledge that I had a chance to resume my football career, I decided to resign.

I went before the board of directors to tell them I was returning to football. I told them I was upset about being passed over and I was told that the other guy had more experience in menswear. I told them it wasn't my fault that I hadn't been cross-trained, and I also told them they were heading for trouble in their mills down South. In addition to everything else, I made a lot of goodwill trips for the company and spent time touring the mills, meeting the workers.

Some of these people had spent thirty, thirty-five years working one piece of equipment and all they had to show for it was a watch. Some mill managers didn't treat their workers very well. They didn't pay them much, and I warned them that they would have problems if they didn't start to make improvements in wages and working conditions. Of course, a few years later, J. P. Stevens had one of the longest strikes in the history of unions in this country, and it hurt their business badly.

I could see it coming, but don't get me wrong. I'd had a real good experience with that company up until that last disappointment. I had been treated well, but the fact that I was passed over for that job made it a lot easier to give up the business world and get back into football.

A few days after Lombardi was named head coach, I flew down to Washington and met him in the Redskin office.

"Now, Sam," he said, "I run a very tough training camp, tougher than anything you remember in New York. If you want to play, you'll have to do everything everyone else does."

I told him not to worry about it. Hell, I kept thinking

about Jurgensen and that old potbelly of his. If Sonny could get through it, I knew I could, too. Anyway, I'd heard all these wild stories about Lombardi, but I figured he couldn't be that tough.

I was wrong.

The man could drive people harder than anyone I've ever seen. He would yell at you, scream at you at the top of his lungs, get so angry at you that you almost begged for mercy. But he also knew when to stop, and when to build you back up. There was a warm side to him, too. At training camp every day at five o'clock in the afternoon, he and the assistant coaches would meet for a beer or two with the press before dinner. Lombardi loved the give-and-take. It was all off-the-record, and you saw the real Lombardi in action. He loved to tell stories, and he was a very charming man when he wanted to be. He was also deeply religious. In fact, in training camp. he put a priest right next door to him in the dormitory so he wouldn't have to waste time going to church for morning Mass. I always thought Lombardi believed in reincarnation, specifically that he had been General George Patton in another life. And just as the troops feared and admired General Patton, that's how it was with Vincent T. Lombardi. I loved the guy, but I feared him more than any man in my lifetime.

Our team found out about fear not too long after we arrived in training camp.

We had a big fullback named Ray McDonald. Otto had made him the number-one pick out of Idaho in 1967, and he looked like he had it all—six-four, 225 pounds, great build, strong as hell. But he just never panned out as a football player, and certainly not a number-one draft choice. The first time I saw him, he was wearing a beret, and I'd never seen *that* on a football player. He was just a different kind of guy, but we had quite a few intriguing characters on that football team.

Hell, we had a running back named Dave Kopay, and he eventually came out of the closet after he left football in the early 1970s. Mary about dropped the newspaper when she read that one morning. And all of us were stunned when Jerry Smith died of AIDS a couple of years ago. We had heard stories about him for years, too, but Kopay and Smith were my friends and my teammates, and I've always felt that if that's the way they wanted to live, who am I to say it's right or wrong?

I hardly knew McDonald, other than in the locker room. But I did know he was going to have some problems making the football team. Before the start of the 1969 season, the coaching staff was going over our personnel and Lombardi asked my opinion of McDonald. I was a coach, but I was a player, too, and I think he valued my views. "He's not a football player," I said.

"What do you mean?" Lombardi barked. "We had him rated real high when I was in Green Bay. He's a number-one draft choice, how can he not be a player?"

"Coach," I said, "he's not going to be the kind of player you want. If you're looking for another Jimmy Taylor or another Paul Hornung, you've got the wrong guy."

"We'll just see about that, mister," he snapped. "We'll just see."

Lombardi always wanted you to know he was in charge, but in camp, it didn't take him long to see that I was right. Ray spent more time in the training room than any guy on the team. He'd had a sore Achilles tendon the year before, and he complained that it was still bothering him. In practice, Lombardi was really on him, and I think Ray knew he was in serious trouble and might not make the team. Ball players can sense that kind of thing, and when they're that marginal, they also know an injury might keep them around a little longer, might get them a couple of extra paychecks. So Ray came up with a pulled leg muscle, and was spending a lot of time in the training room.

We had a team meeting every night at seven o'clock, but the Redskins ran on Lombardi time. You knew you better be in your seat at 6:45, because whenever Vince walked in the door and started talking, that's when the meeting started. McDonald hadn't practiced that afternoon, and Ray came into the room at five to seven. But Lombardi had already started. "Get up front here, mister," he yelled. "There's plenty of seats up front."

So McDonald walked to the front row and sat down. "By the way, mister, you're late, and that will be a seventy-five-dollar fine."

"I'm not late, Coach, it's five minutes to seven."

"I said you were late, mister, and not only are you late, you're also hurt, isn't that right?"

"Yes, sir."

"And did you see the doctor today?"

As a coach, I knew McDonald hadn't seen Dr. Resta. I also knew exactly what Lombardi was doing. "No sir, I didn't."

At that point, Lombardi flew into a rage in front of the team. Finally, he said, "You're fired, just get the hell out of this room, you disgrace the Green Bay Packer uniform."

"Coach," I whispered, "that's the Redskin uniform."

"You disgrace the Redskin uniform, so get out of here, go play for the Roanoke Buckskins or whatever the hell they call themselves. But you will never wear this uniform again, mister. You're fired."

Never had I ever seen that done to a player at any level of football. The room was dead silent, no one said a word. We had seen the wrath of Vince Lombardi, and we were totally stunned.

Out on the practice field, it was brutal, too.

Don Doll, another assistant, ran calisthenics, and I'm not just talking about jumping jacks. That guy would take you through exercises that could kill you—pushups, duck walks, leg lifts. And then Lombardi would call for his grass drills, the true torture of training camp. You'd start running in place, and he'd holler "on your belly" or "on your back" and you'd hit the dirt, then pop up when he'd yell "on your feet." We'd do fifteen or twenty of those and then he'd look over at me and Sonny. We were usually in the second or third row, not real conspicuous but close enough so that he could see we weren't dogging it. He'd stop the grass drills when he thought Sonny and I were about to die.

After that, he'd want us to run a lap around the field, I guess about 150, 200 yards, and you had better not be last. The last guy usually evoked the wrath of Lombardi, and I did not want that to be me. I used to tell Chris Hanburger and Harold McLinton that if they had to carry me, then carry me, but don't ever let me be last.

After a couple of weeks of this, to the tune of two practices a day, Sonny and I were thin, I mean *thin*. No more potbelly for Jurgensen. Still Vince complained that he didn't think the team was in shape. "Hell," he said in a coaches' meeting, "when they come back from that run, all these guys have their hands on their knees and they're breathing too heavy. I've always believed that most games are won in the last two minutes, and the team that's in the best condition will win those games. No team is going to outcondition mine."

So, I let it be known among my teammates not to look as if they were dying after we ran. The next day, not one guy put his hands on his knees. People were taking deep breaths and turning blue, but we actually looked like a well-conditioned team. That night, Lombardi was smiling. "We're getting there, we're getting there," he kept saying. "They're getting in shape."

Of course with Lombardi, that smile didn't last long. One day he wasn't happy with the grass drills, so he got a group of defensive linemen to move up to the front row so he could see them better. He added some extra grass drills and before long, Bill Briggs, a big defensive end, started throwing up, just heaving up everything in his stomach. But Lombardi wouldn't let up. Briggs was lying there moaning, and Lombardi was still screaming at him, telling him he ought to be ashamed of himself for not being in shape. I was back in the third row, and all I could think was, *Keep yelling, Coach, just let me get my breath.* I mean, it was survival.

Sonny was just as scared of Lombardi as I was. I had roomed with Sonny before and had watched him bolt occasionally after curfew. But not this year. In fact, one of our assistants, Lew Carpenter, sat in his station wagon until three or four o'clock every night trying to catch Sonny, but he never broke curfew, not once. That's how much we respected the man, and feared him, too.

No one escaped Lombardi's fury. Early in camp, we had an intra-squad scrimmage. Harland Svare was going to coach the defense, Bill Austin, the number-one assistant, was going to coach the offense, and Lombardi was going to watch from the press box. The defense just dominated that day, and up in the box, Lombardi was getting hotter by the minute. Toward the end of the workout, someone yelled from the stands "Heeeere he comes," and there was Lombardi stomping down the stairs and going right over to that offensive team. He started yelling, and didn't stop. Then one of the officials we had brought in to work the game came over to the sideline and said, "Coach, you've got two minutes to go," and Lombardi jumped all over him. "Two minutes, what the hell do you mean we got two minutes? I'm running this team, mister, and I'll tell you how much time we've got left."

Once later that year, we were going to Philadelphia to play a game and Marie Lombardi came with us. She made most of the road trips and that day we were taking the bus between the airport and the Philadelphia Marriott. Vince was taking a little catnap and we hit a bump on the road that woke him up. "Vincent," Marie asked him, "where are we going to eat dinner tonight?"

She definitely said the wrong thing. He jumped up and said, "Lady, let me tell you something, when you travel with this team, you get treated like the players, do you understand? You're going to eat with the team and you're going to eat exactly what they eat. *Do you understand?*"

Another time, I was walking in New Orleans before a Super Bowl with Vince and Marie, and Lombardi spotted one of his old players, Marv Fleming, a tight end who had been traded by then to the Miami Dolphins. Fleming had let his hair grow and had real long sideburns, and Lombardi literally pinned him against a wall and started giving him hell because he thought his hair was too long. Right there on the street, and the guy didn't even play for him.

Still, there was another side to the man. He definitely agonized over our football team, and early in camp he started to doubt his ability to motivate us. After a few weeks in training camp, he was really down. We had just finished a coaches' meeting and were heading back to our rooms. We were talking and he said, "Sam, I don't think I've got it anymore."

"What are you talking about, Coach?" I couldn't believe I was hearing this.

"I can't coach anymore, goddammit. These guys don't know what the hell they're doing. I'm not getting through to them, and they're all over hell on that practice field."

"Coach, that's not true," I said. "You're the greatest football coach that's ever been."

"Well, if I'm so goddamned great, why in the hell isn't this team coming together?"

"I'll tell you, Coach. When you were in Green Bay and I was with the New York Giants, we knew what you were going to do, but we couldn't stop you. We knew you were going to run off tackle with Jimmy Taylor and we couldn't stop it. We knew you were going to run that sweep with Paul Hornung and we couldn't stop it. And we knew Bart Starr was going to throw that post pattern to Max McGee, and we couldn't stop that either. We couldn't stop you because that team was so fundamentally sound. You could have thrown a football out in the middle of the field and those guys would have known exactly what to do with it.

"Now these Redskins want to perform for you, they really do. But every day you're out there yelling and screaming, and your assistant coaches are yelling and screaming. No one is teaching. These ball players want to be exactly like the Packers, and they'll give you everything they've got, but you gotta teach 'em."

"You're right, Sam," he said. "Do you know what's happened to me? I've become so damned successful that I forgot what made me successful, and that's teaching people. Tomorrow, we go back to teaching."

I'm not going to tell you that he eased off on the conditioning. This was a man who posted a sign in the dressing room that said "Fatigue makes cowards of us all." But the Redskins went back to fundamentals, and it was the best thing that could have happened to us.

That summer, Larry Brown learned the fundamentals of carrying a football, though he learned it the hard way. Brown was an unheralded eighth-round draft choice from Kansas State, but Lombardi liked him almost from the first day Larry came to camp. He used to tell George Dickson, the running-back coach, to ease off on Brown because he appeared to be such a natural talent. But in camp, Larry was having difficulty holding onto the football. And Lombardi did not like to turn the ball over. One day in practice, Larry fumbled, and Lombardi was all over him.

"Mister, you never fumble the football on me," he said. Everything with Lombardi was "me" or "I." That way, if you screwed up, you felt like he was taking it personally.

"From now on, mister, you will eat with this ball, you will sleep with this ball, you will shower with this ball if necessary until you learn how to handle it." It was embarrassing for Larry. There were pictures of him in the papers walking through the cafeteria line with his tray in one hand and that football in the other. But in truth, I can hardly remember Larry Brown fumbling the football again that year, or any other year. He became a guy who almost never fumbled.

By the time the regular season started, a lot of us were starting to think things were coming together. There was no question we were in the best shape of our lives, and the team had a lot of optimism, if only because we were being led by the greatest coach in the history of the game. Lombardi may not have had the talent he had in Green Bay, but he certainly had the mystique and that couldn't hurt.

We did have some talent on that team. Bobby Mitchell had retired by then, but Sonny was still throwing to Charley Taylor and Jerry Smith. Brown was going to start at running back, and Vince had picked up Charley Harraway, a good blocking fullback, off the waiver wire from Cleveland. The offensive line was anchored by an All-Pro, Len Hauss, at center, and our kicking game wasn't too shabby either with punter Mike Bragg and place-kicker Curt Knight. On defense, our line wasn't much, as usual, and I was a thirty-five-year-old man playing middle linebacker. But I was surrounded by outstanding talent—Hanburger on my right side and a kid named Tom Roussel, who had lots of promise, on the left. We had Pat Fischer, one of the toughest little hitters in the game, at one cornerback, and Mike Bass, a pretty good cover man, at the other corner. The safeties were Brig Owens, a very steady, heady player, and Tom Brown, a guy who came over from Green Bay and one of the few people Lombardi never could seem to motivate. Brown hurt his shoulder in the first game, and was eventually replaced by Rickie Harris, a pretty fair return man, too. We weren't great, but we weren't going to embarrass ourselves, either.

I will never forget that first game. We went down to New Orleans to play the Saints, with Billy Kilmer starting at quarterback for them. Right away, they opened up a 10–0 lead and things were looking grim. I also remember just leveling Kilmer on a play he reminds me of every time I see him. Kilmer could still run a little in those days and we had flushed him out of the pocket. He ran toward one sideline, then looped back across the field and was heading to the other side.

I'd been chasing him every step of the way, and just as he got in front of the Saints' bench, he stepped out of bounds.

I hit him a shot anyway. He wasn't that far out, maybe a step. I was tired from chasing him, so I thought, *What the hell, I'll just make sure he's all the way out.* I knocked him straight up in the air and threw him back so far he landed on a table in front of the bench. He broke the table and bruised his hip, and all the Saints came after me. Hell, John Mecom, the owner of the team at the time, came after me, too. These guys were just pounding me, and the officials came over to try to stop it. They kept saying, "Get out of here, Sam," and I was thinking, *What the hell do you think I'm trying to do?* To this day, Kilmer says I cheap-shotted him.

"Damn you," he'll say, "I was out of bounds."

I always tell him, "Next time, you make sure you get all the way out of bounds."

He told me a few years later that he put a reward on my head after that hit—that's right, a bounty on me. Anyone who knocked me out of the game would collect a hundred dollars out of Billy's pocket. He never had to pay it, though.

Anyway, we came back on the Saints, and late in the fourth quarter we led, 26–20. I don't know how, but we managed to keep them from getting the ball in the final two minutes, and we walked off the field with the first victory in the Lombardi Era. It wasn't pretty; we had given up 217 yards rushing, but Lombardi would be smiling at least until he saw the game films. I don't remember his speech after the game. Hell, I was exhausted. I made 19 tackles that day, and I was just glad to get to the locker room.

Lombardi wasn't much for great pregame speeches. Before games, he never really went into his Gipper routine. But during the week, that's when he'd fire you up. He believed preparation and conditioning won football games, not pep talks, and at the end of the practice week, he'd always try to wind down. "The hay is in the barn," he'd tell the assistants, and after our practice on Friday, we'd usually all meet at Duke Zeibert's restaurant, Washington's version of Toots Shor's, and have a nice meal and a couple of drinks.

The next week, it was the Cleveland Browns, the defending Eastern Conference champions, and we more than held our own. The Browns won it, 27–24, but not before we had scared the hell out of them. On the last play of the game, from our own thirty-four, Sonny couldn't find anyone open and even managed to waddle twenty-eight yards before someone dragged him down at the final gun.

I don't remember much about this game because I was knocked out twice. In the first half, I was trying to tackle their running back, Ron Johnson, and he kicked me in the head. Bam, I was out.

I came back in the second half, and we intercepted a pass. I was looking for someone to block and here came Monte Clark, a 265-pound offensive tackle. He used to hold me and a lot of other guys all the time, so now I figured it was time for a little revenge. There was just one problem. He leveled me first, and knocked me out again. When I came to on the sidelines, Dr. Resta looked into my eyes and said, "Sam, you better start thinking about that other career."

I was still a little groggy in the locker room, but I do remember Lombardi just laying into us. He was great after a win, but this was something else. Tom Dowling, a Washington sports writer, spent the season doing a book on Lombardi, and he took notes. "You lost this one for me," Dowling quoted him as saying. "They ran through you people like you were thin air. I needed this one for the title, and you threw it away."

The next week, we tied the Forty-niners, 17–17, and in the home opener at RFK, we played our best so far, routing St. Louis, 33–17. Then it was time for the Giants and we won that game, too. Rickie Harris returned a punt 86 yards for a touchdown and a 20–14 lead and that's how it ended when Pat Fischer and I nailed Fran Tarkenton for a loss as he tried to scramble on their last play of the game.

The next week it was more of the same. We beat Pittsburgh, 14–7, and I got knocked out again, in the third period. Late in the game, though, the Steelers were driving, threatening to tie, and they sent me in again. On third down, a defensive back named Bob Wade, the very same fellow—about 40 pounds heavier now—who coaches the University of Maryland basketball team, knocked down a Terry Hanratty pass, and on fourth down, Wade tackled Earl Gros at the five with an assist from me, and we had won again.

"You people are going to give me a heart attack," Lombardi told us, but he was just as excited as the rest of the team, and the town. Washington was going bonkers over the Redskins because we were now 4–1–1. It really looked like that old Lombardi magic was back.

But not for long. Reality, in the form of the Baltimore Colts, came to town and it was no contest. We gained 357 yards on offense, but we had a punt blocked, we had interceptions, we had fumbles, and we had 89 yards in penalties on the way to a 42–17 humiliation. And over the next four weeks, we were 1–2–1, while Dallas was opening up an insurmountable lead in the division.

The tie against the Eagles was heartbreaking, because it was decided by two bad officiating decisions. We were up, 28–21, with less than two minutes to play, and the Eagles had a fourth and twenty-five at our forty-two. Norm Snead dropped back and threw deep for Ben Hawkins, and Mike Bass was on him all the way. Mike was behind Hawkins, they both went up, and the ball fell incomplete. It was basically an uncatchable pass, but the official threw his flag and Bass was called for pass interference. It was one of the worst calls I've ever seen. They got the ball at the one and scored and it was 28–28. Bass went crazy, and on the sideline, Lombardi was beside himself. But we still had a chance.

We got the ball back with less than a minute to play and on third down with about twenty-five seconds left, Jurgensen spotted Taylor open downfield. He threw it up, but just as Taylor was going to make the catch, he got creamed by two Eagles, Irv Cross and Joe Scarpetti. The official started to reach for his flag, but never pulled it out. If Taylor had caught the ball, or the official had thrown a flag for interference, we would have had the ball at the Eagle thirty-five with enough time to run a few plays and try a field goal. Instead, we had to punt or risk an Eagle field goal.

So it ended 28–28, and as we walked off the field, Lombardi was all over the officiating crew, including my old friend and West Virginia teammate, Fred Wyant, who didn't make either call but was still getting an earful. I finally went over to Lombardi and told him it wasn't Wyant who'd made the call, but Lombardi was so enraged he hardly heard me. In fact, he followed those guys to their dressing room, and people said he screamed at them through the door for a long time afterward. Then he came into our locker room and screamed some more.

By his Tuesday press conference, Lombardi had calmed down. He also told the press corps about a discovery he'd made a few weeks earlier concerning Larry Brown.

In the game films as well as in practice, Lombardi kept noticing that Larry wasn't getting off on the ball right away. When the quarterback tells the team he wants the ball snapped on the count of three, when you hear three, you move. That gives the offense an instant of advantage because you know what the count is and the defense doesn't. Now, everyone was moving at the snap, but Larry was just a bit late.

Lombardi knew something was wrong, but he didn't want to yell at Larry too much. He was a rookie, and Vince saw right away he had some talent. "Mister, you're not getting off the ball," Lombardi told him. "What's the matter with you, can't you hear?"

Larry looked at him and said, "No sir, I'm deaf in one ear." Larry had been having trouble hearing the snap count, particularly with big crowds in the stadium. So he waited until he saw movement before he left his position. Tim Temerario, the team's director of player personnel, came up with the idea of building a hearing aid into Larry's helmet, and Lombardi thought it was worth a try. They got it done, and one day in the locker room, he asked Larry to go to one end of the locker room and put the helmet on. Lombardi went to the other end and asked, "Can you hear me, Larry?"

"Coach," Brown said, "I never did have any trouble hearing you."

A few weeks later we got a little revenge on the Eagles with a 34–29 win. Brown gained 136 yards and we were 6–4–2, guaranteeing at least a .500 season. But at that point, the goal was a winning season. Lombardi had never had a losing season in fifteen years as an assistant or head coach in the NFL, and the Redskins hadn't finished over .500 since 1955.

The Saints were the next opponent, and we went after them from the start. We opened up a 17–0 lead, then held on for dear life before we finally prevailed, 17–14. The defense stiffened in the final two minutes and Jurgensen was able to run out the clock. Once again, it wasn't an artistic success, but a winning season was assured. Though we lost the season finale to the Cowboys, there was a great feeling of satisfaction at what this team had accomplished.

The Cowboy game was my last as a professional football player. I knew I wasn't going to be playing again, but I was grateful for that last opportunity.

Lombardi had always been a little bit absentminded, and he especially had trouble with names. One time he called me in and said, "Go tell whatshisname I want to see him." When Lombardi spoke, you moved, so I was heading out the door when it dawned on me.

"Coach, I really want to go, but you've got to tell me who whatshisname is. I don't know who you want me to get."

"Well, goddammit," he said, "he coaches the goddamned defense, you ought to know who I'm talking about.'' He wanted me to get Harland Svare, but he couldn't remember his name.

Anyway, late in the 1969 season we were going over the film, and all of a sudden, Lombardi yelled out, "Who the hell is number seventy? We've got to replace him.''

"Hey, wait a minute, Coach, that's me," I said.

"Oh, I didn't realize that was you, Sam.''

Of course he did, but there was no apology. In his own way, Lombardi had gotten his message across, just in case I was thinking about prolonging my career. No way. I was getting knocked out with alarming regularity, and this time I really knew it was time to give it up.

Late that season, we had already begun training Marlin McKeever to play middle linebacker, and by the end of the year, I wasn't playing very much. I was standing on the sidelines at the end of the last game against Dallas, when my friend Harland did the nicest thing any coach ever did for me.

"Sam," he said, "you're too great a player to go out standing on the sideline. Why don't you just go in there and finish up the game.''

I can't tell you anything about my last play, my last hit, or my last tackle. I can only tell you that in my last game, I was still the man in the middle right to the end.

16
● ● ● ● ● ●

My playing days were over now, but all during the 1969 season I had been giving a lot of thought to the future. At the time, I thought eventually I'd want to coach at some level, preferably in the National Football League, and I was prepared to do whatever was necessary to serve an apprenticeship as an assistant coach.

I'd been working with the Redskins' younger linebackers all season—John Didion, Harold McLinton, and Tom Roussel—and I was going to be a full-time assistant under Lombardi in 1970. Almost as soon as our schedule ended, we started getting ready for the next season, reviewing film, scouting college players in the postseason all-star games, and going over the personnel lists to see who would be available to shore up our problem areas.

One day late in the 1969 season, I got a call from Wesley Bagby, a political science professor at West Virginia University. He had followed my career from my college days at Morgantown, and he knew I was about to retire as an active player. He wanted to know if I might be interested in running against Senator Robert Byrd, then the most powerful politician in the state, now the Senate majority leader. Bagby headed up a fairly liberal outfit with over a thousand members called the "Coalition for Alternatives to Senator Byrd," and they wanted me to run. I was flattered, and it also got the juices flowing. Politics had always fascinated me; I had campaigned for John F. Kennedy in the West Virginia primary in 1960, and the history books will tell you that his victory was a major breakthrough on the way to the Democratic nomination, and eventually the presidency.

I can remember the first time I met Kennedy. My friend, John Manchin, was involved in Democratic politics in Farmington, and he asked me if I might introduce Kennedy at a function back home. I've been a Democrat all my life; hell, the only Republicans in West Virginia other than Arch Moore, the governor now, owned the coal companies, and I told him I'd be proud to do it.

One afternoon a few days later, I met the Kennedy entourage out on the road and climbed into the backseat with the candidate for the drive into Fairmont. This was the first time I had met the man, and he was obviously the most brilliant person I'd ever talked to. "Sam," he said, "these are your people, you were born and raised here, you understand them. What do you think I ought to talk about?"

At the time, Kennedy's religion was still a very big issue. No Catholic had ever won the presidency, and it was becoming a major topic of discussion, not only in West Virginia, but all across the country.

"Senator Kennedy," I said, "when my dad found out I was going to introduce you today, he asked me why I'd want to do a thing like that. I told him I thought you were a good man and that you could help the people of West Virginia. My dad said to me, 'Son, I don't want the Pope running the country.' That rang a bell in my head. Here was a typical West Virginian, a coal miner, and that's what was on his mind. Senator, I really do believe these people will think a whole lot more of you if you talk about being Catholic and what that means. It's like baseball: if a guy's going to throw you a fastball, be set to hit the fastball, don't be guessing, don't be wondering. Just be truthful with them."

Now, maybe some of his other advisers were telling him the same thing. I don't know. But I do know on that day he gave a magnificent speech and got right to the point we had discussed on the drive into town. "I want to tell you good people that when I joined the service of our country, no one asked me if I was a Catholic, a Protestant, or a Jew because I was there to fight a war," he said. And this was all off the cuff, nothing prepared, and the audience really seemed to respond. As we traveled around the state over the next week, he kept saying the same thing, confronting the religion question almost every step of the way, and by primary day, he had won over the people of West Virginia. He beat Hubert Humphrey and went on to win the nomination. I'm not going to tell you that our little chat was directly responsible for winning him the presidency, but it sure didn't hurt him in West Virginia.

I campaigned all over the state for JFK, and also got to know Bobby and Ethel and Teddy. They were such a dynamic group, a great family, and such nice people. Funny thing, I'd be working the coal mines with Teddy—and we're talking about one of the richest families in America—and I'm the one who was buying all the coffee and sandwiches. Finally, I told Teddy, "This has got to stop. I don't have this kind of money." He laughed and said, "Well, Sam, rich people never carry any money with them."

I answered, "Then rich people are going to go hungry, because I've bought you your last sandwich."

The last time I saw John F. Kennedy was at the college football Hall of Fame dinner in New York. I had gone with Howard Cosell, who in those days was doing a lot of local radio work. We had gotten friendly because he was always sticking his microphone into the Giant locker room, but at this point in his career, hardly anyone knew Cosell. The President was up on the dais and Howard asked me why I didn't go up and say hello to him. He knew I'd worked for him in 1960 and kept telling me to just walk up and renew old acquaintances. Even then, Howard was a little pushy.

Before I could get anywhere near the President, though, I was stopped by a Secret Service guy. He recognized me, but wouldn't let me go up because I didn't have an identification pin they used for security purposes. Bill Shea, the man they named Shea Stadium after, was sitting up there and when he left his seat to see some friends, I asked him if he'd lend me his pin so I could go up. I finally got through the security and walked up to the President. Right away, he stood up, shook my hand, and asked me what had taken me so long to get there; he'd been expecting me. We stood and talked for fifteen minutes and he even invited me to the White House. When I came down, the same Secret Service man who had originally stopped me told me: "You know, my boss doesn't stand up and talk to anyone for that long. You really must be a good friend."

I'd like to think so. And that was the last time I ever saw John Kennedy alive.

But let's push ahead, to West Virginia in 1969. Ever since that experience with the Kennedys, politics had always been in the back of my mind. I've always been proud of my heritage and proud to call West Virginia home. Maybe I could do something to help fight poverty, bad government, and corrupt politicians. The professor's offer was definitely intriguing, but the more I looked at it, the more obvious it became that no one could beat Senator Byrd, he was simply too powerful. I went back home and talked to John Manchin and some other friends, and I decided I would run instead for Congress in the First Congressional District. Now, almost twenty years later, when I give speeches and someone asks me if I'd ever consider running again, I tell them if I did, please hit me over the head with a two-by-four. Never again, but I had to find that out the hard way.

I went to Lombardi after the season and told him what I was planning to do. He was a very patriotic man, loved the country and the flag, and he was very enthusiastic about it and gave me his blessing. He even made some appearances for me during the campaign and helped raise funds back in Washington, and he told me if things didn't work out, I could always come back and rejoin his staff.

I was going to enter the Democratic primary, and my opponent was the incumbent sixty-one-year-old congressman, Robert H. Mollohan. In truth, though, my real opponent was the long-time, all-powerful Democratic party machine. Mr. Mollohan, who had served in Congress in the early 1950s and later went on to become a United Mine Workers executive, was the machine's man. As far as I was concerned, he was also a no-good congressman who never did a damned thing for the district. Over the years, I had heard all kinds of stories about his political wheeling and dealing. Back in the forties, he had been superintendent of the Boys' Industrial School at Pruntytown and there were allegations that he used his influence to obtain leases from the state for a coal company to mine coal on state-owned school property. There were canceled checks made out to him personally from the coal company, and it also was alleged that the coal company gave him free use of a car and a house. That came out when he ran for governor in 1956, and I'm told he was never prosecuted because the local district attorney figured the statute of limitations had expired. In any case, the words "corrupt politician" seemed perfectly suited to Bob Mollohan.

I found out right away what I was up against when I decided to make the announcement of my candidacy. I wanted to do it at my old high school in Farmington, but one day I got a phone call from the superintendent of schools in Marion County begging me not to. I didn't want to hear it; I knew who was pulling the strings. So I went to see the principal of the high school, a Mr. Dodrill, and I took John Manchin with me. We were both steamed because they weren't going to let us use the gymnasium for the press conference.

John started yelling at Dodrill. "Who the hell do you think put the carpet on this floor? I did, that's who!" I thought he was going to slug the guy.

"Mr. Dodrill," I said, "I get a lump in my throat

217

whenever I walk into this school. I love this place, and neither you or any other cheap politician is going to stop me from making my announcement here. If you intend to stop me, you'd better call out the National Guard because that's what it will take."

On February 7, I made my formal announcement at Farmington High School. We had a big media crowd, all the major networks showed up, reporters were everywhere. The high-school band was there, too. But there was just one problem. I later learned that the band director had gotten word from higher-ups not to twirl his baton for the national anthem. So when it came time to strike up the band, the kids kept looking for their band leader, Mr. Moore. He was back in the crowd, and the kids kept looking over at him. Finally, he came up front and led the band. It doesn't sound like much, but that was a very brave thing for that man to do, and I called him that night and thanked him for it.

Over the next three months, I hit every nook and cranny in that district, which stretched 220 miles north to south. Usually, John Machin or his son Joe, a physical therapist, came along, and another childhood friend, Buck Basile, was with me every step of the way. He'd grown up in Grantown and had been teaching high school in suburban Maryland. He wrote me a letter, asking if he could join us and write a book about the campaign. He never did get it published, but at the time, I was glad to have him along, if only to witness some of the bizarre happenings.

I wore out two pairs of shoes, a couple of sets of tires, and my own voice before that three-month campaign was over, but it really was a futile effort, because the machine was not going to let their man get beat.

They put out all these stories and rumors about me. I was called a carpetbagger, even though I owned a house in the district in Rock Lake that I lived in during the off-season. After I met with my friend, Arch Moore, the Republican governor of the state, to get his opinion on my political options before I decided to run for Congress, they said I was a traitor to the Democratic party and wanted me to repudiate our friendship. They put out the word that I wasn't taking care of my parents in their old age. They even started rumors that I was divorcing my wife and having an affair with Ethel Kennedy. Mary kidded me about that when she heard it. "If it's true," she'd say, "I'll be the richest divorcee in the country." I mean, we're talking about some very serious mud-slinging. Even some of my old friends turned against me.

The unions in West Virginia—the UMW, the Teamsters, the AFL-CIO—basically controlled politics in the state. And it seemed like in every town, there was a mini-godfather in charge. They'd have control of the numbers racket or the pinball machines, and they doled out cash to the churches and the Little Leagues and all the local charities to keep things going their way. It was quite an effective system, and I definitely wasn't their man because I wasn't going to play by their rules.

I can recall talking to a high-ranking official of the Teamsters about getting some support from his union. "Sam, I'm going to tell you the truth," he said at one point in the conversation. "I've known you since you were a little boy, I've admired you and followed you through your whole football career, and there's no doubt in my mind you'd make a great congressman. But that's not what we want. We have what we want in Bob Mollohan. When we say jump, he jumps. You've never done that, and you never will. You've made it tough for me because I have to work like hell to make sure you don't get elected. I don't like it, but I have to do it."

There was another guy, Dominick Romino, a lawyer from Fairmont who was the head of the Marion County Democratic party. His wife Libby was my teacher in the second grade. Early in the campaign, I read in the papers that the Marion County Democrats were endorsing Mollohan, so I called him up. "Dominick," I said, "I've been a

Democrat all my life, my father was a Democrat all his life, and how can your organization endorse one Democrat over another in a primary election? Shouldn't we let the people decide?"

He got very angry. "You have no business running for Congress," he charged. "No business at all."

"Dominick," I said, "it says in the Constitution that everybody has a right to run for political office, and if I'm wrong about the Constitution, it's because your wife taught me wrong in the second grade. And I think she's a hell of a lot smarter than you are."

One time I was campaigning in downtown Mannington, West Virginia, and I started talking with the chief of police. At first, he didn't want to have much to do with me. Finally, he came out with it.

"Sam, I can't back you," he said. "At night, I work at the drive-in theater. I run the projector. My boss there is a strong Mollohan man. If I back you, I lose that job."

"When you step in that voting booth, buddy, nobody knows how you'll vote," I told him. "Not even your boss at the theater."

But that's what I was up against. The whole theme of my campaign was that Mollohan hadn't done anything for his district.

I kept pointing out that the state had more people killed in wars based on percentage of population than any other state in the union, and yet we also had less defense spending than any state. People were even starting to take a little notice.

Before too long, I got a call from one of my neighbors back home in Alexandria, Virginia, who worked in the Navy Department. "We just had an emergency meeting today, Sam," he said. "We're going to come to West Virginia in a couple of weeks to start planning a helicopter plant in Clarksburg."

What happened? I asked him, knowing exactly what had happened.

"Well," he said, "you keep talking about no defense spending in your campaign, and I guess your opponent figured he'd better do something about it. The pressure was definitely on."

I went to a function in Clarksburg the day they were going to spring their plans for the new plant. Mollohan was going to be introduced, and I showed up totally unannounced. He didn't appreciate my being there—in fact, he was madder than hell, but I didn't really care. Politics was tough stuff, too, and I wanted him to know he was going to have to fight for every last vote.

A month before the election, I went to the sports banquet at Fairmont State College. My little brother John had played on the football team there, and had kicked a field goal that won the national small college championship for the school that season. I sat with John in the audience, and not only didn't they introduce me, they wouldn't even introduce my brother. The master of ceremonies was L. O. Bickle, a local businessman who was one of the school's big boosters, and he never acknowledged our presence. Bickle also was deeply involved in the Democratic party and of course, he was backing Mollohan. After the dinner, he came up to me, shook my hand, and said, "I'm sure you understand." I squeezed that man's hand so hard he almost had tears in his eyes. "I will never understand how one West Virginian can treat another like this," I told him. "You didn't have to acknowledge my presence, but you also short-changed my brother, and I'm going to get even. Some day, I'll pay you back for this because you embarrassed me and my family."

I had another interesting experience at Fairmont State. I wanted to give a major policy address on Vietnam, and I figured a college campus would be the ideal place to do it. My campaign people got out the word and we were hoping for a crowd of two hundred and fifty people. When I got to the student union, there were six kids in the audience, and one of my campaign aides spent the first half of my speech rounding up students to come in. By the time I had finished, there were twenty kids in the room. One of them wore a Mollohan button.

I also had been invited across the campus that day to talk about the environment and pollution. This time, about forty people were in the crowd, and when the session was over, one of the students asked me to pose for a picture with a couple of the professors who had invited me to speak.

"Glad to," I said, trying to get the professors to join me on the stage.

"No, no pictures," one professor said.

"Why not, this isn't for the press, the kid just wants a picture for his scrapbook."

"No pictures," he insisted. "We don't want to get involved."

That's when I lost it.

"Don't want to get involved?" I yelled. "You guys stand up here and show slides and movies about the environment going to hell, and you don't want to get involved to do something about it? If you guys had any guts, you'd come down out of your ivory tower and start telling the truth."

Clearly, I was getting very little satisfaction from that campaign. I could barely get my name in the papers; meanwhile Mollohan was all over radio, television, newspapers. I even had a Washington political consulting firm, Dave Hackett Associates, working with me. We had a guy named Mike Casey, who was our advance man to set up meetings and speeches. But it didn't do much good. I spent about $35,000 of my own money, and the whole campaign probably cost about $100,000; what a waste.

Still, not everyone was against me. Harry Hoffman, an editorial writer for the *Charleston Gazette* and a man who was considered the David Broder of the state of West Virginia, was very complimentary. "On the credit side for Huff," he wrote, "are reports from the First District that he is showing surprising ability as a campaigner, projecting strength, honesty, and a personality that has been described in such terms as dynamic and magnetic. He doesn't promise miracles, but he offers an alternative that looks mighty good in comparison with Bob Mollohan."

The voters had other ideas. The longer the campaign went, the more I knew I was in serious trouble. On election day, I found out just how much. I visited several polling places, and everywhere I went there were people working for Mollohan, driving people to vote, who couldn't get to the polling places. For every car I had to pick up people, Mollohan had five.

At the Carolina coal camp, I saw a friend of mine, Dale Kane, a guy I had grown up with, a guy who used to pitch on my sandlot baseball teams. I was his catcher. And now, he was handing out brochures for Bob Mollohan and driving one of his cars.

"Dale, you know me, my God, you're a friend of mine and you're working for him?" I couldn't believe what I was seeing.

He looked at me and shrugged his shoulders. "I'm not against you, Sam, I'm really not," he said. "I love you like a brother, but I get fifty bucks for operating this precinct every election, and I get it from the Democratic party. I know fifty dollars isn't a lot of money to you, but it is to me. And they tell me you're not the guy, so I can't be for you and keep this job."

"Dale, you mean our friendship and what I stand for isn't worth fifty dollars?"

"I'm sorry, Sam, that's just the way it has to be."

At that point, I knew it was all over. They didn't even have to count the votes.

But they did. The first returns on the radio reported that Mollohan had 800 votes to my 400, and that trend continued long into the night. I lost the election by a margin of two to one. I even lost in my home town of Farmington, and that hurt, it really did hurt. I shed some tears, most definitely. It was a devastating experience that leaves a bitter taste in my mouth to this day.

A few months later, I went back home for my father's funeral, and a guy I'd known since I was a kid—his name's not important—came up and said he wanted to talk to me privately.

This was the very same fellow who had really upset me during the campaign. We had gone to a mining camp at Rachel, West Virginia, and were shaking hands with the miners as they headed for the parking lot. Well, this guy, a man who used to drive our high-school football team to games around the state when I was playing, walked by and never even acknowledged my presence. I'm not talking about a casual acquaintance; I'd known him all my life. I couldn't figure it out, and it really bothered me. What had I possibly done to deserve this?

At my dad's funeral, I found out.

"A lot of people were wondering why I wasn't for you," he told me. "Well, I wanted to tell you why. You remember your senior year you played Romney in the last game of the season. You picked up a fumble and you ran it back for the only touchdown in that game. Well, Sam, when you scored, you turned your back on me, and I took an oath that some day I was going to get even with you."

I couldn't believe what I was hearing.

"You mean to tell me that because a sixteen-year-old kid didn't spot you in a crowd and walked back to his team's bench, that's why I didn't get a handshake or a vote?"

"That's right, Sam, that's exactly right."

Incredible. But in West Virginia politics, nothing will ever surprise me again.

17

A few weeks after I re-upped with the Redskins, I was working at the team's downtown office, preparing for the 1970 season. One day I happened to pass Vince Lombardi in the hallway. He always walked around with his head down and his hands behind his back, so he very seldom knew who was coming or going. But on this day, it seemed to me that he didn't look very good. There was an odd color to his face, and I asked him if he was feeling all right.

He said he thought he had the flu, and I told him that he ought to go see Dr. Resta, our team physician. "I better do that," he said, "I'm not feeling well at all."

At first, they really did think he had the flu, but then they decided to put him in Georgetown University Hospital and run some tests. That's when they discovered he had cancer. The great irony is that Lombardi, a man who probably knew more about his players' physical condition than any coach who ever lived, didn't like physical examinations, particularly the proctology exam to check for colon cancer. He just refused to take it, and in the end that's probably what cost him his life. He told me that himself before he died, and at my annual physical, I always insist on having that test done. It's a lifesaver.

Almost immediately Lombardi had surgery to remove a section of his colon, and not long after that, I went to visit him in the hospital. He could barely talk, but he always believed he was going to whip it. He was such a strong man, so religious. We sat out on the patio overlooking the Georgetown football field, and we talked about the team, about his coming back to coach again, about the good old days in New York, where he'd always wanted to return to coach. "The timing was just never right," he told me that day, "but I have no regrets."

The next time I saw him, we were in Baltimore, playing a rookie scrimmage against the Colts. He had been out of the hospital a couple of weeks, but he was still weak and when he came into the locker room, he looked very bad. He'd lost about forty pounds, and you could barely hear him talk. But he gathered the team around him, and he directed his remarks at the younger guys, the players he'd drafted that spring.

"You're my people, I've selected you," he told them. "You're going to wear this uniform with pride. You're now a member of the Washington Redskins, and there's a lot of responsibility that goes along with that. Don't you ever forget it."

He was straining to talk, you could see that, and it was a very moving experience for anyone who was in that room that night. It was also the last time I ever saw him alive. The next day, he entered Georgetown Hospital for a second operation. A few weeks later, on September 3, 1970, Vince Lombardi died, and all over America, people mourned his passing.

"He had a covenant with greatness," Edward Bennett Williams said in his eulogy. "He was committed to excellence in everything he attempted. Our country has lost one of its great men. The world of sport has lost its first citizen. The Redskins have lost their leader. I personally have lost a friend."

What made the man so special? He had a great desire to excel, but a lot of people have that same desire. Lombardi knew how to get it out of himself, and he knew how to get it out of his players. When he talked to the football team during the week, he sold us on his game plan. He would tell you, "We will win if we do this, this, and this." And you always believed him. He was a great salesman, a great motivator, a great general. And yet, he also was a human being, a man who loved life, who loved his family, who loved to laugh with that big toothy grin. He really was like a father to a lot of players, and you did everything for him, not yourself. No one was selfish around Vince Lombardi. Nobody ever complained about not getting enough playing time or having to go down on kickoffs or punts.

Technically, he was a smart coach, but anyone can draw X's and O's. He believed in fundamentals. He always used to say, "I don't care what you do offensively, you can go in motion, put up an I-formation, use a triple-flanker set, but the team that blocks the hardest and tackles the hardest is going to win this game." When you played a game, you were so completely prepared, there were almost no surprises, not from your team or from the opposition. Anything that happened on the field, you were ready to respond to it.

In 1969, he had taken a team and literally willed it to a winning season, and I honestly believe if he had lived, the Redskins would have gone on to be a dominant football team for as long as Lombardi was there.

There is no question the man had flaws, but who doesn't? He also made mistakes. One of them was appointing Bill Austin, his number-one assistant both in Green Bay and Washington, as the interim coach of the 1970 Redskins. He did that from his hospital bed in August at the time when he believed he would lick his illness and rejoin the team.

Lombardi died two weeks before the regular season started, and Austin and the rest of us stayed on for the year. After the initial shock of learning about his illness, the team was in turmoil all summer. Every day there was another rumor in the locker room—he'll be back, he needs another operation, he'll never coach again, he's terminal.

When he died, we were all devastated and Williams surely had to know that making a major staff change at that point would have been disastrous for our team, although the season soon deteriorated anyway.

Austin had been fine as an assistant coach, a second lieutenant. But he was a gruff guy, with a real negative streak and the players weren't exactly crazy about him. We did have an excellent staff. Mike McCormack, a Hall of Fame lineman and now general manager of the Seattle Seahawks, was an assistant on that team. We had Don Doll, George Dickson, Harland Svare, and Lew Carpenter, basically the same staff from the year before. We also had a great offense, and a defense that still hadn't improved much. In fact, we really couldn't stop anyone.

It was so bad that before our fourth game of the year against the Lions, Dickson came into a coaches' meeting and said, "There's no way we can win this game, absolutely no way." The Lions had just come off a big win on "Monday Night Football," and they looked awesome. I had never in my life heard a coach make a statement like that. I always felt there had to be some way to win, and damned if we didn't change our defenses and beat the Lions anyway.

Still, as the season wore on, it became clear that we really couldn't stop many teams. It got to the point where Austin would come into our defensive meeting rooms and snidely ask the coaches, "Well, how are you guys gonna screw up this week?" Austin was the offensive coordinator and he had some players—Jurgensen, Larry Brown, Charley Taylor, Jerry Smith. We had almost nothing, and we coaches were killing ourselves week after week to come up with something that might outsmart somebody.

One time Austin started to get on us again and I'd had it. We were about to play the Cowboys, and we knew it was a lost cause, but you have to try something. "You know, Austin," I said to him at one point, "you were a jerk in high school, you were a jerk in college, you were a jerk when we played together in New York, and you'll be a jerk all your life. So let's see how great a coach you are. Why don't we switch this week. Let us coach your offense and you coach the defense, and we'll see how damned great you are."

Normally, that sort of remark would be enough to get you fired, but what the hell, I knew we were going to be gone at the end of the season, anyway. I knew Edward Bennett Williams would go out and get himself a name coach and fire Austin and the rest of us.

Austin wasn't at all pleased, and my friend, Harland Svare, was very upset with me for jumping on Bill. In fact, when Austin left the room, Harland started chewing me out. But I didn't want to hear that, either. "I'm tired of people picking on us with the kind of players we have," I told Harland. "I'm not about to sit here and take that. I never in my life pulled against my own team, but it wouldn't bother me a bit if the Cowboys shut that offense out." And that's exactly what happened. Dallas 34, Redskins 0, and I don't think we made a first down the entire second half.

Later in the season, Harland and I were driving into practice from Alexandria and I told him I hoped he had another job lined up.

"What are you talking about, Sam? Just because you don't get along with Austin doesn't mean that I don't."

"Harland," I said, "Bill's history, he won't have a job here next year."

"Well, I think the man can do the job."

"He won't have a chance to do the job," I said. "Just look at Ed Williams' track record. He fired McPeak and he brought in a big name, Otto Graham. He fired Graham, and he brought in a big name, Vince Lombardi. This team is going nowhere, and I guarantee you it's over for all of us."

"We'll see," he said.

And we did see.

Not too long after the season ended, Williams met with Austin and told him he'd been fired. Austin came back to our office that afternoon and told anyone who happened to be around. I was there, and I took it upon myself to clean out our offices. I took everything. I took all the film, offense and defense, all the overlays for the slide projectors with the plays and patterns on them, all the playbooks. I just loaded 'em in my car. I didn't steal them, I just wanted our work to stay with the people who had done it. Anyone who wanted it had to come to my house in Alexandria to get it.

On January 6, Williams did exactly what I thought he would. He hired George Allen as his next head coach. Allen came over from the Los Angeles Rams and made a big deal out of interviewing most of Lombardi's staff, but he never really had any intention of hiring me. He coached the linebackers; he didn't need me around. But that didn't stop him from trying to pick my brain. George interviewed everybody, asked us about every player and took notes. Then he brought his own staff in. Typical George.

At that point I was beginning to have my doubts as to whether I wanted to stay in football. I started calling around the league to see if anything was available. Ed Hughes got the Houston head coaching job, and my old teammate never even had the courtesy to return my phone calls. Then he went out and hired George Dickson, one of the best running-back coaches in the league, to coach his linebackers. I even put in a call to John Madden in Oakland. He was great, but he had no openings. In fact, John still kids me about it. He says the night I called, he went back home and said to his wife, Virginia, "You'll never guess who called me today, Sam Huff." He said he was honored; meanwhile, I was still unemployed.

By now it was February, and I was still looking for a job. I never made a lot of money playing football and I had house payments. One friend offered me a job in the printing business. Another guy wanted me to get in on a computer operation, but I knew nothing about either business, so I kept looking.

I also had an idea in the back of my mind. When I first came to the Redskins, we occasionally stayed at Marriott hotels. I liked them enough that I'd bought a hundred shares of stock in the company, but I didn't know much about Marriott other than I enjoyed staying in their hotels.

One day, I was driving down River Road in Washington and saw a sign for Marriott's corporate headquarters. I didn't even know they were located in Washington, but that sign started me thinking. Because I had been getting their corporate information as a stockholder, I also remembered reading that the biggest problem they were having was filling their hotels on weekends—Fridays, Saturdays, and Sundays. That set off another bell and got me thinking some more.

I also recalled that as a player with the Giants, we always flew on United, and they assigned one person as a company representative to the team. They did that for a lot of teams. That rep would take care of all the details, and they gave us great service. We had the same pilots, the same crew, and it always went smoothly. They'd take care of all the bags, the buses were on time, there was no holdup in the airport or at the hotel. I even used to help them serve the food and drinks because I couldn't sit still.

Anyway, I put all these things together and started thinking about adapting United's program to the hotel industry for sports teams. I'd had a lot of experience in marketing with Philip Morris and J. P. Stevens, so I put together a plan based on getting college and professional football teams to stay at the hotels on the weekends when they played their games.

But I still needed an entree to the corporation, and I really didn't know anyone there. So I asked the Redskin publicity man, Joe Blair, if he knew anyone in the organization who might be able to help me. He told me that Bill Marriott, the son of the original founder, J. W. Marriott, and now the man in charge, was a big Redskin fan and that I really ought to call him.

That's exactly what I did. On the first call, his secretary, Mary Harne, answered the phone. He wasn't there, so I left my name and asked him to call.

"Are you the Sam Huff who played for the Redskins?" she said.

"Yes ma'am."

"I can't believe it, Mr. Huff. I'm a very big Redskin fan. Don't worry, he'll get the message."

To this day, I always give her credit for getting me in to see Bill Marriott. She calls me number seventy; I call her number one.

The next week I met with Bill Marriott. At first, I think he thought I was there to complain about the stock dividends I was getting. But when I presented him with my plan, he was very enthusiastic. We got along real well— we're about the same age and he told me he liked the way I'd played. He even reminded me about a preseason game against the Bears when I got thrown out for kicking some rookie in the ribs after he'd hit me from behind about 20 yards from the play. "You raised him about three feet off the ground," he said.

Then we got down to business. Before I left the office, Bill Marriott picked up the phone, got the head of the hotel division, Jim Durbin, on the line, and said, "Sam Huff's in here and he's got a plan to help us with these weekend problems. I want you to hire him."

Just like that.

The first interview.

The next day I met with Durbin, told him I needed $30,000 a year, a secretary, an office, and a company car, and he agreed. In fact, they paid me $35,000. He also told me I'd be working with a fellow named Al LeFaivre, who would train me in the hotel business.

LeFaivre was not a football fan. The first time I met him, he told me he knew nothing about the game, so I told him I'd teach him about football if he'd teach me about hotels. In the beginning, we had some problems. He didn't want to give me an office or a secretary. I'd get a desk and a telephone, and I was supposed to use his secretary. I wasn't happy about it, but that's how I started at the company. I made all my own calls, and it got to the point that every time I walked down the corridor, the secretaries would find an excuse to go to the water cooler just to avoid me.

I didn't get all that much training, so I started doing things on my own. I called Frank Gifford, and he suggested trying to get the television crews working the games to stay at Marriotts. The "Monday Night" crew usually arrived in town on Thursday to set up and they'd number forty-five to fifty people. That's a lot of people using a lot of rooms. Multiply that by all the NFL teams and all the colleges, and you understand why Bill Marriott liked my idea.

I've been with the Marriott Corporation ever since, and it's been a great relationship. I came in as a salesman, director of sports marketing, and now I'm a vice-president. I've even got my own parking space, which didn't come easily.

When Marriott moved into our headquarters in Bethesda, Bill Marriott didn't have a very big parking lot. Land was just too expensive to pave it over for parking, so only the corporate vice-presidents had their own spaces near the building. Everyone else had to fend for themselves. I was always after them to get me a space, but Bill was adamant. The day the company honored me for getting into the Hall of Fame, Bill finally gave in. He gave a little speech, and when he was finished, he told the crowd that he had decided to amend the company rules. "The only people who will get their own parking spaces are corporate vice-presidents, and members of the Professional Football Hall of Fame," he said.

Marriott has been very good to me, and I like to think I've done good work for them. In 1987, we had forty to fifty million dollars in revenue just from sports-related business. We did 316,000 room nights alone. When you figure that one room night is about a hundred dollars, right there that's thirty million dollars. We're talking about teams, television crews, school bands, letterman's clubs. We do all the sports, colleges and professional. And if teams are staying in your hotel, that's going to attract even more business. People want to eat dinner at your restaurant because they might see Doug Williams or Lawrence Taylor at the next table. People traveling from Washington to Philadelphia to see the Redskins play the Eagles will stay at your hotel just to glimpse Joe Gibbs walk through the lobby. It's a great business, and I've been fortunate to have had the help of two great secretaries. Linda Dunkley served a six-year tenure, and Del Nylec has been with me for the past seven years. Del is the best there is, bar none; my life would probably be chaos without her. And I also have to give credit to so many young, aggressive, sports-oriented sales people who have dedicated their weekends to serving all the teams.

I'm sure when I first started, there was some jealousy in the company. You know, big-time football hero walks in the door and gets carte blanche. But let me tell you, I hit the ground running at Marriott, and I'm still running. No one ever outworked me, on the football field or in the office, and no one ever will.

My career after football could have gone several different ways. In November 1970, the entire Marshall University football team—seventy-five players, coaches, and some fans—were killed in a plane crash. Marshall is located in Huntington, West Virginia, and I always had it in the back of my mind that I might go back home and coach. I preferred West Virginia University, but at the time, that job wasn't open. So I talked to the people at Marshall about being coach and athletic director, because I figured that was the only way I could afford to make the move. I'd be able to command a bigger salary with both jobs, and I'd also be in charge. Things started off badly, though. The first time I flew into Huntington on a plane chartered for me, we got caught in a storm and had to turn around and go back. It was a single-engine plane, and one of the scariest flights of my life.

In preparing for the interview, I had put together a five-year plan for the school; once again my marketing background was a big help. I was going to put players into junior college for two years, then bring them back to Marshall for three years to keep some continuity. I'd worked up a scouting system based on the NFL scouting combines that would use Marshall alumni all over the state and even around the country to help search out and scout prospects. But the university didn't know what to make of it, and they definitely wanted to separate the coaching and athletic director jobs. They told me it was too big a job for one person. Then I asked them if they thought it was too big a job for Bear Bryant at Alabama.

I finally got a call from one of their officials telling me they had decided not to hire me. He told me they were not going to hire a football coach unless he had his master's degree. I had to laugh. "Do me a favor," I told him. "Let's just forget I've even applied for the job. The way I figure it, I've got my doctorate in football, starting at Farmington High School, West Virginia University, the New York Giants and the Redskins with professors Landry and Lombardi. That's where I learned my football, but if you want someone with a master's degree, I guess I'm not your man."

In the mid-1970s, I also was interested in coaching at West Virginia University. Bobby Bowden had left to take the job at Florida State in 1975, and I knew the job was open. I was at a convention of college athletic directors as a Marriott representative in 1975, and spoke to the West Virginia athletic director, Leland Byrd, about the job.

"Truthfully, Sam, you're supposed to send in an application and interview with the athletic council, but you'd be wasting your time," he told me.

"Why is that?" I asked.

"I'm the one making the decision," he said, "and I'm probably going to give the job to our offensive coordinator. We've had some success here the last few years, and I want to keep some continuity."

So they hired Frank Cignetti, and they started to have

some problems. Bowden was a great head coach and Frank Cignetti was a fine assistant. But he wasn't Bowden, and the program started to slide. Frank also got very sick. He had cancer, and after three years, he had to step down and leave the program. He was a good guy, a fine man, and a pretty good coach, but before it was over, Cignetti was gone, and Leland Byrd resigned under pressure and they had to rebuild again.

When they hired Cignetti, my coaching aspirations ended for all intents and purposes. Don't get me wrong, I still support the program at West Virginia. The coach, Don Nehlen, is outstanding. He's gotten them back in the bowl picture and that was a major accomplishment. I helped them start a letterman's club and that organization now has a dire-need fund for former West Virginia athletes who need financial help. I got them to build a "Wall of Fame" to honor all the old players who had contributed so much to the program. We also have an annual golf and tennis tournament to raise funds for the university, and we've contributed $100,000 to pay for the lobby of the cancer facility at the university hospital. I give speeches for the school, I go to alumni functions, and I contribute to the scholarship funds, as well. But I no longer have any desire to coach there or anywhere else.

I'm much happier these days following football from the radio booth. You don't have to deal with eighteen-year-old kids, you don't have to deal with their parents, you don't have to deal with alumni—all you have to do is avoid all those people who are constantly trying to second-guess you.

My radio days began in Washington while I was still playing. I did some locker-room shows for WMAL radio, and I started a Redskin report that they still use today. In my year off after the 1967 season, I also did some sports shows for ABC radio in New York, including a scoreboard show that gave me some good experience. They even hired a speech coach to work on my diction and pronunciation, and that was a great help.

At one point, I was offered a job as a sportscaster with the ABC affiliate in New York, and I was told later that if I had taken that job, I probably would have been in on the original "Monday Night Football" team. But I was working for J. P. Stevens at the time and turned it down.

After Austin and the staff got fired, WNEW in New York hired me to do color on Giants games. By that time, Allie Sherman had been fired, replaced by my teammate, Alex Webster, and Wellington Mara and I had settled our differences. In fact, he encouraged me to take the job. I worked with a great old pro, Marty Glickman, and a guy named Chip Cipolla, who knew almost nothing about the game but was a popular local sportscaster, so they stuck him up in the booth, too. Cipolla infuriated the Giants because he was constantly taking cheap shots at them. One of the reasons I was hired was to do the postgame locker-room show, because if Cipolla had gone down there, he might have been lynched. He and I never did get along, and we got into some hellacious arguments on the air. One time he was supposed to interview Neil Armstrong, the first man to walk on the moon, on our halftime show. He actually forgot Armstrong's name on the air. Glickman was listening and got so angry he ripped off his headset and threw it against the wall.

Still, overall, my experience with WNEW was great. Glickman worked with me on timing, taught me how to prepare, and spent a lot of time just talking about the business, and his advice has proved invaluable over the years. I helped them, too. Marv Albert, then the voice of the Knicks and the Rangers, was just starting to do football in the early 1970s. He replaced Marty Glickman on play-by-play in 1973, and I'd try to teach him all about the pro game. We'd sit in hotel lobbies and I'd draw plays for him so he could recognize formations. He was a guy who could broadcast anything, a real quick study, and we had a good year together. I loved that job because it gave me a chance to keep my hand in the game. For me, that's always been the best part of it.

The worst part was the travel. After a while, doing the Giants games began to become a grind. I was still living in Virginia and I'd be gone twenty weekends a year between the preseason and regular season. Every weekend was a road trip. It finally got to be too much, and in 1974, I was asked to join WMAL radio in Washington. Andy Ockershausen ran the station, and he modeled the coverage after WNEW, with one exception. "I like what you've been doing in New York," he told me, "but this is not New York and we're not paying New York salaries." In the beginning, it was a shoestring operation. They wouldn't even send an engineer with us. Finally, I talked them into letting me bring along Rick Hunt to do the statistics. He's a Ford dealer in Warrenton, Virginia, a big football fan and a great stat man, even if I'm always kidding him on the air.

In the first couple of years, I worked with several different play-by-play guys, and when Sonny Jurgensen left CBS in the mid-1970s, Jim Gallant, WMAL's director of operations, asked me what I thought about adding him in the booth. I was all for it—anything to get a better product—and that's how we started. Sonny and I and Frank Herzog, as good a play-by-play man as there is in the business. We've been together now for years, and we clicked right away. Sonny needles me, I needle Sonny, and Frank keeps everything straight.

I'm also the first to admit it's a biased broadcast. It has to be because all of our listeners are Redskins fans. But we try not to be cheerleaders, and we try to have respect for the other teams. We also have no qualms about criticizing the Redskins when they're playing badly. Sonny used to be all over Joe Theismann, and he was not especially complimentary toward Jay Schroeder in 1987.

It's no secret that Sonny and Theismann had their differences. Jurgensen and Billy Kilmer despised Joe and his big mouth when he joined the team in 1974. That's an old story, and I would play devil's advocate. I'd take Joe's side because I basically liked the guy.

Joe also did something for me once that I'll never forget. This was when Jack Pardee was the coach, and the team had reeled off a bunch of wins. Joe was starting to become a hot item in the locker room. After one of those games, there must have been fifty reporters around his locker. I was doing the locker-room show by myself, and I kept hearing in my ear piece, "You gotta get Theismann, you gotta get Theismann." I had no chance, really. But then I looked around, and there was Joe. "Do you need me, Sam?" he asked, and he came on the broadcast and saved my rear end. I've always appreciated that.

I've had some great experiences in the booth, and some bad ones. One time, I was working a Sugar Bowl game for Mutual Radio with Al Wester, an old pro who had done Notre Dame football for years. I didn't know him at all, and when we met, he started giving me orders, telling me what to do, who I could and couldn't talk to. And this was after the people at Mutual in Washington had told me exactly what they wanted me to do. I don't take orders from a whole lot of people, and I had to straighten that out right away with Mr. Wester. Then we got on the air, and I probably was talking a little too much when he started giving me the "hurry up, hurry up" sign. During the next time-out, he said to me, "This is my broadcast and you're talking too much. When I give you the signal, I want you to throw it back to me."

"Al," I said, "let me tell you something. We're going to have some dead air on this broadcast because if you ever hurry me again, I'm throwing you out of the booth, headfirst. I hope you understand what I'm telling you." After that, we had no problems. And to this day, the guy still calls me and asks me to make reservations for him in our hotels.

In my first year doing the Redskins, I was working with another fine play-by-play man, Len Hathaway. During a game, when I see a penalty flag drop, I'll try to explain it as soon as I can. But on this day, I saw the flag and then I saw the official give a signal I'd never seen before. So I didn't say anything, and the spotter and I were frantically looking through the program to see what the call was.

Hathaway looked over at us and he said, "What are you dummies looking for?" On the air.

Now calling a football player dumb is in my book the equivalent of a racial slur. I hate it. Nobody calls me dumb or stupid, nobody.

"You're not talking to me, are you," I asked him, still on the air, "because I didn't hear you say that, did I?" I gave him a very dirty look.

At the next break, Len apologized. "I'm absolutely sorry," he said. "I have no idea what made me say that."

"Listen, Len," I said, "I accept your apology, but if you ever do it again, even off the air, I'll throw your rear end outta here. Don't you ever call me a dummy."

That never happened again, either, and Len Hathaway and I became very good friends. I learned from him, and I guarantee you he learned something from me about football players.

As a broadcaster, I have a simple philosophy in doing a football game. We have a wonderful announcer in Washington, Ed Walker. He's blind, reads his commercials from braille, and may be the most talented guy I've ever known. He once told me that when Sonny and I are doing Redskin games, we make him see football—he can see in his mind what's happening. That's the highest compliment I've ever been paid, and that's what I try to do. If I can make all of our listeners understand the game, I've done my job.

If I don't, they can throw me out of the booth, too.

18
●●●●●●●

They are the great days of our lives: the college graduation, the wedding, the birth of a child. And for me, the day I was inducted into the Professional Football Hall of Fame in Canton, Ohio, ranks right up there with anything I've ever experienced.

It happened after I started to think it would never happen. Five years after I stopped playing, I became eligible, but it took eight more years, until 1982, when I was finally voted in.

A panel of sportswriters from every National Football League city selects the players to be inducted. There are specific rules, but basically you have to get something like eighty percent of the votes to qualify. The writers meet every year at the Super Bowl to make their final selections, and every time the voting came up and I didn't get in, there was a pain in my heart.

It wouldn't have been so bad if there had been no middle linebackers from my era in the Hall. But as the years went by, Bill George got in. Dick Butkus got in. Ray Nitschke got in. All of them in the first year they were eligible.

After a while, I started to wonder about myself. What's wrong with me? I played in six championship games, I played on a world championship team, I probably blocked more kicks than any man in the history of the game. I had

30 career interceptions, more than anyone else. I was on the cover of *Time* and Walter Cronkite narrated my story on national television. I worked hard, I provided for my family, I always cooperated with the media, I never wore white shoes, grew long hair, or shot off my mouth. What's going on here?

There was no question in my mind that some of the voters still remembered my battles with Jimmy Brown and Jimmy Taylor. When I was playing, I was not a very popular guy around the league. A lot of people resented all the attention I got because I happened to play for the New York Giants, a glamour team in a glamour city. I'm sure I was not at the top of the list for the guy voting in Green Bay, or the guy voting in Cleveland, or a lot of other places.

There may have been another factor. A lot of my teammates were also being considered at the same time, people like Emlen Tunnell, Y. A. Tittle, Frank Gifford, Andy Robustelli, and Roosevelt Brown. They all got in before I did, and I'm sure there was a feeling among the writers that they didn't want to make this the New York Giant Hall of Fame.

In any case, when I went to the Super Bowl in Pontiac, Michigan, in 1982, I was prepared for yet another frustrating week. It was not exactly the greatest place in the world to hold a Super Bowl. The temperature never got out of the teens, and everyone spent a lot of time sitting in hotel lobbies. For me, that made the wait for the Hall of Fame vote even longer.

The day of the voting, I happened to run into Nitschke. He still goes to all the games and we've become friendly over the years. "Sam," he said, "you deserve to be in the Hall of Fame, and I think this is the year you're going to make it, I can feel it."

That made me feel good, but the knot in my stomach had been getting tighter all week. The morning of the voting, Mary and I were in the hotel elevator and as we got off, we saw Pete Elliott, the executive director of the Hall of Fame. He had just come out of the meeting and he was smiling. "You made it," he said, and I want to tell you, that was the most electrifying moment of my life.

I started crying. Mary started crying, too. We were sitting there in the lobby, with tears running down our faces. That's how much it meant to me. At that point, you feel like you want to get a loudspeaker and start telling the world, but the official announcement wasn't supposed to be made until the next week at the Pro Bowl, and I was asked not to tell anyone. Can you imagine keeping something like that a secret for a whole week? They've since changed the procedure. Now, they announce a list of final candidates on the day of the voting the Saturday before the Super Bowl, then they announce the inductees three days after the game.

In 1982, I wasn't supposed to say anything. But I couldn't help myself. A Washington reporter, Mo Siegel, was doing some television work after his newspaper, *The Washington Star,* had folded and I guess some of his buddies on the selection committee told him I'd been voted in. Hell, he knew it before I knew it. He called me and said he wanted to do a story on my being elected, and that he'd keep it in the can until the formal announcement. That was fine with me.

I also felt I had to tell Frank Herzog about it. Frank worked for a different television station than Siegel, but he and I were doing the Redskin radio broadcasts, and I owed it to him. So he sent a crew over, and I thought we had the same understanding—no story until the Hall of Fame made its announcement. But Frank went with it right away, and the phone started ringing off the hook. One of the first calls was from Siegel, who was very upset about getting beat on the story. Then Pete Elliott called, and they were upset that it had leaked out. And I was upset for a long time with Frank Herzog for breaking the release date.

But really, when it comes right down to it, it was unrealistic of them to expect me to hold that in. It was just too big, one of the most important moments of your life.

The next week they flew Mary and me out to Hawaii to be introduced at the Pro Bowl game. The induction came the following summer at Canton, Ohio. There were thousands and thousands of people there, including my entire family and what seemed like half the state of West Virginia. It's a spectacular weekend—parties, receptions, and of course the induction ceremony itself at the Hall.

I asked Tom Landry to introduce me, and he actually left his team in training camp in Thousand Oaks, California, to fly across the country for the ceremony. "I never had any trouble with Sam," Tom said in his introductory speech, "because any time he started to goof off, I would give him the choice of getting the job done for the Giants, or going back to the coal fields of West Virginia. It was amazing how quick he got his act together again. . . . When the decision was made to move Sam to middle linebacker, I wasn't sure he could make the transition. However, it wasn't long before I realized that his dedication and competitive attitude were ideally suited for the position. . . . It wasn't long before we realized Sam was something special."

Then it was my turn to talk, and quite honestly, I can't really remember what I said. But I do remember looking down into the crowd and seeing my whole family there. Mary, the kids, my brothers and sisters, people from back home, even Dominick Romino, the lawyer who didn't want me to run for Congress, and his wife Libby, my second-grade teacher. My brother-in-law, Billy Maxwell, was there, too. He was blind and had been fighting multiple sclerosis for years. Now, he was sitting there in the broiling sun in a wheelchair, and I kept thinking, *You don't want to go over your five minutes because this poor man is sitting there and suffering in this heat.* I also remember thinking that this was a guy with more guts than I could ever hope to have.

So many thoughts run through your mind at a time like

that, so many emotions. A lot of guys can't get through that speech without getting choked up. It didn't happen to me, but I was close. I thought about my parents, both of them gone now and how much they had sacrificed for me, and about Ray Kelly and Art Lewis, and how proud they all would have been. I thought about Landry and Lombardi, about all the friends I had made, all my teammates, Little Mo and Rosey, Yat and Andy, Kat and Gifford, my roommates, Don Chandler and Sonny Jurgensen.

It was an emotional moment, and every time I look at the Hall of Fame ring on my finger, I realize how lucky I am, how fortunate I've been.

I've also been fortunate to have been associated with the Washington Redskins over the last twenty-five years, first as a player, then as a coach, and for the last fifteen years as a broadcaster. So many interesting people, so many fascinating personalities.

After Bill Austin, in came George Allen, a great defensive coach, but a man who would do anything to win and a man I never really trusted. This is a guy who once traded the same draft choice to two different teams. He also used to say that losing was like death, and I never quite believed in taking it to that extreme. I liked Lombardi's theory. He always said there's nothing like winning and there's nothing like losing, and when you do lose, all you can do is rededicate yourself to the proposition that you won't lose again.

For George, everything was right now. He never talked about a long-range rebuilding program because he didn't have time for that. He wanted to win immediately. He knew he wasn't going to be around forever, so he went out and got the ball players he needed for that year, no matter the price. I also never thought the future of the franchise meant much to him because he didn't sell his house on the West Coast. That told me he never planned to stay long.

He was a defensive coach, and he was good for the older players. He'd give guys you'd normally think were washed up a chance, and they played hard for him. But he also did some things I didn't agree with. He'd want you to take Novocain and play hurt. He made players feel like the team couldn't win unless they were out there on the field. That probably cost Bill Brundige, a good young defensive tackle, several years of his career. At the end of George's last season, Brundige was on crutches all week before an important game against the Cardinals. Nobody thought he could play because he'd really hurt his foot the week before. But he took a shot, numbed it up, and went out there and played. In the off-season, he needed surgery to repair that foot, and he never played again.

When Allen left to coach the Rams after the 1977 season, it didn't surprise me at all. I think he saw that his policy of trading draft choices for veterans had finally put the Redskins in a position where the cupboard was pretty much bare. The older guys were now getting very old, and there was not much left to trade. So he got out, went to Los Angeles and got fired by Carroll Rosenbloom, the owner, even before the regular season started. Leaving Washington was the biggest mistake of his life; he's never coached again in the NFL probably because no owner wanted to trust him with his franchise. You could hardly blame them.

His replacement, Jack Pardee, was a good man and a good coach. In his second year, the team finished 10–6 and just missed going to the playoffs. He also made some mistakes. He had a Hall of Fame safety on his team, Ken Houston, and in 1980, the year Kenny was going to retire, Jack never put him into his last game at RFK Stadium. The Redskins were out of playoff contention at that point, and Ken Houston should have been on that field. Jack took a lot of heat for that, and it was justified.

He and Bobby Beathard also had some differences of opinion. That seemed inevitable. After Allen left, Edward Bennett Williams hired his coach first, and then brought in Beathard. Pardee moved right into Allen's old office, and

Bobby got relegated to a smaller office, the old public relations room. So almost from the beginning there was a split. At the end, Bobby wanted to go with the younger players but Jack, knowing that he had to win to keep his job, didn't want to risk it. By 1980, Jack Kent Cooke had taken over day-to-day operation of the club from Williams, and he basically sided with Beathard. When his team finished 6–10 in 1980, Pardee was gone, replaced by a young assistant from San Diego named Joe Gibbs.

In the seven years since then, all Gibbs has done is this: three Super Bowl appearances and two world championships. In my mind, this guy just may be the equal of Lombardi. I think he has that kind of credibility with his players. He's an amazing guy, especially when you consider how he's been able to adjust to almost any kind of situation and how he's been able to get the most out of so many different personalities.

Take John Riggins, one of my favorite ball players of all time. He laid it on the line for you every time he played. A great competitor, but also a great character. When he wasn't playing, he did some stupid things. John always liked to have a good time, and he also never knew when to stop.

I'm not going to sit here and make character judgments, but John probably regrets some of the things he's done. Did Riggins have a drinking problem? Only John can answer that. I can tell you that it bothered me when he drank, just like it used to bother me when Sonny had too much to drink a few years ago. Sonny hasn't had a drink in over a year, and I think that's great. I also think John is starting to think a little beyond the next day. He's got enough money to live comfortably the rest of his life, but I believe he's getting bored and wants to do something a little more productive than just clip coupons. He's called me and asked for advice on what to do now that he's out of football, and I've told him that he really should try to get into broadcasting. He's a natural, glib and funny, and he knows the game.

Like I said, he's a terrific guy, and one of the greatest competitors I've ever seen.

I could say the same thing for Theismann. What an athlete, and what a competitor. Here's a guy who wanted to play so much, he volunteered to return punts for that team.

But I always believed Joe was his own worst enemy. He was a brash young man, a real child of the "me generation," a guy who would run onto the field and want the spotlight focused on him. "I'm the greatest." "I want to be seen, I want to be heard." People of my generation were a little more laid-back. We believed that if you were good, people would notice you. You didn't have to wear white shoes or get a Mohawk.

Still, he was a great success. He took that team to back-to-back Super Bowls, and while the Redskins of that era followed Riggins, Joe still managed to get the job done, even if a lot of his teammates couldn't stand him.

No matter how you felt about Joe, though, you have to cringe when you think about his last game as a professional football player. That injury, on a "Monday Night" game against the Giants in 1985, had to be one of the ugliest things I've ever seen on a football field. I knew he was hurt bad as soon as I saw it. When they kept showing the replays, it got to the point where I couldn't even watch. I remember what it felt like to have Spain Musgrove fall on my ankle in 1967. That was just awful. Whatever else you might think about the guy, he deserved better.

A lot of people are also down on Dexter Manley these days. I'm not one of them. Once again, we're talking about a guy who is a fabulous athlete on the field, and a strange case off it. Dexter wants everyone to believe he's a tough guy, but I think down deep he's got a real big heart. He's worked hard at being a great player, and he's also gone through the star syndrome. He's had a lot of attention paid to him, his name is all over the media, and for a while, he had some real problems with it. You're talking about a poor kid from Houston, and now all of a sudden the whole world is at his feet. Some people have a hard time dealing with that, and Dexter was no exception. He had a drinking problem, too, and I hope that's behind him.

He and I have always gotten along, though I could have strangled him during the 1987 season when he got on the radio in our locker-room show and started cursing into a live microphone while I was interviewing him. Dexter hadn't been talking to anyone, and now that they'd just won, he decided it was time to break his silence. So he got on and said, "Yeah, we really kicked their ass."

"Dexter, we're on the air, you can't say that," I told him. That did no good, because a few seconds later, he was talking about "bungholes." When we got off the air, I told him I wasn't happy, and it would not happen again. So far, it hasn't, but with Dexter, you never know. He gets carried away, but I'm going to tell you something. Dexter, for the most part, knows exactly what he's doing. Some people around town talk about how dumb he is. Not true.

Of course I kid him all the time. Once he said to me, "You know, Sam Huff, the ball player of today is bigger, faster, and smarter than they were in your day."

"Is that right, Dexter?"

"That's right, Sam."

"Well, first of all, Dexter, they may be bigger and faster, but I can't remember anyone ever driving a car through the gates of the team's practice facility, tearing it down, speeding around the practice field, then running it into an eighteen-wheel tractor-trailer truck on the street like you did. Now how damned smart is that?"

The point I'm trying to make is this. Joe Gibbs has all kinds of personalities on his football team, and every year he manages to blend them into a solid unit that is right in it. Every week, his team is in the game. Last year, Joe seemed to have two different game plans for each opponent. If you shut the Redskins down in the first half, they went into that locker room and changed everything and tore you up in the second half.

Joe also has great credibility. He's so organized, and he

treats his players like men. He has some of the best practices I've ever seen. No one really stands around much, but there are none of those silly rules about having to wear your headgear all the time, or standing at attention while you're watching from the sideline.

He's also got a temper, most definitely. He's a religious guy, that's absolutely genuine, and he really doesn't swear, at least I've never heard him. He'll give a "goldangit," but that's about as bad as it gets.

Once, he got furious with us at the Dulles Marriott, where the team stays before home games. He had kept the team in a meeting about twenty minutes longer than usual, and when they came out for their snack before curfew the night before the game, the hamburgers were too well done. He almost switched hotels because of that, especially after they lost in the playoffs the next day to the Bears. The hotel manager went to talk to him a few days later when he heard Joe was upset about the service, and the poor guy got chewed out as if he'd dropped a pass. Joe even talked to Bill Marriott about it. Bill comes out to watch practice every once in a while and is a great fan of the team. He told Joe Gibbs that if he wanted to switch to another hotel, and he honestly felt it would help the Redskins' effort, then by all means he should do it. Of course the Redskins stayed with us, but it was touch and go for a while, all because of well-done hamburgers that were Joe Gibbs' fault in the first place. We can laugh about it now, but at the time, Joe was pretty upset.

The bottom line, though, is the man can coach. What he did with that team last year was so typical. Wasn't Joe Gibbs the only coach in the league willing to take a chance on Doug Williams? And look how that paid off.

He had a running attack that never really got going. George Rogers was banged up all year, Kelvin Bryant was nicked and inconsistent. And he never even played the best back on his team, Timmy Smith, until the end of the season. The Super Bowl was the first game he started, and he broke the rushing record with 204 yards. They put together the best strike team in the NFL and they survived a terrible quarterback controversy that would have ripped most teams apart.

Gibbs is the best coach in the league in a crisis situation because his players believe in him. They know that it doesn't matter who has the biggest contract or who is the big star—the guy who produces is going to play. There's no politics on that team, nobody telling Gibbs who he has to play or doesn't have to play. Joe Gibbs wouldn't have benched Sonny Jurgensen for Dick Shiner, I can tell you that.

He's also got the advantage of having an excellent front office. They have an owner in Jack Kent Cooke who cares passionately about his team. And he's there all the time. As much as I admired and respected Edward Bennett Williams, he was basically an absentee owner. You'd see him on Sundays and that was about it. Cooke and his son John run that football team, and their front office is as good as any in the NFL. I know it's fashionable not to like Jack Kent Cooke. How can you like one of the world's richest men? But I do. He reminds me of an older Theismann in that he's so hyper. It's always, "I gotta go, I gotta do this, I gotta do that." When I see him and he tells me that, I ask him where he has to go. When you've got as much money as he does, you can go whenever and wherever you please, move at whatever pace you want. I've had some long conversations with him and he's one of the smartest men I've ever been fortunate to be around. I admire the heck out of the guy. I really do. And all you have to do is look at the people he hires to understand why the Redskins are so successful.

Joe Gibbs is the best coach in the league right now, no question. Against everybody but maybe Shula and Landry, he's probably worth seven points going into every game his team plays. And Bobby Beathard is the best personnel man in the business. He could spend a month in the Sahara

Desert and find himself a football player. They've spared no expense in their coaching staff. Last year, when their special teams were falling apart, they brought in an extra special-teams coach, Paul Lanham, and they liked him so much, they kept him for 1988. When I was playing, the idea of a special-teams coach would have gotten you laughed out of the league. But no one laughs anymore.

And that brings me to another point. People ask me all the time if players from my era could play the game today. My answer is always the same. There is no question in my mind that every man in the Hall of Fame could play the game, and probably be a star. And a lot of players who never made the Hall, too. Just look at the record books. How long did it take to break Jimmy Brown's records, and for most of his career, he was playing twelve-game seasons. His 5.2 yard-per-carry average may never be broken. Sammy Baugh, a guy some people say was one of the greatest quarterbacks ever, had the punting record for years, at least until domed stadiums with no wind became fashionable. And Baugh did the punting while he was playing both ways.

The biggest difference I can see is in conditioning. In my day, we had big guys, and most of us had a little beef on us. You look at these kids coming out of college now, and they're one solid hunk of muscle. I really believe that's one of the reasons there are so many injuries. In addition to the artificial turf, you get collisions now with muscle against muscle, and there's no give. In my day, we hit just as hard—ask Jimmy Taylor if you don't believe me—but there was a little padding there to cushion the shock.

I also think that more guys get hurt because there aren't as many great athletes out there on the field. It's an age of specialization. You have forty-five players on the roster. You have maybe seven to ten great players on each team. The rest of them are average. I've always felt that the great players rarely get hurt because they're not the guys running down on punts and kickoff returns, where so many injuries seem to happen.

And these guys now are playing so many more games. Four preseason, sixteen regular season, and if you get to the Super Bowl, three or four more. That's a lot of collisions.

They're also getting paid quite a bit more, and that's led to some disturbing trends. Football players have become big-time entertainers. Frank Sinatra can make a million a year singing and people think that's all right. Now linebackers make a million a year, and people are accepting that. A lot of these players also become prima donnas. Second-team tackles won't talk to the media. In my day, if you didn't like a certain reporter, you just went on and talked to someone else. Now these guys hide in the training room, and I believe that's a mistake on their part. Their careers are so short, an average of about four years. Why not take advantage of all this exposure to get a job in the off-season, to start another career?

In my time, the quarterback or the star running back would get most of the publicity; now you go into a locker room after a game and there are fifteen reporters around every player. They've even got women covering football teams. That just amazes me.

The game obviously has exploded. These guys are making hundreds of thousands of dollars. You look in the parking lot and they're driving Mercedes and Jaguars. The players have a different attitude. You book them for a speech, and sometimes they won't even show up for the $500. I would have driven halfway across the country for that kind of money. But these guys don't care; they're not as reliable. Some won't even sign an autograph. They should be honored anyone even asks.

They all belong to a union, but I've always wondered why they need a union and an agent, too. The two seem incompatible to me. The union is the National Football League Players Association, and that's how it started out, as an association that was concerned with player safety, getting reasonable per diems, insurance benefits, and pensions. But player salaries should not be a major concern of that union now. That's what they have agents for.

Their strike last year was ludicrous. The day the owners decided to field replacement teams was the day that strike ended because half of these guys were hearing from their agents that it was crazy to sit out while other guys were playing the games on national television. The owners broke that union last year, and I'd be very surprised if the players ever threatened to strike again.

But the game will go on, and it seems to get bigger all the time. You also have to admire the people who play pro football, because it's gotten so sophisticated, so complex, and so specialized. There's so much classroom work involved, but in the end, I really do believe the best athletes prevail.

It's like that in another sport I've been following closely over the last few years. Ever since the days when I listened to Roy Rogers and Gene Autry on the radio, I've been fascinated by horses.

I've gone to the last fifteen or sixteen Kentucky Derbys, and it's as much a spectacle as any Super Bowl I've ever seen. If I hadn't been a football player, I'd have loved to have been a jockey. I admire the heck out of those little guys for sitting on top of those huge animals and riding like the wind. Talk about great athletes.

About five years ago, I visited a stud farm in Lexington, Kentucky, and fell in love with a thoroughbred. I bought a third of it for $15,000 and when I told Mary—she always wrote the checks—she wasn't smiling. But that was a big thrill for me, and since then, I've got shares in about fifteen horses. It's a part of my life that gives me great pleasure and satisfaction.

There is also a part of my life that has caused me great pain and anguish. Mary and I are no longer together. When we split up in 1987, it was one of the saddest days in my life and certainly, it's my greatest failure and disappointment. Over the years, we just started drifting apart. What I liked to do, she didn't. I wanted to move to the country, she preferred our house in Alexandria. I liked the horses, she never got very interested. These things happen. And once the kids started going off to college and getting married, we grew even further apart.

I never wanted to separate, never wanted to get a divorce, but in reality, we were destroying each other. We had been together since high school, and we raised our family and did what we had to do. In truth, Mary raised the family. I was off playing football or working at a job trying to keep it all together, trying to provide for the family and help out our parents and our relatives. We started with twenty dollars between us, and it was her twenty. Mary paid the price, and I paid the price, and over the last few years we were just not getting along.

My kids are not happy about the situation, and we're dealing with it as best we can. I'm very proud of all of them. Sam Jr. is a businessman in Atlanta and has a son, my grandson Nicholas. Cathy lives in Alexandria and works for a doctor, and J. D. works for Marriott at their computer center in Frederick, Maryland, and has a daughter, Mary Carmen, named after his mother, with a third grandchild on the way any day now.

I live on twenty-two acres in Middleburg, Virginia, right in the middle of horse country in a house I designed myself. When I was a kid sharing a bed with my brother Don, I dreamed about a house like this, and now I'm living my dream. My partner in the horse business is Carol Holden, who loves horses as much as I do. She's also helped get me through some very difficult times, and I don't know what I'd do without her. Together we're trying to upgrade racing in West Virginia. In 1987, we put on the West Virginia Breeders Classic, the first $100,000 horse race in the history of the state—an annual event that will only get bigger and bigger.

I'll keep working at Marriott for as long as they'll have me. I'll be busy doing radio and television work, giving speeches, and raising money for West Virginia University, the NFL Alumni, the Hall of Fame, and so many other causes I've always supported. And maybe one day, I'll even come up with a horse that will run in the Kentucky Derby.

I'm working at it; I've been working at it since the days I used to sweep out John Manchin's grocery store back in Farmington. I grew up in a coal camp, and I always knew I wanted something better for me and my children, and their children. Ask anyone who's ever known me and they'll tell you that no man ever outworked me in anything I ever set my mind to—football, politics, broadcasting, or the business world.

The way I figure it, I've been the man in the middle all my life. Why stop now?